Up from Puerto Rico

Up from

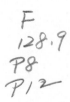

Puerto Rico

By ELENA PADILLA

NEW YORK AND LONDON

COLUMBIA UNIVERSITY PRESS

—In all my borned days I is never seed
Nothin' unto like this here a-fore!

'Course I ain't really been lookin'
For nothin' like this either

POGO, 1955

Nature hath made men so equal, in the
faculties of the body and mind; as that,
though there be found one man some-
times manifestly stronger in body or
of quicker mind than another, yet
when all is reckoned together, the dif-
ference between man and man is not
so considerable.

THOMAS HOBBES, 1651

Preface

SINCE the end of the Second World War, Puerto Rican migration to New York City has increased manifold. Partly a product of the social and economic developments that followed the war, it also reflects the sense of hope and the greater aspirations of Puerto Ricans in search of new frontiers for living. The monumental expansion of air transportation that followed the war helped to make possible what Clarence Senior has called "the first airborne migration in history." A unique kind of movement to the United States, the Puerto Rican migration is comparable to interstate migrations within the country, yet at the same time quite like the past immigrations from Europe in that American life is culturally foreign to Puerto Ricans. Hence the mass migration and settlement of some 650,000 Puerto Ricans in New York has been an object of much attention both in this country and abroad. For New Yorkers, this migration has both created bewilderment and concern and refreshed their memories and old attitudes toward foreign newcomers.

Up from Puerto Rico is an attempt by an anthropologist to provide a new way of looking at some of these issues, memories, and attitudes. It provides a detailed description of the ways of life and changing culture of Puerto Ricans in a New York City slum. A documentary story written for the general reader, it is based on two and a half years of intensive fieldwork in a neighborhood that I have called Eastville to insure the privacy of its inhabitants. These people generously permitted me to participate in many activities of the neighborhood, visit their homes, and intrude into many aspects of their private lives. The book tells about Puerto Ricans who live in the slums and who with their other American neighbors experience the lives of the underprivileged. It has to do with living in poverty, with coming to New York, with what happens to the uprooted family, the children, health, and friends, and with the changing traditions and values of Puerto Ricans.

Only in relatively recent years have anthropologists started to study urban life and the culture of city people. Many have spoken and written of the difficulties and shortcomings anthropologists experience in approaching urban life. In this I join, and confess that while in bringing understanding of the workings of the society and culture of city dwellers we anthropologists have a unique contribution to make, we must also be willing to borrow theories, methods, and techniques from other behavioral sciences, particularly sociology and psychology. This explains why the influence of Parsons, Merton, Hyman, Homans, Whyte, and Lewin is reflected throughout these pages. Anthropological approaches for the study of modern societies tried by Steward and his associates in Puerto Rico [1] also have had a definite influence in shaping the research on which this book is based.

I planned the study of Eastville as an exploration or pilot study of the social adaptations of Puerto Ricans to American slum life. I wanted to find out how Puerto Ricans were living and how they were changing, if at all, in the setting of a lower-class New York neighborhood. From January, 1954, to July, 1957, I did fieldwork in Eastville. For one year of that period I was assisted by Joan Campbell, Vera Green, Joan P. Mencher,

---

[1] Julian H. Steward and others, *People of Puerto Rico: A Study in Social Anthropology* (Urbana, Ill., University of Illinois Press, 1956).

George Wee, and Muriel White, graduate students of the Anthropology Department of Columbia University. Edwin Seda, now of the faculty of the Social Sciences at the University of Puerto Rico, and I planned together and undertook a special intensive investigation of the migrant family. James Gallagher of Teachers College, Columbia University, assisted me with a special study of the schools of the neighborhood.

While doing the study, we became personally acquainted with over five hundred persons living in the neighborhood. Our relationships with them ranged from very casual acquaintances to sustained personal friendships that lasted throughout the two and a half years of fieldwork. We did not live in Eastville, but our home base at Columbia University being only some twenty minutes away by bus, we could visit there regularly day or night, and we did. We visited people in their homes, shared their food, and attended their parties. We strolled around the streets and alleys, climbed to the roofs of buildings, and like Eastvillers, we sat, listened, and talked to people on the sidewalks and stoops, and in the stores. We attended church services, and accompanied residents of the neighborhood when they had business to attend to outside of Eastville. Many a warm evening we went with them to the near-by parks to "catch air." We visited their sick at home and in hospitals, and attended services for their dead. We visited the schools where the children received their education, and we talked with their teachers and principals. We also met the attendance officers whose job is primarily to see that schoolchildren do not play hooky. We visited the community centers where family and youth recreation programs are undertaken, and we talked with social workers and other professional people who run such activities. We also talked to clergymen, politicians, social investigators, physicians, lawyers, and other people whose work places them in contact with Eastville. We wanted to find out about their attitudes, the kinds of relationships, and the personal experiences they had had with

Puerto Ricans. We listened as well to many non-Puerto Ricans in Eastville to find out how they got along and what their troubles with Puerto Ricans were. We talked and listened to Puerto Ricans. We followed this approach to gain more insight and knowledge about Puerto Rican life. While concentrating our interest on Puerto Rican respondents, we felt that Puerto Ricans in New York could be understood only in relation to their neighbors and to other contexts of the society in which they participate. Their lives are not isolated but enmeshed in the social and cultural matrices of the city.

Thus we could not rely solely on the techniques of participant observation and informal or hidden interviews. Focused interviews also had to be used, and specific areas for investigation had to be decided upon early in the formulation of the research plan. Yet the research had a broad enough scope to permit the exploration and following up of leads and hunches. Weekly staff meetings were helpful in bringing about necessary changes in the strategy of investigation. After having worked for eighteen months in Eastville we administered questionnaires to forty-eight Puerto Rican family heads, selected on the basis of residence in every third apartment of each fifth building. These questionnaires, of the open-ended type, covered over two hundred items pertaining to family history.

Working in Eastville, we gradually learned that to do research among the people of the neighborhood we had to adapt our techniques to be within their reach. For instance, when we discovered that those who joined conversation groups in the streets or stores need not know the others' names or have been formally introduced, we just walked up, listened, and participated like others in the conversations. We also learned that in Eastville it was a waste of time to schedule appointments for interviews unless it was raining or snowing. So we started to drop in on people at their homes, or we looked for them at their favorite stores, street corners, or neighbors' homes, as is commonly done by Eastvillers when they want to locate someone. Interviews were conducted in a variety of situations. We could occasionally interview people in the neighborhood health clinic or in a small apartment we rented in Eastville. But many times we had to sit on lids of garbage cans, on stoops, in candy stores, or alleys while interviewing. Frequently an interview conducted in somebody's home was carried on while trying not to interrupt a woman's chores and in between the streams of visitors who, like the anthropologist, had dropped in and stayed for hours. We also learned that we could not rush answers to our questions, but that we had to time carefully comments or questions to receive reliable answers. We realized that despite the limited time available, our research would take long and unspecified hours, of both day and night, and a great deal of patience. Interviews and casual conversations were conducted either in Spanish or in English depending on the language preferred by the respondent. Fieldworkers who were not conversant in Spanish would use an interpreter, generally a schoolchild, when the respondent claimed he did not speak English. Or, the respondent was shifted to a Spanish-speaking fieldworker. Many times, Spanish-speaking fieldworkers had to conduct interviews in English with Puerto Ricans who grew up in this country and who had a language handicap when speaking Spanish. Being Puerto Rican or American was no major advantage or disadvantage to establishing rapport or to the quality of fieldwork achieved. As a whole, success as a fieldworker depended on the training, flexibility, and skills in human relations of the individual fieldworker. Formal interviews were recorded in front of respondents and details filled in after the interviews were completed. Observations and informal interviews were written up either in a restaurant, or as soon as possible after leaving Eastville. Each fieldworker kept a diary of his research activities. Some formal interviews were tape-recorded, such as group interviews with children in the schools and recreation centers and individual interviews with drug addicts.

During the time we spent working in Eastville we never encountered situations in which we had unpleasant interpersonal experiences or in which aggressions were directed against us. At first apprehensive and suspicious, anticipating that it was "dangerous" to work in a slum, we soon found acceptance and friendship among many people in the neighborhood. Our worst occupational hazards were accidental, such as getting spit on our heads, or having garbage being thrown out of a window land on us, but these incidents were part of the routine of Eastville life. On such occasions, we could always count on finding some kindly person who would invite the fieldworker to come into his apartment and wash, the while commenting unfavorably on the culprit.

We got to be part of "the sight" of Eastville; we were seen individually in its streets, alleys, dark dance halls, bars, restaurants, schools, and candy stores. We mingled with many Eastvillers with confidence and passed no judgment on them nor volunteered unsolicited advice. Our roles as anthropologists were not understood in the same terms as we understood them, but this was no obstacle to our work. Though we were a team of researchers, work was divided among us in such a way that many respondents could not associate us as a group. Each fieldworker was assigned a special load of work to do, and was responsible for working with a number of respondents not to be interviewed by other fieldworkers. We acknowledged that we were professional persons doing a study, but as such we tried to relate with respondents on their own social terms, respecting their attitudes and feelings whether the respondent was a prominent educator, a housewife, or a drug peddler. Many people called us by our first names and we reciprocated, but when respondents required more formality in our relations with them, we complied. In other words, we tried to adapt ourselves to our respondents without losing our objectivity or perspective on our status.

I have written this book for people interested in the quiet dramas of anonymous lives. It is neither an apology nor a condemnation. Rather, I hope that it will serve the cause of offering the general public access to the findings of the scientific study of society, with the additional hope that this kind of knowledge may be applicable to more skillful living and human understanding.

ACKNOWLEDGMENTS

Thanks are due to Joan Campbell, James Gallagher, Vera Green, Joan P. Mencher, Edwin Seda, George Wee, and Muriel White, who helped me with the toil of fieldwork. Charles Wagley, Professor of Anthropology at Columbia University, was most helpful with his advice and interest in the research. Beatrice B. Berle, M.D., is also to be thanked for her encouragement. The Foresight Foundation of New York supported financially the research through a grant made to the Anthropology Department of Columbia University. To both, my appreciation is here expressed. Edwin Seda discussed with me several sections of the book, and many of his ideas have been incorporated in it. I also wish to thank Michael D. Ciavolino, Jr., who took most of the pictures in the book. Dr. William Bridgwater and Miss Barbara Melissa Voorhis of Columbia University Press are to be thanked for their interest and careful editing. My deepest gratitude is to the people of Eastville who provided the information on which this book is based.

ELENA PADILLA

New York City
April, 1958

Contents

Up from Puerto Rico

Where they live

IN New York City on Manhattan Island there is a neighborhood which we shall call Eastville. It is a slum, and as in many another slum of urban America, the people who live there can trace their ancestry, recent or remote, to all the four corners of the earth. But in Eastville many are newcomers not only to this city, but also to this country. This makes the neighborhood distinctive. Among these are large numbers of Puerto Ricans. The forebears of many others came so long ago that they have lost touch with their past national origins. Nevertheless, regardless of how long they have been melting in the pot, the people of Eastville are seldom identified as just plain Americans. They are designated "Hungarians," "Puerto Ricans," "American Negroes," "American Indians," "East Indians," "Russians," "Italians," "Chinese"—and all of these group labels are conceived as indicating something about the personal, social, and biological traits of the various group members. It makes little difference in this categorizing whether or not individuals were born and have lived all their lives in this country if they still possess characteristics—real or assumed—in physical appearance, in styles of wearing apparel, in knowledge of another language than English, and in their names, that allow them to be distinguished from "real" Americans. The term "American" is used, as a rule, with reference to outsiders who do not live in the neighborhood and who, although they themselves may be members of ethnic groups, do not meet the criteria that suggest to Eastvillers membership in any particular ethnic group with which they are familiar.

Eastville is a patchwork of ethnic groups framed in slum tenement buildings. A stretch of twelve city blocks comprises this enclave, which is flanked by new housing developments, a hospital, warehouses, city housing projects, garages, and a more prosperous and well-preserved neighborhood where businessmen, skilled and white-collar workers dwell. Like Eastville, this other neighborhood is the home of Italians, Puerto Ricans, and members of other ethnic groups, but they contrast sharply with Eastvillers in their standard of living, which is reflected in the tone and appearance of their neighborhood. The landscape of Eastville proper, the 1950 census of the United States tells us, consists of buildings, most of which were put up over fifty years ago. They have deteriorated and are now in various stages of neglect and disrepair.

Through the years the picture of the neighborhood has changed in more ways than one. Once a prosperous area of pleasant flats, Eastville has turned into what is now one of New York's darkest niches of poverty and blight. In the earlier part of the century it was tenanted by recently arrived European immigrants. Once Germans predominated. Afterward, Central European and Russian Jews were followed by the Irish, the Slovaks, and the Hungarians. Then Italians, spreading from the northern fringes of the neighborhood, started to move in, and Eastville became known as an Italian neighborhood. Later on came American Negroes, who soon predominated, and in recent years —those since the Second World War—Puerto Ricans have appeared in ever larger numbers. Of the 13,575 inhabitants reported by the 1950 census, 4,610 were Puerto Ricans and the children of Puerto Rican migrants. Today American Negroes still predominate, but Eastville becomes increasingly attractive as time passes to recent migrants from the island.

One cannot help noticing that the social history of Eastville has been similar to that of other urban neighborhoods in America, especially those neighborhoods whose housing has undergone inadequate maintenance and progressive decay while it was being rented to people of low income. In time, those who have made good have moved out of Eastville, but many other Eastvillers have remained. They have been unable to follow the ideal of moving up in the world. Getting out of Eastville, which is almost synonymous with moving up and a sign of being better off, is still in process there. The population turnover suggests that this is a place where people come to live while they can find no better, but that it by no means represents what they want in terms of housing and living conditions.

The imprints of the past and its human movements delineate the character of the neighborhood. The old synagogue has given way to the Christian Family Center, but the six-pointed Star of David remains untouched above the sign of the new organization. Aging individuals who came to this country in their youth are the conservative remainders and reminders of the Old World immigrations. Some buildings in the neighborhood are occupied exclusively by members of one ethnic group; there are certain streets in which members of one or another ethnic group predominate; and there are even particular spots on the sidewalk, in the streets, and in the parks near by which serve as landmarks where members of given ethnic groups get together.

Church membership is also aligned according to ethnic group, and churches of the same religion tend to proselytize on this basis. One of the Catholic churches appealing to Italians has an Italian priest and sermons are rendered in Italian; another appealing to Puerto Ricans has a Spanish-speaking priest who conducts the vernacular part of the services in Spanish. In addition, stores, bars, restaurants, and other local businesses are adapted to the different ethnic groups. Even the chain-owned supermarkets operating in the neighborhood, such as the A & P, have adapted themselves to the demands of the local consumers by setting aside special shelves for the display of exotic imported products used in the diets of Puerto Ricans, Italians, American Negroes, and others. Many a human difference and many a human similarity in Eastville can be explained in terms of the differences among the various ethnic groups and the range of similarities within each.

Eastville is more than just a place where people live. It is like a community where people find much of their social life, have many of their friends, where their churches and a large number of business enterprises in which they can buy the things they need are located. On the average each block of Eastville contains four churches and from six to eight small stores. The storefront churches represent a variety of denominations, with Protestant and Spiritualist sects predominating. A few "social and athletic clubs" for young men are housed in the neighborhood. Under the sponsorship of churches and social agencies, premises for family and youth recreation are allocated. Numerous small stores owned by individual proprietors not only sell goods, but also serve as recreation centers. Laundries, tailors, plumbing equipment and hardware stores, beauty salons, barber shops, bakeries, luncheonettes, bars, groceries, clothing shops, vegetable markets, and candy stores, often occupying only a few square feet of space, continually mushroom and decline. Peddlers with horse-drawn wagons and pushcarts ply the neighborhood streets selling vegetables and fruits. In spring and summer improvised stands displaying iced watermelon cuts are set up on the sidewalks. Fish are hawked from vans stationed at street corners. Door-to-door salesmen canvass apartments in the evenings and on holidays, offering their merchandise on credit.

The people of Eastville nonetheless must leave the neighborhood for many of the essentials of life. They have to seek work outside it, frequently in Brooklyn, the Bronx, and Long Island, for the few small factories and the businesses in and around the neighborhood provide very little employment for its residents. While grammar and junior high school children attend school in or near the neighborhood, high school students have to travel by subway or bus to distaint points in the city for their education.

As there are no post offices or banks in the neighborhood, Eastvillers must go beyond its boundaries for the services these institutions offer, although such routine transactions as buying stamps, cashing checks, or purchasing money orders can be attended to in neighborhood stores. In the vicinity there are some movie houses patronized by Eastvillers, but they also go to movies outside Eastville. In summer they journey out to Coney Island and Brighton Beach, or turn to a near-by public swimming pool.

Since medical and other professional services are absent from the neighborhood, except for a small health clinic and a city-operated dental clinic, Eastvillers have to go afield for these also. To shop for many things they need, such as furniture and clothing, they do not depend exclusively on the neighborhood marts. For food and other items, they may go to *la marqueta,* the city-owned market, where fish, meat, vegetables, fruits, clothes, shoes, herbs, and household goods are generally sold at lower prices than in the stores in or near the neighborhood.

Both the services offered locally in the neighborhood and those that Eastvillers seek outside are an indication of how the neighborhood and its people are an integral part of the life of the city. They show how its way of life and the fulfillment of its basic needs are embedded in the matrices of the world of worlds which is New York. In it, Puerto Ricans, Italians, Jews, Russians, American Negroes, and those who have lost track of their foreign ancestry share a commonality of experience in living which is derived in general from dwelling in New York and in particular from the responses they must make to the specific social conditions of the slum.

In terms of American standards, Eastville is a neighborhood of poor people. Its inhabitants grope for sustenance in jobs which, according to the 1950 Census of Occupations, were of unskilled and semiskilled levels in factories and service industries, such as restaurants, hospitals, laundries, and households. Sixty-seven percent of Eastvillers earned less than $2,449 a year, and many Eastvillers depended on Federal, state, and city aid in order to manage. This applies to all who live in Eastville, since there are no major differences there among the ethnic groups in education, employment, and income.

The residents of Eastville consider it a "bad" place. Bitterly complaining of the housing conditions, of nests of delinquency, and of life in general, Puerto Ricans and others alike look forward to leaving it. Mrs. Guzman, a Puerto Rican mother, summarized the anxieties about living in this milieu in words not unlike those of other parents whether from South Carolina, Sicily, or San Juan. "I want so much to move. This is a bad neighborhood. I keep the kids good because I keep them in the house with me. My husband said, 'You can be good even in the middle of twenty bad ones.' But it is hard. . . . I have a niece going to junior high school. She says it is so strict, but even though it is all girls, the boys get in and they bring the dope. They smoke marijuana and even sometimes they inject that stuff in the veins, cocaine, I think. My niece says some of the girls there, they even get pregnant right in the school. She says the school doctors examine the girls every six months . . . to see if any of those habits have started yet. But I hope we can move out of this neighborhood before my daughter goes to [junior high] school."

Commenting on the exodus from the neighborhood during the years of the Second World War and shortly thereafter, the Reverend Joe Kielsen said that at that time "landlords used to give five or six months of rent free to those who were willing to move into their vacant apartments." Today apartments are at a premium. Signs advertising the sale of apartments and furniture are posted in barber shops and grocery stores in both English and Spanish. Upon inquiry, it is not unusual to be told that $1,500 in cash is the price for the furniture in an apartment and the privilege of moving in. Unfurnished apartments are also "sold," and a prospective tenant may be asked up to $800 "for the key." Most sales, however, are not advertised, and apartments are obtained through friends already living in the neighborhood who find out when apartments are to become available. This does not eliminate the so-called "purchase," however, which is a transaction between someone who needs an apartment and either the building superintendent or the tenant occupying the premises. It is defined as the sale of an apartment rather than as the payment of a fee, and among recent migrants it is accepted as one of the ways a private apartment can be obtained in this city. Monthly rentals range from fourteen to eighty dollars in addition to utilities. Apartments, as a rule, are self-contained, having from two to seven rooms, including a closet toilet. A bathtub may be located in the kitchen-dining room, which may also be a passage to the rest of the apartment. The enamel lid covering the tub is frequently the utility table. Some rooms have no windows or any other source of ventilation and are almost as dark in the daytime as at night. The rooms of these apartments are generally so small that they seem overcrowded with only a few pieces of furniture in them. The 1950 census reported that there was an average of three persons to a room in the neighborhood. While two or three persons may use a single room, including the kitchen and the living room, as sleeping quarters, there is actually less crowding in Eastville than in comparable slums in other parts of New York, where a whole family may have only one room as its total housing. The latter is rare in Eastville. There the household consists of an apartment of more than one room. For those occupying rooming houses, Eastville seems a choice place to live, for in Eastville rents are lower, more space and privacy available. For Eastvillers, however, anywhere else is a better place to live than is their own neighborhood.

Often it is up to Eastville tenants themselves to plaster holes in the walls to keep the rats from entering their homes. Alicia Colar, a twelve-year-old girl, was making her bed before going to school one morning. As she shook out the sheets, a rat fell from her bed. She was frightened and ran from the room screaming. Her father simply brought plaster and covered a crack in the wall through which the animal had come into the apartment. Rat extermination campaigns, however, frequently serve only to exacerbate Eastvillers' discontent, for the rodents, trying to quench the thirst produced by the poison they have consumed, go out into the streets, the corridors, and the sidewalks, and there they die. This litter remains to rot and decay. Repairing electric installations and defective plumbing, painting and decorating apartments frequently must be undertaken at the tenant's own expense. Landlords and real-estate agencies managing the houses are absentee, and the superintendents, who are the intermediaries with the landlords, often displace the responsibility onto them for the dilapidated conditions. After successive complaints have failed, tenants may either make the repairs themselves, complain to the city authorities, or just live with conditions as they are. In winter, apartments equipped with central heating may be as cold as those that do not have it. Hot water may be turned off for several hours during the day and the evening. In summer, the sticky weather and the warmth exuded by hot water pipes in the walls of apartments and halls combine with the smell of garbage and defective plumbing to push Eastvillers, like other slum dwellers past and present, out of their homes into the streets where the atmosphere is apt to be cooler and more fragrant.

But no description of Eastville approximates what it is really like if one ignores the role of the street in the lives of its people. Strewn with garbage though they are, the streets and alleys are notable for the number of people of every conceivable ethnic group who spend a considerable part of their time there to get away from their apartments. Day and night the jukeboxes in the candy stores deluge the streets with the tunes of the latest records of the season, and it is not strange to see youngsters or young adults dancing by themselves inside the stores or on the sidewalks to rock 'n' roll rhythms by the Velvets or to Xavier Cugat's mambos and merengues. Others watch and then try the ones they like under the tutelage of those who know the steps and proper motions for the dances. Noise of music and of words in Yiddish, Spanish, Italian, and English, barking dogs, movements of people, and cars' horns, are interwoven in a polyphonic soundtrack which records the pace of the neighborhood. Only very cold weather or news echoed through the grapevine that gang fights are scheduled keep people off the streets. Otherwise, the streets, the sidewalks, the stores, and the bars are filled with people meeting, chatting, and relaxing.

Many languages are spoken in Eastville, and walking through its streets one hears shouts from the windows in Italian, Slovak, Spanish, or Hungarian. But rarely ever are the tongues pure; into each are mixed English words and phrases. English itself, which is used here by native speakers in preference to any other language, also comes in such a variety of accents and with so many nuances of tones that it sometimes sounds as if it were yet another strange, exotic tongue. Eastvillers are generally to some degree bilingual, except for American Negroes and British West Indians. There are even children and adults who are not fully conversant in any particular language but whose vocabulary is made up of a number of words from two or more languages. Puerto Rican children growing up here are the most distinctive among these nowadays. Streams of sentences pour from them in a bastard tongue that well might be called "Spanglish."

As in other slum areas, Eastvillers are well aware of the number of drunken old women, prostitutes, narcotics addicts, dope peddlers, perverts, thieves, and other delinquents who invade their streets. But they are also aware of the many law-abiding citizens, of the puritans, of the conservatives and the radicals in fashion and in custom, of those who work hard and those who live by their wits. They recognize among themselves those who are fearful of sin and evil, and those who are daringly defiant of the laws of men and religion. There are many confirmed churchgoers and many who never set foot inside a church. There are those who are sensitive and those who are crude and insensate. In short, Eastville has most of what makes humanity what it is—in various doses and strengths, without regard for color, religion, or national origins. This is the America that Puerto Ricans get to know through Eastville: one of variety in languages, in views of life, and in peoples. It is an America where uniformity is unknown, where diversity of standards marks the stage.

The sudden influx of large numbers of Puerto Ricans into Eastville has added new ingredients to the variety of its life. Distinguishing Puerto Ricans as Spanish-speaking from other groups, they are referred to as "Spanish" or "Puerto Rican" as against "English," which includes people who are not native speakers of Spanish and who are not conversant in Spanish. Puerto Ricans and their descendants in turn refer to themselves as "Hispanos," "Spanish," or "Latinos."

Not all persons who identify themselves as Hispanos or are considered to be Puerto Ricans by outsiders and by non-Puerto Ricans in Eastville are from Puerto Rico or descendants of Puerto Ricans. A number of individuals who have come from other Spanish-speaking countries are assumed to be Puerto Rican and among these are some who claim to be from Puerto

Rico. One day while sitting in the waiting room of the health clinic in Eastville, a woman started a conversation with three other women. She bemoaned her absence from Puerto Rico, making remarks about the beauty of the island, mentioning names of towns there, and expressing her homesickness. Her manner of speech, however, was somewhat unusual for an Eastville Puerto Rican migrant, and observing this a member of the field team asked her if she had ever been to Puerto Rico. The woman replied "no," and added that even if she had not been there she liked it very much and had heard a lot about it. She later admitted to being from Ecuador. Among recent migrants it is said that other Latins who are not American citizens like to claim that they are from Puerto Rico in order to take advantage of the privileges of American citizenship bestowed on Puerto Ricans, and that many crimes and antisocial acts of which Puerto Ricans are accused are actually committed by these other Latins. Scapegoating among Eastvillers, both Puerto Ricans and non-Puerto Ricans, is widespread.

Unlike El Barrio Latino, or Spanish Harlem as it is referred to by the press, Eastville is a "mixed" neighborhood, in which Puerto Ricans interact in daily affairs with non-Puerto Ricans, and where they have direct interpersonal relationships with members of other ethnic groups, involving both tensions and conflicts, friendship and understanding.

Among Eastvillers there are levels on which feelings of neighborhood solidarity bind members of all ethnic groups together. By the process of discrimination and dislike people get involved in relationships of conflict, and by common understandings and participation in common activities sentiments of solidarity develop. Both the positive feelings and the negative ones work together to shape the social body that is the neighborhood. The idea that the neighborhood is a bad place in which to live is a shared one among Eastvillers. So is their attitude toward discrimination by outsiders against them.

When a noted magazine carried an article featuring the missionary work of some religious leaders among Eastvillers, resentment against it was voiced in terms of discrimination against the people of the neighborhood. An American Negro woman, who is outspoken in her disapproval of Puerto Ricans, toned down her feelings about them to express disapproval of the article, which, in her opinion, demeaned Negroes as well as Puerto Ricans. Her target was her own church and the church leaders who she said had discredited both the church members and the people of the neighborhood. She also expressed disapproval of articles in the current press that have told of the conditions in which the people of Eastville live and have generalized about social problems there, pointing to these as insulting.

On the other hand, it is difficult to organize programs of social action in Eastville when ethnic group barriers are ignored or when the sources of loyalties within an ethnic group are not recognized. Beneath the intergroup tensions and conflicts among the ethnic groups are working interpersonal relationships among individuals, which override ethnic group affiliations. These are characterized by mutual assistance, friendship, love, and acceptance. Interpersonal relationships are highly prized in Eastville, and the proliferation of cliques and close personal relationships in the neighborhood are suggestive of their over-all importance as techniques for ameliorating some of the tensions and loneliness of the individual in modern urban society. First and last names are seldom known or recognized in Eastville. People are identified according to whatever characteristic they are best known by in the neighborhood—the man from Italy, the lady who owns the candy store, the woman from Ponce—and interpreting information given or received about others is conditioned by one's own characteristics. Since interpersonal relations are the primary ones in the neighborhood, an outsider is soon spotted. He is stared at and inspected carefully in the street, and guesses are made as to his identifica-

tion: "He works for the electric company." "He is a salesman."
"He is from Welfare."

That ethnic barriers are not strong on the level of informal,
face-to-face interpersonal relationships is illustrated by the following story. Mrs. Tie, an American woman in her fifties, was
hospitalized. While in the hospital she was visited by two
middle-aged American Southern Negro women. Some time
afterward, Mrs. Tie was in the street and saw the two women
who had visited her in the hospital. She commented, "Oh,
these are the ladies who visited me at the hospital. Thank you!"
One of the visitors replied, "Oh, you know how these things
are. . . ." These women knew one another only by sight before the hospital visit and were not friends in any formal sense.
Yet, in a moment of crisis, ethnic barriers broke down to give
way to human relationships on an individual, person-to-person
basis.

Eastvillers, as a whole, receive in their homes as guests and
visitors, persons they consider their friends and persons who
have some professional status which they respect. When one
knocks at a door, the resident asks for identification before it
is opened. If he is not convinced by your identification that
you are acceptable to him, or if your voice is not a familiar
one, the door remains closed. The informal meetings in the
streets and the many hours of day and evening spent in them
provide ample opportunities for socializing, gossiping, seeing
who is doing what, and getting to know about each other. The
street-life of Eastvillers follows distinctive and routine patterns.

From dawn or before, regardless of the weather, a stream of
young and middle-aged adult men and women carrying lunch
boxes can be seen walking quickly out of the neighborhood on
their way to work. This stream continues until eight or eight-
thirty. The people go either in groups of two or three, or individually. Among those who pass through Second Street, some
stop at Mrs. Penny's newspaper stand, which is improvised out

of an empty wooden grocery box. She sells the *Mirror,* the *News* and *El Diario de Nueva York.* Mrs. Penny hands a paper to a customer who pays her for it and continues on his way. Apparently she makes no error as to who reads what. Occasionally she asks about a sick child, or something else pertaining to the customer, who, while walking away, briefly replies. Mrs. Penny's business practices are not unusual for Eastville, for, with the exception of the large supermarket, buyer and storekeeper are involved in a more than business relationship; they are friends and neighbors. The storekeeper knows his customers' tastes and is acquainted with their lives. Both exchange personal questions and information as they transact their business. In addition, the storekeeper provides credit which contributes to making the relationship between him and his patrons one of trust, understanding, and mutual obligation.

After eight or eight-thirty, the children start out to school. Among the teen-age crowds there are various groups. Second-generation Puerto Rican girls, and those who have lived in New York most of their lives, usually go together with boys, either recent migrants, second-generation, or those who migrated as small children. In some of these groups, particularly those in which there are colored Puerto Ricans, are American Negro girls and boys who attend the same schools. These groups are different in composition and overt behavior from those of recent migrants. They speak English among themselves. Their clothes, kind of conversation, and social manners distinguish them from recent migrant children of the same age and social class. They blend into comparable teen-age groups in American society. In winter they wear woolen skirts, socks, long athlete's sweaters with letters, and sports coats and jackets. Only by knowing them and their families personally would one know whether they were Puerto Ricans. Recent migrant girls especially are more noticeable, however. Ordinarily they walk to school by themselves or in small groups, and are rarely accompanied by boys. They wear cottons and rayons the entire year round, sweaters, and princess or other fitted coats in winter. Also to be seen are the crowds of Italian boys, recently arrived Puerto Rican boys, and American Negro boys. Those who go to school alone, whether boys or girls, are generally the ones who are also seen alone on other occasions, or in the company of their brothers, sisters, or parents, but seldom with friends. In Eastville friends are considered by some as sources of evil, and a significant sector of Eastville life has to do with protection of oneself and of those one loves from becoming "bad."

Junior high school children follow a somewhat different pattern: among these the groups are formed by children of the same sex. Girls and boys are seldom seen together unless they are brothers and sisters. The Puerto Rican girls especially are accompanied by other Puerto Rican girls, or else by their brothers. This is particularly true of those who have arrived recently, and seldom does one see such a girl with one who has been born or brought up in New York, unless she is the daughter of a relative or friend with whom the parents maintain a close social relationship.

Of children attending grammar school, the youngest, who are starting their first year, are accompanied by an adult, older brothers or sisters, or older children known to the parents. The older boys and girls who do not have to be taken care of in the street, or who do not have to look after younger children, go by themselves or in small groups of two or three, boys and girls not mixing. Among recently arrived Puerto Ricans one sees many of the nonemployed mothers accompanying their daughters to grammar school regardless of the girls' age. Some of these mothers then stand by the school buildings while the classes are in session, others go away, returning to pick up the children when the classes are dismissed. These parents regard their presence as necessary to protect their daughters from men and boys, to prevent other children from beating them up, and to protect the younger children from the added hazard of traffic accidents.

After the school crowd has gone in the morning, housewives emerge into the streets, some to undertake the shopping for the day, some "to catch the sun," others "just to breathe." Those receiving welfare aid remain upstairs on the days the investigator is expected. From this time of morning until one o'clock in the afternoon the bets on the numbers are also placed, on the sidewalk, in the stores, and on the stoops.

At noon the children start coming home from school. Even those who have had lunch at school return to their block. Some of those who attend morning classes in double-session schools then commence their play in the alleys and the streets with people of various ages. In Eastville groups of playmates at times involve children of six to adults of nineteen or twenty who, during warm weather, play together such games as baseball, punch ball, and handball. In games requiring teamwork, ethnic barriers do not operate, particularly for those who speak English. One also sees horseplay in the street among groups of children of more or less the same age. Peer groups, however, may range from children in middle childhood to teen-agers and young adults. Grammar school boys also play other seasonal games—top spinning during June and marbles in the early spring. Teen-agers visit the candy stores where they listen to their favorite tunes. One may see a conversation among eight or ten adolescents broken off suddenly by the movement of all of them into the candy store where someone has dropped a nickel in the jukebox to play a rock 'n' roll tune, such as *The Ship of Love, Sexy Ways,* or *Good Night, Good Night Sweetheart,* which rated high with Eastville youth. Recent migrant girls from Puerto Rico are seldom seen in these groups or even standing on the sidewalks or stoops by themselves. Rather, they are at home.

In the afternoon the street is also a place of recreation for adult men and recent migrant boys. Various groups sit here and there over a game of checkers, cards, or dominoes. The corner of Second Street, for instance, is a spot where young American Negro men stand watching passers-by and a game of checkers in which American Negro players participate. On Fifth Street there is a spot next to an alley where Puerto Rican men play cards or dominoes. Down Avenue B a group of old Italian men play checkers next to a restaurant, where one can see aged Italian immigrants meeting for coffee. Other games also run on during these hours of the day and beyond: for example, in some bodegas—Puerto Rican grocery stores— games of dominoes are played continuously for hours and hours, even late into the night. Then there are the illegal gambling hideouts from which the public is barred.

After three o'clock in the afternoon one rarely sees an adult woman in the street. By this time cooking for the evening meal has started, and most children are out of school. The streets then are flooded with children of all ages, playing, singing, and shouting, while some, however, just gaze longingly from their windows at the streets and alleys below. Employed men and women also start returning to the neighborhood, and many take a bit of time to stop and chat for a short while in the street. By six or seven o'clock in the evening, dinner over, mothers and housewives are again on the sidewalks, perched perhaps on top of garbage can covers, chatting with neighbors who have also come down to watch the children. It is not uncommon to see a number of small Puerto Rican, American Negro, and other children, two or three years old, all being cared for by a five- or six-year-old girl of any ethnic group. On the other hand, one may also see a number of children whose mothers maintain a close watch to prevent children of other ethnic groups from playing with them and who warn them not to play with "Puerto Ricans" or "Italians" or "Negroes" because these are "bad" and will harm them. As night falls, particularly during summer, one of the avenues of Eastville is so jammed with people of all ages, including babies in carriages, that it is very difficult to walk there at all. Even at midnight on a summer night the stores of Eastville are open, the jukeboxes are blaring loudly, the men are gambling and chatting in the social and athletic clubs, cars drive by, children play and sing, men and women and whole families sit on stoops telling stories and drinking soda pop. North of Fifth and south of First Street, Eastville fades. Beyond its borders there are no crowds in the streets, and the whole tone of life—day and night—conditions, and standards of living are different.

At the end of August an outstanding annual social event takes place in Eastville, when one of the civic-minded churches of the neighborhood holds its bazaar. Various residents of the neighborhood operate the booths that sell hot dogs, pigs feet, *pasteles, pastelillos, alcapurrias,* and candies, or the games, gypsy tent, and dancing, all for the benefit of the church. On such a night, youth dances in the streets to rock 'n' roll and mambo music, the dancers of the different ethnic groups tending to occupy separate but contiguous parts of the street.

When fall comes with cooler days, some of the old Puerto Rican women of Eastville, as on similar days of spring, watch the strollers in the streets with a towel draped around their arms like a stole. Gradually, the crowds grow thinner as the weather grows colder. Winter keeps Eastvillers more to their homes. Fewer people congregate on the sidewalks and stoops. But they do run down to the stores, which become the bad-weather centers for informal visiting with neighbors.

As winter pales and spring begins to soften once again, Easter marks a season for new clothes. The girls and women appear in light, bright colors, the young men and boys sport new suits and hats. Eastville has its own Easter parade, with Eastvillers snapping pictures of their friends and family members. On

Easter Sunday afternoon little girls of grade school age, in pink or blue or white dresses, ruffled and wide-skirted, with their new spring coats, bonnets, and white gloves, may be seen wandering aimlessly through the alleys where beans have started to sprout out of five or six inches of fertile garbage.

The Puerto Ricans
of Eastville

THE majority of Puerto Ricans living in Eastville today are recent migrants. The Puerto Ricans of Eastville also include, however, those who came thirty or forty years ago, when they were young adults or children, and those who were born and have lived in New York all their lives. Unlike their predecessors from the island of years ago, Puerto Ricans who consider migrating now do not have to wonder in a vacuum how they will manage to survive in a strange and complex new world. Flying over the Atlantic to New York has become a routine matter, and with direct, nonstop flights New York is now only a few hours from Puerto Rico. In fact, it takes only as much time to fly from San Juan to New York as it does to travel by bus or *línea* (scheduled jitney) between San Juan and Mayaguez in the island itself.

For over a hundred years Puerto Ricans have been migrating to the United States, but it is only since the end of the Second World War that migration to the United States has taken on social and economic significance for both the island and this country. Between 1900 and 1940 the number of Puerto Ricans coming to live on the mainland was relatively small;

yet there were Puerto Ricans in thirty-nine of the forty-eight states by 1910—seven years before Federal law was to declare that Puerto Ricans are citizens of the United States by birth. Between 1940 and 1950, the trend toward spreading out from New York City and migrating directly to other parts of the country was firmly established, and figures show that while during this period the migration to New York increased 206 percent, that to other states increased 443 percent.[1] In 1955, it was estimated that there were from 160,000 to 175,000 Puerto Ricans in the United States outside of New York [2] and from 500,000 to 550,000 in New York City.[3]

For years now Puerto Ricans have been hearing about New York City, have read about it in the local papers, heard about it on the radio, and seen some of its scenery in the movies. To have relatives, friends, and acquaintances already living in New York may even be more common than to have relatives and friends in other parts of Puerto Rico. New York is regarded as a place where many other Puerto Ricans live, and where they have improved their conditions of life, their health, and their general welfare. Many Puerto Ricans in the island have known New York migrants who have returned to Puerto Rico and boasted of their "good life" in New York, of their high standard of living, and of the employment opportunities for men and women in this city. They have personally known or heard stories about many who, with a few dollars and a plane ticket, came to "adventure," to search for a better life, and who

[1] Arthur C. Gernes, Implications of Puerto Rican Migration to the Continent Outside New York City, Address before the Ninth Annual Convention on Social Orientation, University of Puerto Rico, Río Piedras, December 10, 1955 (New York, Commonwealth of Puerto Rico, Migration Division, Department of Labor; mimeographed), p. 10.

[2] Clarence Senior, Puerto Rican Migration, Spontaneous and Organized (New York, Commonwealth of Puerto Rico, Migration Division, Department of Labor, 1955; mimeographed), p. 2; reproduced from "Puerto Rico, Migration to the Mainland," *Monthly Labor Review* (U.S. Department of Labor), 78, No. 12, 1354–58.

[3] *Ibid.*, p. 4.

found it. They may know personally those who failed on their first or second attempt and returned in discouragement to Puerto Rico "because things were bad in New York," but who shortly afterward undertook another trip with renewed hopes. New York has become a very important element in the hopes and dreams of the islanders for a better life and in the realization of their life-aspirations. As part of this dream pattern New York has also been brought into the geographic picture of the world with which Puerto Ricans are familiar. Names of such places as Brooklyn, the Bronx, and Manhattan are commonly known on the island.

In line with this, New York has been interwoven into the network of social relationships of many Puerto Ricans in the island, and continued and frequent personal communication is maintained through visits back and forth, correspondence, and the exchange of gifts. Obligations to immediate family members and friends are carried out almost as if the 1,400 air miles between the island and the city did not exist. According to Joseph Monserrat, director of the Labor Department Office of the Commonwealth of Puerto Rico in New York, 30 million dollars were sent from New York to Puerto Rico by postal money orders alone in 1954. This figure does not, of course, include the amounts in cash and presents sent from New York Puerto Ricans to their families and friends in the island.

Transportation facilities have long been a powerful ally of Puerto Rican migration to New York. For decades, New York has been the main outlet for Puerto Rican trade, and most steamship companies taking passengers and cargo to and from the island sail the route between the ports of Puerto Rico and New York. During the years of the Second World War, migration to New York was still small, but a new device was then being essayed in mass transportation—the airplane. With the close of the war, the unprecedented increase in airplane transport facilities in the world did not exclude Puerto Rico. An increase in the number of airlines, the direct flights between the island and New York City, the aircoach and unscheduled planes' low-cost fares, all helped to broaden the corridor between New York and Puerto Rico, making it a common skyway and relocating Puerto Rico from five days far away by steamship to a few hours near New York. Direct air routes between the island and other cities in the United States also shortened distances and brought more Puerto Ricans to the mainland.

Why Puerto Rican migration has received such impetus since the end of the Second World War, however, is more than just a matter of increased transportation and low fares. Over a period of years statisticians observed a mathematical correlation of .82 between net migration from Puerto Rico and national income in the United States.[4] This high correlation has linked Puerto Rican migration out of the island with favorable business and employment conditions in the United States. In turn, throughout periods of economic recession in the United States, many Puerto Ricans have returned to the island.[5] The vast social and economic changes which Puerto Rico began to undergo during the early 1940s, the increased income per capita, the broadening of employment opportunities, the improvement in health and general welfare, all combined to develop greater aspirations to higher levels of living among Puerto Ricans. If these could not be achieved in the island, they might be sought in the States, for migration had become one of the possible routes to social mobility. The increase in employment opportunities and the prosperity that followed the war in the United States opened up jobs for Puerto Ricans and pulled them not only into New York City but into other parts of the country as well.

Yet economic factors do not completely explain the motiva-

[4] Clarence Senior, "Migration and Economic Development in Puerto Rico," *Journal of Educational Sociology*, 28, No. 54, 152.
[5] *Ibid.*

tions for the great postwar migration either, for not all persons
of lower income groups in Puerto Rico are leaving the island,
nor can we say that they desire to do so. Puerto Rican outmigra-
tion clearly has an economic aspect, but this is linked to income
both as an economic reality and as a symbol of achievement of
the migrants' aspirations and hopes, which are social and psychological realities. Migration, then, can be looked upon as
one of the possible responses or actions developed to cope
with dissatisfaction—whether real or imaginary—with the
conditions of life that operate to frustrate achievement of desired goals.

For those who leave the island, New York is a Puerto
Rican frontier and not a foreign place. The airplane has helped
to make this so, and the familiarity migrants already have with
the city, plus the relative security they find here, helps to
keep it so. Looking at a neighborhood like Eastville, one can
learn to distinguish many facets of the Puerto Rican migration
to New York—the attraction it has, the elements of hope and
despair in it, its consequences in the lives of the migrants,
and their techniques for making sense out of living in New
York. All in all, the lives of Eastville Puerto Ricans present a
human story, of people who are making a satisfactory go of their
lives, of people who are struggling toward this goal, and of people who have already lost hope. Understanding Eastville, one
can understand many aspects of Puerto Rican life in New York,
but more than that, perhaps one can also gain more insight into
social processes of American society through seeing how these
are experienced by a minority group in a slum.

American slums are inhabited by underprivileged people
who identify as members of minority groups. Their definition
of the American way of life is based on their experience of
living in a slum. Slums represent a segment of American society which is characterized by low income, inadequate housing, and deprivation. They are one of the modes of adaptation of

a society that emphasizes success, abundance, and equality of opportunity, while at the same time it promotes mechanisms that effect inequality of opportunity and scarcity of material and emotional fulfillments, often through techniques of discrimination and prejudice. These factors affect the life-chances and the ways of life of many individuals and groups in the society. Bennett and Tumin in examining the consequences of inequalities in life-chances in the United States posed this issue for thought when they wrote:

> No society can reasonably expect standard performance and observance of rules where it does not provide equal opportunity to do so. If the meaning of democracy rests firmly on equality of opportunity, then our society has squarely before it the task of eliminating these disfunctional differences in life-chances. . . .
>
> Our traditional approach to social problems has tended to view these "problematic" phenomena as accidents and exceptions. Closer analysis would reveal their regularity and normality in a society structured as ours.[6]

Slum-dwelling people, whether Puerto Rican or not, are among those saddled with inequality of life-chances in the United States. Their ways of life and cultural adaptations are profoundly affected by this.

Coming to New York

For Puerto Ricans coming to New York today, their initial residence in the city may have been prearranged by friends and relatives already living here. Visiting Idlewild or Newark Airport, one sees, day or night, a number of persons who await the arrivals from Puerto Rico. On the other hand, there are those seeing off migrants who are going back to Puerto Rico for a visit or who perhaps, still in quest of a better life, have decided to return to the island to seek it there. Among the new

[6] John W. Bennett and Melvin M. Tumin, *Social Life: Structure and Function* (New York, Knopf, 1949), p. 183.

arrivals are those who have a job promised, or an offer of help to find a job. An individual may have found out that someone employed in the same factory where he works is leaving his job, or that the factory is taking on extra help. He may pass this information on by air mail to a friend or close relative who is willing to come if he can be assured of a job. Others may leave their jobs in the island to take the chance of the "adventure" in New York. Some receive tickets or advances from a close relative—a sister, brother, or parent—and little by little, the family reunites in New York. There are also those who decide to drop in, and arrive unexpectedly from Puerto Rico, feeling secure in the knowledge that they will be put up in the home of some relative or friend until they find a job and a place of their own to live, for, after all, this is what is to be expected from good relatives and friends.

As time passes and the years of separation increase between migrants and their relatives and friends in Puerto Rico, the bonds of affection and obligation start to weaken. There are instances in which kin and kin, and friend and friend are strangers to each other when they meet in New York. Time is a factor that operates both to ally and to separate groups of Puerto Ricans, and in Eastville one can see how recent migrants would be lumped together, while "older" migrants who "know the country" would form another distinct group, and those who were born and reared in New York or came in early childhood (*de muchacho*) would be regarded as a third separate group. A recently arrived migrant may have relatives in all these categories, but it is not until after he has been in New York for a while that he starts to experience the consequences of these groupings. Coming into what is superficially a "Puerto Rican neighborhood," recent migrants are to a certain extent spared some of the fears and anxieties about leaving their homeland and loved ones and facing a new country and a new life. The transition from living in Puerto Rico to living in the social settings of Puerto Ricans in New York, however, does not carry the character of continuity that may be implied at first glance. Profound changes have been taking place among Puerto Ricans in New York, in their ways of life and their cultural orientation, and the general tone and character of these are, to a large degree, responses or adaptations to the immediate conditions of life or the social contexts in which they live in New York City.

Here Puerto Ricans operate within at least three major social contexts: their particular socioeconomic class, the Hispano ethnic group, and the institutions of the larger society. In any class-structured society the individual has a position, rights, and privileges, which are granted to him by virtue of his class. His way of life and kinds of social relationships are conditioned by his position in the social hierarchy. Among Puerto Ricans in New York there are differences in income, occupation, and level of education, which are reflected in the way they live and in their values and social attitudes. The socioeconomic background of the individual in Puerto Rico also affects what is likely to happen to him should he migrate to New York, for his educational, occupational, and income standards will help to condition his choices and chances in this city. Partly, this is because his social set in New York will be determined, at least in the earlier years of migration, by his own previous set in Puerto Rico. So it is likely that if a Puerto Rican lawyer moves to New York, he will participate and be associated with persons of comparable status and occupation. His life will be substantially different from that of a bus boy, regardless of whether the lawyer has difficulty speaking English or of whether he prefers to associate with other Spanish-speaking individuals. Along the same lines, it is likely that persons who come to New York and live in a slum will be those from lower socioeconomic groups in the island. It is also probable that because of their particular social position the pressures of discrimination by the larger society will be greater toward the lower class and will restrict their opportunities more than they will those of the professional or business groups.

The second important context in which Puerto Ricans operate, and which acts to influence and control their behavior, is the Hispano ethnic group subculture. Many norms of behavior and social attitudes are associated with being a Hispano, and to this extent the body of standards provided by the Hispano group is an important factor in conditioning the social beliefs and ways of conduct of Puerto Rican migrants.

The third context in which they participate is that of the larger society of New York, the more distinctly American institutions, with their own norms, social attitudes, and standards of behavior.

These three levels of participation and cultural variation represent the noncontinuous span of cultural adaptations within which Puerto Rican migrants make their way in New York. Before migrating they form certain expectations about their lives in the city, and while they are aware that "things in this country are not like in Puerto Rico," rarely does the reality match their beliefs about New York.

In other words, both the social class and the extent of participation in the social activities of the ethnic group must be taken into account in understanding the social behavior of members of any ethnic group in a country like the United States. Such a group are the Puerto Ricans, who, while they may have shared similar standards of living, income, and socioeconomic background in Puerto Rico, have in New York developed certain important differences in their social attitudes, life goals, and standards of behavior. These differences are recognized among Puerto Ricans themselves, and are very much related to their experiences in New York City.

Soon after settling in New York, Puerto Rican migrants find that many of the expectations they have nursed about New York and their future lives here begin to shatter. For example, the norms and values they hold concerning "proper" and "correct" behavior are not the same as those held in New York—even among Hispanos. Here, many children, women, and men behave in ways that are "not proper" from the migrants' point of view. Individuals who left the island as adults and have been in New York for many years do not conform to their expectations either; they act differently and have learned to look at and weigh things differently from the ways in which such things are done in the island. Those who came to New York in childhood and those who were born and reared in New York deviate still more than those who came as adults many years ago. Puerto Ricans in New York do not help each other as they do in Puerto Rico and are not "united." New migrants speak frequently of the lack of consensus and solidarity among Puerto Ricans as reflected in the weakening and lack of recognition of mutual obligations among friends, relatives, and countrymen. This is a matter of particular concern when other people who are not Puerto Ricans, such as Italians, Jews, Germans, Russians, Irish, and Negroes, live in the neighborhood. These are perceived as forming groups of their own kind, and the members of these groups, which "are united," protect one another. Puerto Ricans are said to be considered "worthless" (*que no valen na'*) in this country because of their "lack of unity," which means lack of self-protection as a group. Furthermore, living in a slum presents threats of its own against which unity is needed for protection: Eastville is said to be a hangout for drug addicts and dope peddlers. The streets and alleys which serve as recreation grounds for children are considered dangerous to their moral welfare, because it is in these places that they meet "bad" children and are exposed to delinquent behavior.

As for jobs, total wages in New York are higher than in Puerto Rico, but now unexpected taxes and other deductions are made, and real income is not as large as anticipated. In their eagerness to obtain jobs in New York, migrants may accept employment for which wages are, dollarwise, higher than those they earned in Puerto Rico, but which are considered low-paying jobs when measured against prevailing wage scales in New York. These jobs are often seasonal or created to meet the requirements of production schedules and so terminate as soon as these have been met. Unemployment through dismissal is regarded as a reflection on the workers who are laid off, or, on the other hand, as unfair treatment to Puerto Ricans. It also affects the self-appraisal of the unemployed worker, as it is hard for him to believe that he is not being judged as a bad worker, because hard work is to be rewarded with permanent employment.

In New York living expenses are higher than in Puerto Rico and economic needs spiral. More things can be bought in New York, and many, such as furniture, clothes, and appliances that ease housework, can be obtained on the installment plan. Not only do such articles become necessities, they are also regarded as symbols of general welfare and success. In Puerto Rico these were considered to be available only to the rich. In New York lending companies offer loans through circular letters and suggest borrowing a lump sum to pay off small, separate debts. Unexpected layoffs and underemployment point up the ephemeral quality of Puerto Ricans' economic security and well-being, and while the search for another job continues, welfare aid may have to be secured or severe hardships faced.

These are only a few of the disappointments in New York that face recent migrants when they start to meet the problems of living here. In order to make it possible to continue living in New York with fewer difficulties, they must commence to learn how to cope with the realities of the life they find in New York. This is, of course, a matter of social learning. It is part of a struggle that touches upon every aspect of their lives in the city. There are social and cultural adaptations to be made on all sides if their goals are to be obtained, if they are to be able to bridge into American society from their position as members of an ethnic minority in a lower-class slum.

For Eastville Puerto Rican migrants the process of bridging into the larger American society has, to a great degree, been taking place in the context of social relationships with other Puerto Ricans both in and out of Eastville. These social relationships are like "schools" from which migrants learn informally about life in New York through information and example. In addition, Spanish-language radio, television, and newspapers provide guides to New York. This does not mean that there are no social relationships between Puerto Rican migrants and non-Puerto Ricans in New York, for in order to carry out their business of living here, such relationships are an essential. In other words, Puerto Ricans do not form an exclusive group, but are involved as neighbors, as coworkers, as employees, consumers, and in many other ways with non-Puerto Ricans. New York, in turn, has been making adaptations to its growing Puerto Rican population, and among others, city government services, a large number of business enterprises, and private social, medical, and religious agencies have been taking steps in that direction.

The culture of Puerto Ricans in New York cannot be characterized as "Puerto Rican," for it is not the same as that of Puerto Ricans in Puerto Rico. Rather, the culture of Puerto Ricans in New York has developed in accordance with the circumstances of their lives in this city. Even the Spanish language spoken in New York differs from that of Puerto Rico. Part of the learning that a recent migrant has to accomplish right away involves acquiring words and phrases in Spanish currently used here and not in the island. Many of these are derived from English and assimilated into the Spanish the migrants have brought with them. Nor is the new vocabulary static; it is constantly changing. Furthermore, there are cleavages among Puerto Ricans with reference to the language they speak. Those who grew up in this country ordinarily speak very little Spanish but are fully conversant in English; those who migrated to New York a long time ago have through the years picked up enough words and phrases in English to claim they can "defend themselves" (*defenderse*) in English. Others go to night school to learn English formally from native speakers. Among migrants, Spanish is not totally discarded, for it is the language of the home and the language to be spoken with other Puerto Ricans and Spanish-speaking persons. Children born or reared in New York, though, usually prefer to speak in English to their friends and parents.

Having other Puerto Rican friends and relying on other Puerto Ricans involves much more than just speaking in Spanish, however. By migrants the Puerto Rican group is seen as sharing common understandings, as pointing toward changes that are acceptable to Puerto Ricans, as well as against changes which would interfere with living lives of order guided by principles that are acceptable and understood. Participation in the Puerto Rican group cushions and eases the process of gearing the life of Puerto Rican migrants to American life.

The Puerto Ricans Define Themselves

The Spanish-language press, radio, and television refer to New York Puerto Ricans as the "Latin" or "Spanish colony" (Colonia Latina or Hispana), or sometimes as the "Puerto Rican colony" (Colonia Puertorriqueña). Occasionally the term "Boricua" (a derivative from Borinquen, the Indian name of the island, according to the Spanish conquerors) is used. Among Puerto Ricans who belong to the Spanish or Latin colony, the terms "Hispano" and "Latino" are used and preferred to "Puerto Rican" for self-identification.

Hispano and Latino have been in use for many years in New York, but their references have changed in the course of time.

In the past, Hispanos or Latinos were a small minority of intellectuals and middle-class professionals from Puerto Rico, Spain, and Latin America who lived in New York. By 1950, the Spanish-speaking, socially mobile persons of lower-class origins, who now considered themselves in a higher social position than the recent lower-class migrants from Puerto Rico, were calling themselves Hispanos.[7] More recently, the term has been extended to include all Spanish-speaking persons who reside in New York, regardless of their social and economic class.

In Puerto Rico, a Puerto Rican is someone born on the island, which is his country. He may be a member of the upper, the middle, or the lower class; he may come from either country or city; he may be a farmhand, a farmer, or a banker; he may be a millionaire, a salaried employee, or a wage earner. But whatever else he is, he is Puerto Rican and is not regarded as a member of an ethnic or minority group.

In New York, the terms "Hispano" and "Latino" have been substituted for that of "Puerto Rican," because the latter, in more ways than one, has become a "bad public relations" identification for New York Puerto Ricans. It is associated with unfavorable pictures of the behavior and respectability of Puerto Ricans, which are not necessarily true or real. Even when used in Spanish and by Puerto Ricans themselves, it may convey an assumption of undesirable characteristics of the persons referred to, and this, even if they are Puerto Ricans. Throughout this book the term "Puerto Rican" is used alternately with that of "Hispano" to describe persons born in Puerto Rico and their descendants who consider themselves Hispanos and members of the Hispano group of New York.

When referring to friends, or to persons considered "decent and respectable," the term "Hispano" is preferred by Eastville

[7] Edwin Seda, Acculturation of Puerto Ricans in New York: Participation in a Community Center (unpublished Master's essay, School of Education, City College of the City of New York, 1951).

Puerto Ricans. Recently arrived migrants soon learn that they are to call themselves Hispanos and drop their identification as Puerto Rican. They will probably not deny their country, but will resort to the linguistic subterfuge of Hispano to protect themselves from being characterized in a derogatory manner. They will tend to emphasize their particular home towns and municipalities in Puerto Rico, for to be accepted socially among Hispanos, it is important to know something specific about one's past and where one came from.

In Eastville one often hears dialogues like the following between persons who have just met on the stoop of a building, in a church, or a bodega, or while visiting in someone's home.

"I can always tell Hispanos. . . . Where are you from?"

"Puerto Rico."

"On all sides?"

"Yes."

"Where from?"

"San Juan."

"I am from San Juan, Calle de la Cruz, near Norzagaray."

"What family?"

"Rodriguez."

Formal introductions of an unknown person are rarely made unless the social positions of those to be introduced are known to the introducer. For instance, a person who is known to be a doctor is introduced to a brother or sister, or a friend of long standing, but not to a casual acquaintance whom one has met recently and who has not yet established his status clearly with the introducer. One of the common forms of relating personally, however, is by initiating a conversation in which one identifies oneself as being Hispano, in the sense of Puerto Rican, and by establishing this clearly. This particular approach to personal relations suggests three major social features of the Puerto Rican group. First, that being Puerto Rican and referring to oneself as Hispano is an entree for social relationships, and second, that the participants in the relationship have to establish the authenticity of their being Puerto Rican by showing some particular knowledge of the island, such as being conversant with a specific *municipio,* town, or city, and then a particular street there. Thus the identification is narrowed down to a level that no foreigner can reach unless he happens to have lived in the particular *municipio* for a long period of time. Third, the identification also calls for establishing that one belongs to a particular family. One's statuses must be defined and acceptable if a personal relationship of any continuity is to be formed.

Hispanos classify themselves into three major groups with reference to life-experience and time spent in New York City. Those who have lived here for many years (*los que llevan muchos años aquí*) are the first. Those who grew up in this country, including the second generation, *nacidos y criados* (born and brought up), and those born in Puerto Rico who come to New York in early childhood comprise the second. Recent migrants, those who have come in the last several years from Puerto Rico, and who are referred to in derogatory terms by "those who have lived here for many years" and by "those born and brought up" here as "Marine Tigers," are the third. (*Marine Tiger* was the name of one of the Liberty ships which made a number of trips between San Juan and New York after the war, bringing many thousands of Puerto Ricans to the States. It lent its name to the new greenhorns, and the name has continued to stick.) Important social and cultural differences appear among these three subgroups of Hispanos.

Old Residents

"Those who have lived here for many years" form the core of old residents from Puerto Rico in Eastville today. In this group are persons who migrated to New York as adults and who either brought their small children with them or bore their

children here. In general, the members of this group came during
the period between the two world wars. After their arrival they
settled either in Eastville or near by. Though some members of
the interwar migration who settled in Eastville moved out of the
slums eventually, having achieved socioeconomic mobility, others
remained and are still there today. They include a number of
individuals between forty-five and sixty. These old residents are
not unattached but live within family groups and now comprise
a grandparental generation. The strongly cohesive family organizations of which they are a part have contributed to stabilizing
the lives of these people in the context of Eastville, where they
live near or with their married children, their sisters, brothers, or
other relatives. Among these persons are found a number of individuals who are defined as Negroes by the larger community in
New York and who have remained within the neighborhood and
continued to associate and identify with Puerto Ricans as they do
not desire to be identified with American Negroes. They probably
will not be defined as Negroes in the Puerto Rican group, and
they live with their families in which may be found persons who
are distinctly white and are considered white by non-Puerto
Ricans. Such old residents as these respond to the American
social stereotype of Puerto Ricans as racially "mixed," and prefer
being classified as Hispano or Puerto Rican instead of as Negro.
Thus a reaction against what is regarded as a social disadvantage
has been transformed into a source of family and neighborhood
group solidarity which, in turn, serves as a source of emotional
strength, reinforcement, and support for the individual.

Around the old migrants also revolve a number of kin and
friends from their home towns and *barrios* in Puerto Rico who
have migrated at different times and who look to the old migrants
for protection, guidance, and advice. The old migrants have not
broken off their contacts with Puerto Rico, particularly with their
kin and friends there, and are expected to provide hospitality,
assistance, and guidance to new migrants. As a rule, the old mi-

grants in Eastville have picked up English only casually and informally, but they prefer to speak English when dealing with non-Spanish-speaking people. At home and in the intimacy of the family and friends of the Hispano group, however, they like to use Spanish as the language of conversation. The old migrants define their children as Hispanos, but as *nacidos y criados, criados aquí,* or *de muchacho.* To strangers they may identify their children as Americans, and a child born in New York is taught by his family that he is an American as well as a Hispano. These are ways of stating the higher status value and preference for individuals who are born and/or brought up in New York.

The Born-and/or-Brought-Up-in-New York

In Eastville this group consists of individuals ranging from infancy to their early thirties—the young people of a parental and a filial generation. In this category are included Hispanos who have lived in New York since early childhood and who received all or most of their schooling here. Being born and/or brought up in New York is considered significant for an individual on three different scores. The first is that, as a rule, those of this group have more formal education than their parents, and education is highly prized among Eastvillers. Second, recent migrants regard the men of this group as potentially good husbands. A fieldworker asked Margarita about her fiancé, "Is he a good man?", to which she replied, "He was born and brought up [here]," meaning that he must be a good man because such men help women around the house and do not run around. On the other hand, the women are not considered potentially good wives. They are said to have departed too much from what makes a good woman "good." The third factor entering into the positive appraisal of the born-and/or-brought-up is the fact that they are fully conversant in English without a trace of foreign accent and that they have been wholly educated in American schools.

Conversely, part of the disapproval of this group is based on the fact that going to New York schools and being exposed to life in this city have resulted in conflicts between them and their parents and between them and the Puerto Rican ethnic group over cultural expectations and ideals. One of the most frequently voiced discontents with life in New York concerns the children, particularly the daughters. Parents talk about how they have lost control over youth here. The young men in this subgroup, however, seem to subscribe to their parents' ideas about women, for they regard as preferred wives those of recent migration, and age is no barrier to this choice. Hence, it is not at all strange to run across a middle-aged woman, in her mid-thirties or early forties, being courted by a young man in his late teens or early twenties. Women migrants are supposed to be "good," in contrast to those who were born and/or brought up here, who do not respond to the cultural ideals of women as homemakers, dedicated to the interests of their husbands and children, and subordinating themselves to the demands of their homes. Male or female, when not conforming to the standards of behavior considered desirable by the Puerto Ricans of Eastville, the born-and/or-brought-up-here are termed "Puerto Rican," rather than Hispano, by other members of the group, even if they have never been to Puerto Rico.

The born-and/or-brought-up-group does not look toward Puerto Rico as "home." Its reference is New York City where social mobility can operate regardless of ethnic group. The self-identity of members of this group is not Puerto Rican. They regard themselves as different from their parents and the new migrants. As Lita Norte, a Hispano born and raised in Eastville, said—echoing her religious advisor—concerning her recent migrant husband, "We have a cultural conflict [in our marriage]. The Spanish men are different; I don't understand them."

Recent Migrants

Los que hace poco que estan aquí are at the bottom of the scale in the Puerto Rican group as it is represented in Eastville. Recent migrants include a large number of persons who do not speak English and who lack relatives or kin on whom to rely in case of need. As a whole, Hispanos born and/or brought up in New York regard the recent migrants as undesirable, particularly those who have no "respectable" relatives to protect them, and therefore have no way of obtaining acceptability through the status of their relatives and friends in the neighborhood. Those migrants who are illiterate and who look poverty-stricken because of their clothes and homes are considered ignorant and are the most undesirable of all. On the other hand, the Hispano group highly approves those who obtain employment, keep a clean, well-furnished apartment, and acquire other material symbols of well-being as these are recognized in Eastville. From the standpoint of social composition the recent migrants can be subdivided into the following categories.

Nuclear families. These are composed of father, mother, and their children, and perhaps the mother's mother. The pattern of migration is one in which the family is usually initially split, since the father often comes to New York first, obtains a job, and then later sends for the rest of the family. The father may stay at a brother's, a sister's, or a close friend's home. If the father has not secured an apartment for his family when they arrive, they, too, will stay temporarily with the relative or friend. As guests, they are not expected to pay for their keep, but they are expected to show their appreciation by reciprocating with gifts of money or goods, by verbal expressions of gratitude, and by approving of the ways of their hosts without complaints or criticisms. The hosts are expected to help the father secure an apartment for his family. This requires that the host accompany the father and explain to the landlord or superintendent the need of the family for an apartment, advising the father as to the payment of a fee for the apartment and as to the rental asked. If the father is unemployable because of a physical handicap, his kin are expected to aid in obtaining information about agencies and hospitals which can help in his case and to accompany him in his search for them.

Able-bodied, unmarried, young men. These migrate to New York after being directly asked by kin or assisted financially to come, or they come on their own and invite themselves to stay. They are expected to work and help support their families in Puerto Rico and perhaps, in turn, to assist them financially to migrate to New York. Here they settle in the home of a relative of either the immediate family or the extended familial group, or with special friends. That is, they stay in the home of a brother or sister, a niece or nephew, a cousin, or a godmother or godfather. These young men are to obtain employment through the help of relatives who are already employed. Relatives, bound by such obligations, try to locate employment opportunities through interpersonal channels—through contacts with their friends, their relatives, or their employers. Even if jobs are heard of through the press—usually the Spanish press or radio—the good relative still accompanies the newcomer personally or arranges for someone else to assist him in getting to places outside the neighborhood. These persons locate addresses, act as interpreters, and often speak for the newcomer in job interviews. The recent migrant is thus a protégé who is thought to need such personalized assistance. He is offered hospitality, but he is expected to take advantage of it only temporarily. From the standpoint of the migrant, on the other hand, he can help his kin in Puerto Rico because, since he is staying with persons with whom his family maintains relations, he has no expenses other than those connected with his job, his clothes, and his miscellaneous personal expenses.

Unmarried young women. These are a smaller category, the "daughters of family," maidens and virgins, señoritas, who have recently left school or poorly paid employment in Puerto Rico. Either they come at the request of female kin in New York who pay their fare, or they are sent to New York entrusted to the care of a female relative or godmother who is supposed to assume a parental role and protect them from men and "bad company." These young women may be expected either to seek employment and help their family in Puerto Rico, perhaps assisting them to migrate eventually to New York, or else they may be expected to help out in the household of the relative who sent for them and to take care of the children while the other adults of the household go to work. For the latter kind of work the young woman is not to receive wages, but she is provided for as a "daughter of the family," is considered a part of the family, and, as such, receives the supervision and sanctions of a daughter. She is expected to ask permission when she goes out and to obey and comply with her elder kin's orders. If she is gainfully employed, she is supposed to help her host financially and share in the household tasks with the rest of the women.

Mujeres (*women*). This social category, also a smaller one, is derived from the status evaluation, roles, and treatment that differentiate a virgin or maiden from a woman who has experienced sex, and who, even if she was legally married and a good wife at one time, is now unmarried either through widowhood or divorce. These women fall into three classes. The first is maidens who have lost their virginity; the second, divorced, widowed, and other women who had marital arrangements in Puerto Rico and no children; the third, husbandless mothers who are thereby heads of families.

In the first group are "daughters of family" who "made a mistake," or "to whom wrong was done." They may not have become pregnant, or even have had sexual intercourse, but simply engaged in intimacies with a man, perhaps only once. But if this has become known, as it usually does, either through the girl's confession to her mother or friends, or through the man's boasting of it to his friends, the girl will have lost her "honor." In the event that the parents cannot get the "wrongdoer" to marry their daughter, they may send her to New York in the care of a female relative or a godmother. In this way she is protected from the future social consequences of her "mistake," for example, becoming the prey of other men who will not marry her because she is not a virgin. This course of action protects the family's honor and saves face for them. Here these girls are expected to become gainfully employed, to help their families in Puerto Rico, to "mend their ways," and to try to marry properly.

The women who had marital arrangements in Puerto Rico but no children come to live in the home of a relative or a special friend. They are expected to become employed, for example, in a factory, and their personal independence is acknowledged, although they are supposed to behave as "good women." They are also expected to help the household financially, but not to "pay," and to share in the chores.

The husbandless mothers who are heads of families, the most numerous in this category, include unwed mothers, divorced and widowed mothers, and their children. These mothers migrate with one or more of their children, generally leaving the older ones in Puerto Rico in the care of their mothers, sisters, or close friends until they can send for them. They stay with relatives or friends in New York temporarily, where they are considered guests. They are expected to start their own households as soon as possible, either by seeking employment or by securing welfare aid for their dependent children, if they have small children, and they are to care for and support them fully without aid from the earlier migrants. Their migration is connected with trying to better their families, educate their children, and "live their own lives."

Disorganized persons. A small number of these, some chronically ill, some with severe emotional illnesses, deviants, unemployables, and so forth comprise the last category of recent migrants. They are sent here by their families in Puerto Rico to be taken care of by other members of the immediate family in New York. It is assumed that in this city they can not only receive better care than in Puerto Rico, but also that members of the family here are in a better financial position to care for them.

The "we feeling" among Puerto Ricans

IN the winter of 1955, August Robles, a noted hoodlum of the Eastern seaboard, was in serious trouble with the law. An ex-convict and much sought-after criminal in Maryland and New York, he was suspected of being the hired killer of a state witness against a former police magistrate accused of conspiracy for armed robbery. Robles was reported as hiding out in New York City. For three days hundreds of policemen searched the city for him in what the New York *Times* described as "one of the most dramatic manhunts in the city's history." [1] Then he was discovered in an apartment in El Barrio within walking distance of Eastville. Tipped off by a frightened woman, the police surrounded the building one Sunday afternoon, and for several hours there was a gun battle between the bandit and the police. It ended with Robles's death.

Hundreds of people had congregated to watch the battle from the streets, the rooftops, fire escapes, and windows near by. The battle, covered by local television stations, also made headlines in the New York press. Among the many people who went to watch the manhunt were Eastvillers, Puerto Ricans and non-

[1] New York *Times,* February 21, 1955.

Puerto Ricans alike. The well-publicized Robles incident caught
the imagination of many New Yorkers. Among Puerto Ricans
it posed many questions and mobilized social behavior that
revealed in dramatic form some of their basic attitudes toward
themselves, as well as their reactions to the larger American
society.

For days afterward the Robles case was a frequent subject of
conversation and comment in the homes of many Eastville
Puerto Ricans. It was also discussed by shoppers in the stores,
by friends and passers-by in the streets and on building stoops.
Robles was not from Eastville, and had been a total stranger
to Eastville Hispanos until the press made him a public figure.
The press did not identify Robles as Puerto Rican, yet Eastville
Hispanos identified him as such. His career of crime and its
end were described not as experiences of a particular individual,
but as having overtones and consequences for the Hispanos in
New York. Robles's actions were talked about as if they reflected upon Hispanos. Similar effects had already been evoked
by other cases of antisocial behavior involving Hispanos or individuals assumed to be so, even if the culprits had never been
known about before they achieved public notoriety.

After the Robles incident Hispano public opinion was mobilized. Among the reactions noted were those expressed by
recent migrant mothers who talked about the importance of
teaching children to respect, of how punishment—scoldings
and beatings—were necessary in order to prevent children from
growing up into Robleses. His life conduct was regarded as
something calling for moral indignation and as an example of
the result of improper ways of bringing up children in this
country. Other comments centered upon the broader implications of the Robles case for Hispanos in the city. It was said that
the police had been embarrassed at having had to call upon
three hundred men just to capture one. And now the police
could be expected to avenge this affront by being tougher toward

Puerto Ricans. But within this same framework, Robles was also regarded as a hero, whose conduct with the police attested to manliness and courage.

The corpse rested in a funeral chapel near Eastville. Hundreds of curious people—large numbers of Hispanos, among others—massed in queues, in between police horses and lines, for a chance to look at the bier. Among these were Gloria, a Hispano teen-ager born and brought up in New York, some of her friends, and a member of the field team. On seeing a cruising police car, Gloria commented wryly, "We had better be careful because now they'll [the police] do anything to the Puerto Ricans." Laughter from the other youngsters echoed her words while she continued in the same vein, "Puerto Ricans do everything wrong anyway—now they're [the police] going to be on the lookout."

After having had a look at the corpse, the youngsters continued their discussion of Robles. Mary said that now that Robles was dead and had made such a fool of the detectives it would go hard on Puerto Ricans, to which Jay replied, "Yes, I was surprised that they didn't have it all over the headlines that he was Puerto Rican. Yes, now they [the Puerto Ricans] better be careful because anything they do will be twice as bad."

The particular ways in which the Robles incident was talked about reflected many aspects of feelings of identification and solidarity, as well as conflicts about being a Puerto Rican in New York. On one level, the Robles issue was one of special concern for all Hispanos, regardless of how long they had been in New York. It had been seen as a "proof" of why Puerto Ricans are not considered acceptable in New York City, and it had also been seen as the way the unacceptable actions of a particular individual can be utilized by the larger society to justify and intensify prejudice against Hispanos. On another level, statements, like those quoted above, from young people born and/or reared in New York concerning Robles illustrate a set of attitudes that is widespread among youth and adults who have grown up in New York. That is, they consider themselves Hispanos or Puerto Ricans as they are so defined from the point of view of the larger society, but as outside the Hispano group when seen from the standpoint of the Hispano social group itself. These attitudes are simply manifestations of the social and cultural schisms running through the matrices of the Hispano group in Eastville, which, in turn, are aspects of the social and cultural divisions among Puerto Ricans in New York.

From the standpoint of American society, Puerto Ricans form a group. This is defined either as a racial group, an ethnic group, or a cultural group. From the point of view of official statistical sources, Puerto Ricans are individuals born in Puerto Rico and children of Puerto Rican-born women. But this criterion for identifying Puerto Ricans is not consistent: miscellaneous Spanish-speaking individuals, and odd assortments of dark-skinned individuals are frequently assumed to be Puerto Ricans. In general, Puerto Ricans are assumed to have a common and uniform culture and to share in individual and social behavior. There is a tendency to ignore individuality and to obliterate social and cultural differences among Puerto Ricans. From the standpoint of Puerto Ricans, there is a Hispano group in New York, but this is defined differently from the usually prevailing definitions of Puerto Ricans expressed by non-Puerto Ricans. The Hispano group includes Puerto Ricans, their descendants who may or may not be Spanish-speaking individuals, and also Spanish-speaking persons from Latin America and Spain. In this sense the Hispano group includes peoples who share elements of a common Hispanic historical heritage. The Hispano group is a communal form of adaptation of peoples of such heritage in the context of American life. Basically, the Hispano group, nonetheless, is formed by the Puerto Rican migrants and their descendants, and in some contexts "Puerto Rican" and "Hispano" are equivalent terms, to the point that

"Hispano" is a preferred term to "Puerto Rican" when referring
to Puerto Ricans.

The group owes its existence both to its own internal structure and *esprit de corps* and to the external social and cultural
pressures of the larger society upon Hispanos. Sources of solidarity and bonds of understandings among Hispanos are partly
derived from the historical common general cultural traditions
of the peoples who are considered Hispanos. But partly, too,
they are a reaction against the position of the group as an ethnic
minority in New York. In this sense the group exists as a social
body that protects its members from the hazards, strains, and
psychological dislocations that can be effected by lack of social
acceptance and by the handicaps to life fulfillments that act
upon members of minority groups, who are targets for prejudice
and bigotry. The bonds of solidarity among Hispanos, nonetheless, are not so effective as to offer foolproof protection to the
members of the group, for being incorporated within the larger
society, the Hispano group also shares and incorporates within
itself values, standards, and orientations of the larger society.
The culture of Puerto Ricans in Eastville is a slum adaptation
of the Hispano subculture of New York.

In a cultural sense, cleavages within the Hispano group of
New York mark sharp differences in ways of life, values, and
cultural orientations among the group members. In a social
sense, however, members of the Hispano group can be spoken of
as sharing many common sentiments of solidarity, as well as
feelings of belonging and being part of a social group. There are
ideals of behavior, standards of values, and rules for living that
are considered appropriate to Hispanos, rather than to others,
and there are forms of social control—sanctions and standards
of approval and disapproval—that emerge from the body of
ideals of behavior expected from Hispanos. In fact, many cultural diversities and behavioral expectations cluster within subgroups of the larger Hispano group, and each subgroup is

geared to the others as if they were all parts of a system, a system we can call the Hispano social group. This, in turn, is part of the larger system and the sets of subsystems that make up American society.

Because of the fluidity of interaction between the Hispano group and the rest of the society, many an irreconcilable duality characterizes the Hispano group. On one hand, bonds of solidarity and loyalty among Hispanos as a minority group are reinforced by "being in the same boat" with each other. They share a common position and common life-chances in American life. On the other, there is a tendency toward fostering separation and fragmentation within the Hispano group which calls for rejection, dislike, intolerance, and critical devaluation of Hispanos simply on grounds of being so. Many Eastville Puerto Ricans are pushed and pulled between these tendencies, though the conflict is more distinctly represented among those born and brought up in New York and by those who came to New York as young children. In other words, the social dissensions within the Hispano group are reflections of the cultural cleavages within the group. It is not possible to speak of a Puerto Rican culture in New York, nor even pretend to understand the culture of Puerto Ricans in New York in the light of the culture of Puerto Rico. To speak of the culture of Puerto Ricans in New York as if it were a uniform and homogeneous body of cultural standards to which all Puerto Ricans respond or adhere only leads to oversimplifying the cultural picture and to distorting and ignoring significant facts. Puerto Ricans participate within different subcultures of the city and within different subcultures of the Hispano group itself. The culture of Puerto Rican migrants in New York City will vary with reference to the socioeconomic class of the individual, which is largely a function of his degree of acculturation, and with reference to his position within the Hispano group, which is also a function of his class and extent of acculturation.

The Hispano society in New York is class structured. Its class system and the culture of its classes are not, however, wholly identical with those of the larger society. There is a tendency for individuals born and brought up in New York and for those who migrated in early childhood to conform to the class culture expectations of the larger society. Individuals who migrated in their adult years, on the other hand, tend to conform more to Hispano values and standards of behavior that are oriented toward bringing recognition and enhancement of self, not only in New York, but also in the island. The latter feature is a consequence of the continuity of migration, the back and forth movements between the island and New York, and the degree of communication between the two places.

It is possible to speak of the Hispano group as an ingroup when viewed from the standpoint of the larger society and its influences on Hispano social life and, in the same sense, of the larger society as an outgroup. The two groups, nevertheless, must be seen as interrelated with each other, neither existing in isolation from the other. This book, however, is concerned only with one of the subcultures of Hispanos in New York, namely, slum dwellers and underemployed or unemployed Puerto Ricans who live at the bottom of the ladder. In Eastville there are no well-to-do or professionals among the Puerto Ricans. A few have become skilled or white-collar workers. Their backgrounds in Puerto Rico were also characterized by poverty and deprivation. Individuals who at one time or another have achieved higher income and economic welfare have generally been moving out of the neighborhood. Old-timers in Eastville speak about former neighbors who improved their economic position and left. Moving out of Eastville is regarded as a step ahead, even if this does not actually accompany any material improvement. Only individuals with real or imagined social disabilities have stayed in Eastville after having improved their economic position substantially. Fear of encountering intolerable prejudice and rejection are given as explanations for not leaving the neighborhood. Yet one of the areas in which Hispanos, as well as other Eastvillers, seemed to show agreement was in judging the neighborhood a bad place in which to live. There was a stated preference to live elsewhere in the city rather than there.

Even within Eastville where all Puerto Ricans share being members of a lower-class slum subculture, significant differences are found among them with reference to the length of time they have resided in the city and the degree of Americanization achieved. These two factors are of basic importance in shaping the culture of Eastville Puerto Ricans and are essential to the formulation of any generalization concerning their cultural behavior.

From the standpoint of length of residence in the city, Hispanos range from those who have lived here all their lives to those who only yesterday, or perhaps only a few hours before coming to Eastville, were in Puerto Rico. In between are those who come and go to Puerto Rico several times a year, and there are also those like Maria Reto's father, who only came to paint her apartment in Eastville. From the standpoint of degree of Americanization Hispanos range from those who are thoroughly oriented toward American society and its values and who are native speakers of English to those who are thoroughly oriented toward Puerto Rican society and its values. While these extremes lie within the boundaries of the Hispano group, the central tendencies in the group represent intermediate kinds of cultural adaptations, or accommodations, to New York society. From the standpoint of acculturation, the Hispano group can be described as the main channel through which this process takes place. It provides a framework and model for adaptations: it has norms and provides social techniques through which Hispanos can channel their relationships with the larger society; at the same time it holds norms that emphasize resistance to change in conformity to demands of the larger society. Other

norms held are in varying degrees of conflict with each other,
bespeaking the consequent conflicts and unsatisfactory rewards
they provide the individuals who ascribe to them. In a sense
the cultural conservatism represented by emphasizing a preference for Hispano values conflicting with those of the larger
society is an aspect of the changing nature and general instability of the Hispano subculture. The conservative elements are
part of the functioning social order which acts to brake over-
whelming changes that could lead to strain, disorganization, and
chaos.

Hispano society is in a constant state of turnover, which adds
to its social and cultural instability. New arrivals from Puerto
Rico enlarge it day after day. Similarly, new departures of those
going back to the island deprive it of members. Other Hispanos who move into the outgroup and become indistinct from
the general American population through acculturation and assimilation are also lost. Despite all this, however, being identified
as a Hispano offers an individual a sense of belonging and stability that strengthens his emotional security. Otherwise, the
individual migrant finds himself outside the social avenue for
adaptation that the larger society proffers him, namely, becoming a part of the Hispano group. But the Hispano society can
only provide emotional and social shelter of a limited nature,
for it is a transitional social order, responding more to the demands of the larger society than toward meeting the needs of
the individual migrants. The frequent complaints of recent migrants that the Hispano group is not a united front are expressions of the migrants' awareness that the group does not respond
to their ideal of it as the bulwark of Hispano institutions, a way
of life, and a set of cultural values.

One of the circumstances in which pan-Hispano solidarity
appears most pronounced among those in Eastville is when an
individual is considered to have been mistreated or abused by
individuals or agencies of the larger society. Such instances

are likely to be judged as prejudice against an individual because of his being Hispano. This calls for sympathy toward the victim, expressed verbally to him, or even to strangers. Unflattering press reports on Puerto Ricans also provoke expressions of anger and disgust against "the Americans," and against persons considered responsible for having written or relayed the information. Prejudice is suspected in relationships with agencies or individuals representing the larger society, and individuals may argue defensively and hostilely with persons who presumably have acted in a prejudiced way.

In part, Hispanos accept indictments of prejudice against their group, as is demonstrated by their own claims that Hispanos "are all bad," that "the Americans are right in hating us," and so on. Yet antiprejudice civic campaigns or political appeals to Hispanos on the basis of civil rights and antidiscrimination legislation do not mobilize Eastville Hispanos to concerted political and social action. Such appeals are interpreted as exposing Hispanos to others, and furthermore, as associating them in the public eye with other minority groups, particularly as placing them in the same position as American Negroes. In this sense attitudes of Hispanos toward American Negroes affect their political behavior.

Another aspect of this behavior is the displacement of actions considered improper, such as criminality or delinquency, on members of other ethnic groups. This is clearly a mechanism of prejudice in itself. For example, when a crime is committed by a person with a Spanish name, it may be said that the accused is not really a Hispano, but someone from Cuba or the Dominican Republic who, purchasing or forging a birth or baptismal certificate, claimed to be from Puerto Rico in order to enter New York without a passport. Occasionally the New York press has carried news about undesirable aliens from those countries who did enter and remain illegally in the United States by claiming birth in Puerto Rico. These accounts have lent vali-

dation to the assumption that a criminal act attributed to a Hispano by non-Hispanos has not been committed by a Hispano
at all, but by some foreigner who claims to be Puerto Rican.
Thus his act is seen as stemming from his national heritage.

Another way of shifting the assumed responsibility of the
Hispano group for the actions of a particular individual is by
saying or implying that that individual, although Hispano, belongs to a subgroup other than one's own. For example, antisocial behavior, delinquency, bad manners, illiteracy, acceptance
of low wages, poor sanitary conditions, and so on are characteristics that New York-born-and-reared Hispanos claim as
those of recent migrants. In turn, recent migrants are likely to
say about a delinquent, a "bad girl," or some other deviant
that "he is from here," implying that he is not Puerto Rican.
Among the New York-reared Hispanos, this is a matter to be
expressed ambivalently. As one of them put it:

"They [my parents] don't like them. . . . They spoiled
everything for us. . . . Yes, because they're Puerto Ricans,
and things are . . . the way people treat Puerto Ricans, the
ones that ain't been here. Well, they thinking that if they're
Puerto Ricans, they ain't no good. They don't give a damn if
you been here, or if you just came over. They just classifies you
like the bad ones. . . . They came over, and the way New
York was, it was all right the way it was, until they all start
coming over. . . . They give the Puerto Ricans a bad name.
. . . Today all you have to do is tell someone you are a Puerto
Rican, and they classifies you with what they read, or what
they say in the papers, that you must be that way also.

"But it's not true because Puerto Ricans is just like any other
nationality. They's good and bad. Well, this, what they did
when they came here, they making it rough on all of us, people
that was born here, that's sorry that they have to say they's
Puerto Ricans. Well, the majority of crimes and all that today
is from Puerto Ricans, they say, and the records . . . the ar-

rests and all that . . . and they print that stuff in the papers,
and the people eats it up. . . . They think that all Puerto
Ricans are like that."

Hispanos, nonetheless, are expected not to harm the reputation of other Hispanos with members of the outgroup. Those
who are known to speak in a derogatory way about other Hispanos to non-Hispanos are criticized, and comments such as
"What kind of Hispano is he?" are made about him. Criticisms
of Hispanos as a group, or of particular Hispano subgroups, are
more permissible and in fact these can be quite deprecatory,
but the criticisms are to remain within the group. Criticisms
from outsiders, whether mild or intense, are not acceptable, and
can result in "putting on ice" or subjecting the critics to severe
criticism in turn.

In seeking and maintaining the cooperation of Hispanos with
the research team, it was necessary to recognize these characteristics of Hispano social solidarity, self-judgment, distrust of outsiders, and conditioned feelings of discrimination against the
group. The intentions of fieldworkers were often questioned. We
were asked if the study was interested solely in Hispanos and
whether Hispanos were being singled out for research. Comments were made about newspaper articles in "the American
paper" said to have insulted and discriminated against Hispanos. The fieldworkers had to be particularly careful not to
provoke feelings of resentment, to reserve their personal opin-
ions and judgments to themselves, and to avoid arguments.
Time—in days, weeks, and months of visiting informally, of
giving and gaining friendship and acceptance—was necessary
to obtain reliable data on materials not revealed otherwise.
Cooperation with the research workers was assured when in-
formants were convinced that it was the truth about Hispanos
the anthropologists were interested in. At first, this truth meant
a denial of the undesirable stereotypes and views of Hispanos
assumed to prevail in New York. Eastville Hispanos would in-

vite non-Puerto Ricans, and particularly professional people, to their homes to show them "we are not like the papers say." It was claimed the newspapers told lies about Hispanos when printing stories on crime and delinquency, conveying the idea that Hispanos as a group were criminals and delinquents. Their eagerness for recognition as "decent people" by the outgroup makes for self-appraisals which emphasize and exaggerate qualities of propriety and correctness. This implies acceptance of a basic premise of social discrimination: that the behavior of selected individuals on selected occasions can be used as a basis for generalizing about the behavior of a whole group. In self-defense Hispanos overemphasize those elements and characteristics of behavior they consider essential for bolstering the integrity and self-esteem of members of the ingroup in the eyes of the outgroup, while those who discriminate against them choose the opposite.

Discrimination on the part of the outgroup has been a powerful mechanism in splitting the Hispano group as a positive and creative source of social and emotional strength. It has operated negatively to increase the internal cohesion of the group as a defense against the threat that discrimination represents. It has also contributed to the acceptance by Hispanos of images of disapproval and devaluation of individuals for being members of their group. So for some Hispanos it is openly accepted and unquestionable that Hispanos are undesirable persons. Juan, a thirty-six-year-old migrant who has been employed in a restaurant since he came to New York in 1949, voiced his feeling when he said, "Our race, the Latin race, has spoiled this country by the use of drugs. That is why the Americans hate us."

There are Puerto Ricans, Hispanos themselves, particularly recent and old migrants, who, having come to this country in adulthood, proclaim the social inferiority of Hispanos. They are also outspokenly disapproving of American Negroes and West

Indians on grounds of their imputed behavior or race. At the same time they disclaim being prejudiced. There are others in this same group, however, particularly those who came from families oriented toward the traditional values of respect and dignity as qualities residing in the properly reared individual, who have no problem of ambivalence about being Hispanos. With pride and assertiveness they speak of the values and traditions of their Puerto Rican backgrounds without fear of being disapproved for being what they are. As an important aspect of their children's growth, these people try to see that the children learn to identify socially as Hispanos. Being Hispano for them revolves around emphasizing the ideals of the good life for Hispanos in New York and the proper and approved methods of achieving them.

For recent migrants, the most important and most desirable life goals and adaptations in New York are: working hard and being a "good" worker; valuing formal education and schooling; learning English while not forgetting how to speak Spanish; cultivating the desire to "progress" and get ahead, or "to get the feet off the dish," particularly through the education of one's children; being brave and assertive; not letting anyone take advantage of oneself, or "take you for a ride" (*no dejarse coger de bobo*); being quiet; being careful in the selection of friends and trusting only a very few; and preferring the unity and continuity of relationships with one's own family and cooperating and helping those relatives and close friends who are in need. With the social preference for white persons above colored ones is joined those of coming from a "good family" in Puerto Rico and restricting one's group of friends to those possessing desirable characteristics.

These social aims are taught to children from an early age. Mike O'Neill, a seven-year-old boy, born in New York of Puerto Rican parents and now attending one of Eastville's grammar schools, was indicating some of the ideals of recent migrant parents that he had already accepted when he said: "Most of my friends are Spanish, but we mostly talk English. When we talk to Spanish people we talk English to help them to learn to talk English. At home my father and mother mostly talk Spanish, but when the book men [credit collectors] come, they talk English."

To reach the approved group goals one may seek the help and alliance of God and saints. Prayers and the forecast of the future through dreams or revelations by spirits and ghosts may also assist in bringing desired goals to fruition or in clarifying what is in stock in the struggle that life presents to every man. Among migrants, destiny (the concept of the inevitable) and chance (the concept of luck or adventure) are seen as playing a part in determining the paths of their lives.

For old migrants, recent migrants represent old-fashioned people with antiquated ideas that the old migrants gave up when they became "modern." These ideas center around methods of rearing children, the definition of a good woman as one who stays home and does all the household work, who is subordinate and obedient to her husband, and the expectation that relatives will feel obligated to take care of them in case of need. For adults who were born or grew up in New York, recent Puerto Rican migrants represent ignorant people who do not know how to live modernly, and who, in their eagerness to be employed, work for low wages in inadequate jobs, get into trouble easily with the law, and contribute in these ways to increasing prejudice and discrimination against all Hispanos.

While actually there are no sharp contrasts in life ideals and social values among old and recent migrants who came to this country as adults, there are sharp differences between persons who migrated as adults and those adults and adolescents who either were born in New York or came to New York in early childhood (*de muchacho*). This gap is acknowledged by both subgroups.

The New York-born-and-reared Puerto Ricans are oriented toward the United States rather than toward Puerto Rico, and consider themselves New Yorkers and the United States their homeland. They place a high value on speaking in English, at the expense of Spanish; they reject identification with recent migrants and often express dislike and criticism of them. They frequently express ideals of success in life in terms of individual accomplishment and initiative without much reliance on fate. Life in New York is not conceived of as an adventure, and while progressing and getting ahead are life goals, their point of reference is American society, rather than Puerto Rican society or the society of other Puerto Ricans in New York, as is the case among migrants.

Looking at how recent migrants view their early experience in Eastville, one can gain insight into the whole Hispano group there, for it is those who are facing New York for the first time who are most affected by and aware of the changes that Puerto Ricans undergo in the city after being here a while. The pattern of Hispanos already established in New York becomes a social model of life in the city for recent migrants to follow. Newcomers from Puerto Rico soon realize that New York Puerto Ricans are not like Puerto Ricans in Puerto Rico. Either they revise their expectations of Hispanos, or else they are due for disappointments. This is one of the lessons they learn while living in New York. Soon after they arrive in the city, they become aware that Hispanos do not conform to how Puerto Ricans "should behave," and it is most clear that adolescents and adults born and reared in New York are much less Puerto Rican than are their migrant parents. Furthermore, the people who came years ago are not any more as they used to be. It is said that men, women, and children change in New York. The men become rascals and shameless (*sinverguenzas*), losing their sense of responsibility toward their wives and children. The women are said to become "free" (meaning morally lost); they smoke and drink without feeling remorse. And the children have no respect for their elders, talking back to adults as if they were their contemporaries. The Hispano group is not "united," Hispanos do not help each other and are not concerned about undermining other Hispanos. They are not like other groups of people, non-Puerto Ricans, that is, who also live in New York, and who give the impression of having unity based on their color, language, or religion—the Italians, Germans, Jews, Irish, American Negroes, and so forth, who to Puerto Ricans are not real Americans.

Relatives and other close family members cannot be counted on in New York to the extent that is necessary. Years of separation have made relatives practically strangers, to the point that if migrants come and stay with their kin here, the latter expect the migrants to pay for their rent and food and encourage them to move out as soon as possible. If one is too poor, one is not really welcome at relatives at all, not even for short visits.

While relatives and close friends usually help recent migrants to find jobs, the expectations from work in New York are not like those one had in Puerto Rico. The income in dollars is higher in New York than that which migrants earned in Puerto Rico, but being employed and earning more cash than in Puerto Rico does not mean that one is going to live better in New York. A larger amount of money is spent here for rent, food, and clothes than in Puerto Rico. Other economic needs also increase in New York: credit outlays are available for furniture, food, and clothes, and these are necessary to maintain the apparent prosperity that bestows social acceptance and a sense of fulfilling the goals of economic progress associated with migration. Yet there is no awareness of the interest increments accrued on debts, and there is great disappointment when a seasonal layoff and termination of employment mean that banks and loan companies will foreclose on the belongings for which partial payments have been made, without taking into consideration the word of honor of the buyer as a guarantee of payment at a future date.

Many services that could be obtained free in Puerto Rico have to be paid for in New York. Migrants find that any number of services that would have been deemed personal obligations and *noblesse oblige* in the island are not acknowledged as such here, not even by relatives. In short, they discover that they cannot rely upon the resources available to them in Puerto Rico to get along satisfactorily here.

In Eastville, or in any other neighborhood where there are large numbers of Puerto Ricans, migrants can get along in Spanish. Unskilled workers can get jobs where they need no English, for most jobs at the unskilled level require no special knowledge of English. Shopping, visiting, or carrying out other activities outside of the neighborhood can also be managed without knowing English. One may ask a friend, a relative, or perhaps one's small child to accompany him when attending to any business requiring English. However, the person asked to accompany one for purposes of translation may know as much or as little English as the one who requests the help. Living in a place like Eastville, migrants find a certain degree of solidarity that cushions and protects them from severe cultural discontinuities. But there are also dysfunctions from living in Eastville. A slum is a threat to the attainment of the desirable life goals. The children's recreation has to take place mostly in streets and alleys or in nonsupervised parks or schoolyards, and parents associate bad behavior with lack of supervision by responsible adults. In this area family controls are seen as breaking down very soon. Traditional techniques of enforcing good behavior "do not work any more," threatening the very existence of family life. Recreational facilities here make it possible for a child to play with other children whose parents are not known personally to migrants. Only when one has first had personal knowledge of a person's behavior and reliability can

he allow his children to play with the other's. Else one is risking that his child will learn bad manners and other forms of misbehavior.

Another threat posed by the slum involves interference not
only with the goals of recent migrants, but in some measure with
those of all who dwell there. Integrated social norms function
poorly in a slum, where people are expected to behave according to the standards of more privileged social groups, which
can seldom be fulfilled in the situations of life available to the
underprivileged. There is a high incidence of violation of norms
because of their ineffectiveness in providing the individual with
suitable personal and social adaptations. The slum has a culture
of its own. It is a way of life whose consistency is partly determined by the standard of living of its people and partly by their
position at the fringe of the larger society. Its code for living
makes allowances for behavior not necessarily tolerated by
other segments of the society, and it condemns behavior considered most appropriate in other circles. It harbors many individuals who lack personal controls and whose aggression is
discharged destructively. This, coupled with low protection by
the police, results in a circular snare for those who live in Eastville.

Recent migrants find in addition that many of their convictions about "how to act" are not approved or just do not work
either in the neighborhood, or among old Hispano residents,
or when they come in contact with the agencies and personnel
of the larger society. If they try to find jobs, buy goods, eat in
restaurants, go to hospitals for medical care, talk to teachers
about their children, and so forth, they encounter a problem in
establishing relationships with those involved. This problem has
been defined as a language barrier. Yet it is more than just communication of words, it is a barrier in frame of reference—a
wall in cultural understanding. New learning has to be acquired,
but unlike the social learning acquired to meet life in Puerto

Rico, it is a cultural learning that requires insight and know-how about more highly complex and heterogeneous kinds of behavior and standards.

From their friends and neighbors they acquire the notion that in this country children cannot be disciplined as they were in Puerto Rico because the police do not permit it, and that here children "belong to the government." Those parents who require obedience and enforce it on their children anyway seem to ignore this "interpretation" of the law, but the interpretation is widespread and effective in shaping the views of many a frightened Hispano parent. Newspaper stories about parents being punished by the law for physical abuse of their children are used to validate the argument that parental authority and even reasonable discipline are forbidden by the law in New York City. Parents who accept this view are likely to see their growing undisciplined child as a "problem," meaning, "he gives me trouble," or, "he does not obey," and they are likely to try to seek placement for the child in some *colegio* ("boarding school") where he can learn good manners and be corrected for his ill-behavior. This is particularly the case among mothers who live alone with their children or those whose husbands who are stepfathers of their children are not regarded as are disciplining fathers by the children.

When migrant mothers discover that their children now do not "respect" them, they claim that they try to secure "fathers" for the children. After they get them, however, they will probably find that these "fathers" are not acceptable to the children, who defy them and do not obey. In New York City such potential husbands are not the providers and the enforcers of paternal roles that the mothers hoped to find, but rather men they may have to support and care for, who will not undertake obligations toward them or their children. There will be a faster "breakdown" of familial controls in such mother-centered families than in those over which a permanent biological or sociological father, regardless of whether he is married legally or not to the mother, is the symbol of authority and respect. This may be so even if he no longer lives with the family.

Parents also find that when their children go to school, they are taught the desirable English language, but at the expense of Spanish, the language of communication in the home. The child is taught norms of behavior, unfamiliar to a parent in themselves, that are handled with techniques which are equally unfamiliar. The school does not teach what parents traditionally have accepted as education, namely the three R's. Their educational aspirations are frustrated when they discover that the schools "don't teach to read, write, or do arithmetic." In addition, the school stimulates individuality in the child, self-assertiveness, means of expressing creative abilities, and other things that do not fit the parents' conceptions of the role of the school, the status of children, or the kinds of knowledge which a child should be taught in order to become a good adult.

When the schools ask parents to let their children go on trips, picnics, and other outings, the parents find that they are expected to sign a waiver stating that they alone are responsible. This is unacceptable to parents, for they expect adults to whom they entrust their children to act as substitute parents and assume full responsibility for their safety and conduct.

The children, on the other hand, soon realize that if they learn conversational English their status in the family will improve. The English-speaking child will now be the interpreter for his father and mother. He will be a major linking factor for his family with the institutions of the larger society. He may have to miss classes to accompany his mother to hospitals and schools, and on errands that require the services of an interpreter.

As husbands, Puerto Rican migrants will find that their wives have acquired ideas about women's "freedom" which call

for the husbands' helping with household duties and granting
their wives greater privileges. Even if the ideas are not put into
practice, they may affect the husband's role as undisputed head
of the family. And if the wives are employed outside the household, the husbands find that their authority over their wives is
seriously threatened.

Migrant wives will find their responsibilities and obligations
increased, even if they explain this in terms of having "greater
freedom." Wives who were confined "inside the house" in
Puerto Rico, and were not expected to have "know-how" in
shopping and dealing with schoolteachers, welfare workers, doctors, and housing agencies, in New York City are delegated
these responsibilities by their husbands, unless the husbands
are unemployed. In that circumstance the husbands can substitute for the wives.

Women also find that the institution of consensual marriage,
a union into which they entered by mutual agreement with a
man, without going through a formal religious or civil cere-
mony, is regarded differently in New York than in Puerto Rico.
Here, such a union is considered immoral and without promise
of stability. The children of it are also cast in an unfavorable
light. While the institution of *querida* (husband's mistress) may
not be a threat to the stability of a legal marriage in Puerto
Rico, here it is likely to mean desertion of both the wife and the
children. Yet widely held is the belief that in New York
women are less helpless, that there is more "government protection" for them and their children than in Puerto Rico, and
that this gives wives power to bargain with their husbands.
Wives here find it easier to take their husbands to court if they
want redress.

When recent migrants arrive here, they find that the evalua-
tions they had made of their families, which were those accepted
in the *barrio* or *pueblo* they came from in Puerto Rico, are
either not used or not taken into account in New York. They

learn that family "connections" and social prestige classified as "poor but decent" do not count any more. Here, when migrants are called "Puerto Rican," it is a term of derogation, so they start referring to themselves as "Hispano." They are often told they are "ignorant"; sometimes people of the outgroup even tell Hispanos that they do not know their own names, or what those of their children are. Migrants are also told that they do not know how to live, how to bring up their children, or how to relate to their husbands or wives. They are expected to be militant Catholics, although they may well be Protestants or have never attended any church service, considering religion a system of beliefs that can be practiced either in or out of church. They are regarded as "irresponsible" if not legally married, even those who have lived in a stable marital union for years, fulfilling the basic obligations expected of them, both as spouses and as parents. They are expected to have a standard grammatical knowledge of Spanish and a large Spanish vocabulary, yet actually they will have had almost no schooling and will have learned their tongue largely from illiterate parents and friends. Migrants are expected to try to learn English, but they consider that only children are capable of learning, and that they just cannot.

Recent migrants regard these expectations of behavior as yardsticks of the larger society to appraise and judge them. In principle, the expectations of Americans are considered sound and good, but it is also admitted that there are ways of behaving that are proper for Americans but not for Hispanos or their children. There are times when a migrant cannot help but say that this is a crazy country; yet conscious efforts are exerted to understand and accept demands made by the larger society. It is particularly in relation to gaining approval for one's growing family that approval from Americans seems most important, for the future of one's children is seen as closely related to this approval. Nonetheless, a person cannot accept everything that "the Americans" say, for "they just don't know." At home one should keep trying to teach the children to speak Spanish, to count, and to appreciate songs and music from Puerto Rico and other Latin countries.

Important also is striving to be accepted by Hispanos, in many more areas than in which the approval of Americans is sought. It is not important to keep up with the Joneses, but it certainly is important to keep up with the Menderos or the Perezes of one's home town and of the Hispano ethnic group. Feeling approved by Hispano standards acts as a bulwark to self-evaluation and is a reflection of how good and proper (*correcto*) one can be. It is also a yardstick of how well or how badly one has done in New York. Sociologically, the Hispano ethnic subculture merges migrants into the culture of the city while sheltering them from many of the stresses and strains inherent in migration and in the social system of the city. But the Hispano subculture is not a stable system. It is also characterized by conflicting values and norms of behavior, so within it, too, migrants will find themselves in situations of conflict.

The high value that the larger society assigns rapid assimilation and the low value that it assigns "looking and acting different" place Hispanos, particularly recently arrived ones, at a disadvantage. While enjoying certain psychological comforts, such as a feeling of belonging in the Hispano group, and finding norms and social values that are compatible, migrants also discover that this kind of adaptation paves the way for conflicts, disapproval, and other discomforts in the New York community. In addition to this, they also find themselves in the midst of the conflicts of the Hispano group itself.

One of the pivotal areas of conflict within the Hispano group and in the relations of Hispanos with the larger community is manifested in the field of racial issues. These are of major importance, for they have a strong impact on the life-careers, self-evaluation, interpersonal relations, and eventual assimilation of

Hispanos. In Puerto Rico, as in the United States and other societies of the world, people are classified for certain social purposes into ethnic, racial, or nationality groups. Such classifica-
tions are used to group people on the basis of what appear to
be physical, linguistic, or cultural characteristics. Social relations, the ways men will be expected to behave toward each
other and think about each other, are permeated with the beliefs they hold about their race, nationality, or language.

One of the outstanding contributions of American anthropology has been to point out the lack of real or logical connection between racial, cultural, and linguistic groups. Still, in
many scientific circles, as well as in popular thought, conceptions about race involving cultural and linguistic elements are
presented without recognizing that these lack scientific reliability, and are assumed to be unquestionable truths and correct statements. The term "race" means something, but it
means one thing to modern biologists and physical anthropologists, and something else to those who speak about race
in any other sense. From the point of view of modern biology,
a race is not a group of people who speak a common language;
nor is it a group which shares a common cultural or religious
tradition; nor is it a group of people who seem to look alike or
to have similar body shapes and skin color. Race is a classi-
ficatory device used with reference to certain aggregates of
inherited characteristics of living organisms, plant or animal.
To biologists, races are based on differences in gene inherit-
ance. The inherited genes of any population of plants or animals are not visible; they cannot be recognized by the naked
human eye; that is, they are not necessarily manifested in the
physical appearance of individuals. While this does not deny
that physical types, based on appearance, can be established
in human or other populations, it also means that physical
types per se are not races in a genetic sense.

Human beings with a common physical appearance do not

necessarily speak the same language, nor must they adhere to the same culture, or vice versa. Human beings who may resemble each other in a number of physical characteristics may be placed in different racial groups, in accordance with how and with which characteristics are considered as criteria for race. This concept of race, then, is relativistic; it reflects cultural definitions, but not necessarily genetic attributes.

When people speak about races as if these were something they see, they are speaking about race in an altogether different way from the modern biologist. Race, however, makes sense to them in terms of their common life experiences, regardless of whether the term is employed in its correct scientific sense or not. For example, the term "race" is used conventionally in the United States and other Western societies to describe and evaluate individuals and groups in connection with what are assumed to be their innate characteristics and behavior. Assumptions or mistaken facts or both can be examined as if they were objective and verifiable phenomena only in terms of what they are—that is, the ideas and beliefs of a society concerning how people are grouped either as races or ethnic groups, or that part of the society's culture which governs rules of behavior that guide interpersonal and intergroup relations with such groups. Within this framework race is a social phenomenon, which can be appropriately called "social race." [2] Because these are aspects of social behavior, they are subjects for study by sociologists and related social scientists.

Both in Puerto Rico and in the United States social race is an important aspect of social life, but race is looked at, defined, and appraised in different ways in the two countries. Racial attitudes, ideas of racial equality, superiority, or inferiority, are all learned behavior. They are neither inherited nor a product of human instinct. Regardless of how deep convictions about

[2] Charles Wagley, ed., *Race and Class in Rural Brazil* (Paris, UNESCO, 1952), p. 11.

race may be, racial attitudes are acquired. They are part of the
lore or social learning of individuals in any society where
they appear.

When ideas about social race in a society convey the notion
that people assigned a certain race share behavior characteristics on account of it, racism is the result. To describe what
happens when individuals who are members of the same linguistic community or the same cultural group are judged to be
characterized by the same personality or behavior responses,
we shall use the term "culturism." Both racism and culturism
are forms of prejudice, each using a different point of reference
for its justification, regardless of whether the members of a
group are all considered to be "good" or all "bad." Culturism
involves the assumption that each individual is representative
of his whole national or minority group culture, and that regardless of the uniqueness of his personality, of changes in
the circumstances of his life, and of the learning situations
available to him, he will continue to be immutably attached
to the standards of behavior of his ancestors and to the cultural
traditions of his group. The basic error in racism is repeated in
culturism: both ignore the fact that social behavior is learned
and not an inborn quality or an instinct. Nor are individuals
replicas of their fellow group members. As members of a society individuals learn standards of behavior and roles to en-
act prescribed ways of action. This makes it possible for the
social order to operate and for individuals to act normally or
in conformity with their society's standards.

Some social groups in a society may have acquired greater
prestige and power than others. Those at the top of the heap
may consider themselves better, and those underneath may
agree. These are value judgments rather than proof of inborn
superiority or inferiority. Some mechanisms such as social discrimination may be resorted to for maintaining power groups

in their position (social discrimination excludes others from
joining their ranks). Discrimination may be practiced against
members of groups even when the characteristics associated with
those group members and used to discriminate against them
have disappeared. That is, individuals may have learned how
to speak American English, just like a native speaker, yet they
may be considered "Italian," "Puerto Rican," or "Jew." Individuals may be born in this country and have experienced their
whole lives here, and still, they may be discriminated against
for being foreign. Persons having some African descent may
look as if they conform to the standard of being white in physical appearance, and yet they are still discriminated against as
Negroes.

Hence one can speak of the grounds for discrimination as
being inconsistent and unrealistic, to say the least. The social
consequences of discrimination are a waste of human resources for a society, as by it, the society is deprived of developing the creative forces of individuals, either because
their opportunities are cut down, or because both those who
discriminate and their victims utilize energies in an irrational
struggle that could be used more fruitfully otherwise. Members
of a group against whom discrimination is practiced, tend to
stay in enclaves of their own to protect themselves from the
trauma and rejection of discrimination. They become partially
isolated from other segments of society, while consolidating
and retaining their own group distinctiveness. Furthermore,
as the discriminated group is part of the larger society, it is
affected by it, and particularly those individuals who adopt
overt symbols of the larger society are likely also to adopt the
same discriminatory attitudes as the larger society toward their
own group, and hence reject and dislike their group wholesale
and themselves for being part of it. These factors make for a
great deal of personal and social dissatisfaction, for they in-

volve conflicts and dilemmas which often have no resolution. As a minority group New York Puerto Ricans exemplify these processes to a remarkable degree.

Among Puerto Ricans there are those who are white and range from blonds, with blue eyes and reddish complexions, to brunets, with light olive skin colors and curly or straight hair. At the opposite pole are those who have the dark brown skin color, kinky hair, broad noses, and thick lips associated with Negroid characteristics. In between are a great variety of combinations in physical appearance and characteristics. Names are no clue either. While most Puerto Ricans have Spanish names, it is not uncommon to be a Puerto Rican and have an English, Irish, French, German, or Italian name. In Puerto Rico being Puerto Rican means having been born on the island; it carries no implication of being a member of an ethnic or a minority group.

As in the United States, however, in the island two major racial groups are recognized socially; they are white and Negro. But the recognition of these two groups does not result in the formation of two distinct subgroups of caste-like separation as it does in the United States. In Puerto Rico the number of categories recognized between the two extremes of Negro and white mark degrees of racial departure from both, but mobility in this continuum is possible even within the lifetime of a particular individual. Much social interaction takes place and many interpersonal relations of an intimate and warm nature occur among individuals regardless of whether or not they have Negro ancestry and whether they look Negroid or white, though there is a stated preference for being white. All other things being equal, it is a social advantage to look white rather than Negro. This is particularly true in the upper and middle classes and is a factor in social mobility. In classifying individuals by race the main physical indices selected are those of skin color, hair type, and width of lips and nose. Having immediate Negro ancestry does not necessarily peg an individual as Negro, for race is more a matter "of appearing to be" than of ancestry. When ancestry is taken into consideration as a criterion of race, reference is made to "being of the white race" or the "colored race." In socially mobile groups, and in the upper classes, a marriage between two white-looking persons known to have Negro ancestry may be discouraged by parents on the grounds that "the race should not be spoiled" by taking a chance on having offspring that may not look white. A white person who has no known Negro ancestors, a *hijo de españoles* (child of Spaniards), may use his whiteness to gain social mobility by marrying someone who is better off and hence in a higher socioeconomic position, whether his appearance is white or Negroid. Children born to parents who appear to be white and yet have Negro ancestors may be considered white and not necessarily Negro, as they would be in the United States.

The existence of intermarriage between people of different racial heritages has long been recognized in Puerto Rico. Since early in the days of Spanish colonial domination, the strongest barriers separating the people of the island have been those of a class system based on wealth. Complementing the many combinations of complexion shades, features, and hair forms that are seen among the people of the island, a number of intermediate categories indicating degrees of either whiteness or "color"[3] are used to classify individuals. The term *trigueño* (brunet) is applied both to white persons who have brown or black hair and tan or light olive skin color and, by extension, to persons whose physical appearance would place them as Negroes if that were the only criterion of race. This not being so, *trigueño* is used to avoid the term "Negro" for persons of respect, because, besides race, there are other

[3] C. Wright Mills, Clarence Senior, and R. Kolsen, *The Puerto Rican Journey* (New York, Harper, 1950), pp. 26 *et seq.*

social and personal factors, such as wealth and education, which determine a man's worth and social position. It is not proper to call persons of respect "Negro." If used in that context, it is considered quite blunt, or even insulting. Yet, the term "Negro" may be used to address a person in a friendly and loving manner, and in this context it has no manifest reference to social race.

Other terms used to describe or classify individuals racially are *indio, grifo,* and "mulatto." An *indio* (literally, Indian, but not to be confused with individuals of East Indian or American Indian ancestry) is characterized by his thin or medium nose and lips, and has either straight or curly hair. The children of *indios* are *indios* only so long as they look like *indios.* Those who want to lower the rank of an *indio* would refer to him as Negro. The main index of the classification *grifo* is hair. *Grifos* may have very light skin color, thin noses and lips, but their hair is kinky, which is synonymous with "bad." Mulatto refers to a person who has kinky hair and dark olive skin.

Whether an individual is to suffer discrimination for not being "white" will be tested on the social ladder. Racial discrimination is one of the many tools used to limit the chances for upward mobility in the society. For poor whites, however, the obverse can be true. They may use their "whiteness" as a technique for achieving upward mobility for themselves by marrying persons who are not considered white but who are in a higher socioeconomic position. For the wealthy who do not look white the society usually overlooks their race, unless they fall within the extremes of darkness of skin color, and often no reference is ever made to their color. But for lower-class persons who do not look white reference to their race or color may be quite open. The term "Negro" is used to describe with contempt a Negroid person considered to have a lower social position, or even to belittle the social importance or rank of a person who is socially white by his wealth but not by his appearance or ancestry. Thus racial attitudes in Puerto Rico involve ambivalences that rotate around the cultural ideal that there is no racial prejudice among Puerto Ricans while social class is strongly associated with race.

If in Puerto Rico social race is subordinate to social class, in New York it is central to Hispano life. As a social factor, race becomes acutely manifested among migrants early in their New York stay, and it continues to be embedded in the matrices of the social relations of Hispanos. Lower-class persons in Puerto Rico are not very much involved in the racial aspects of social mobility, since their mobility is quite limited, but in New York lower-class Hispano society is socially mobile. Struggling for acceptance and accomplishment in New York, Hispanos acquire new meanings for their ideas and beliefs about race, which now assume greater importance and have stronger emotional content.

Among old migrants and individuals who grew up in New York, the term "Hispano" itself is often used to indicate the social race of an individual. This is particularly true if the person is liked and respected. Among recent and old migrants, the terms *trigueño, indio,* and *grifo,* as well as white and Negro, are used with reference to both Puerto Ricans and members of the outgroup. So an Italian may be described as *un Italiano trigueño,* or an American Negro who is a friend, may be spoken of as *un Americano trigueño.* An individual who appears to be white is considered white by Hispanos even if his father or mother looks Negroid, and vice versa. Mulatto is seldom used in New York. Instead, it is Negro or *trigueño,* depending on whether the person referred to is being approved of or belittled. Persons who are being talked about in their absence may be referred to as Negroes, but they will probably be described as *trigueños* in their presence. The term *indio* is also used in Eastville, and as in Puerto Rico, with reference to persons who have brown skin and straight or curly hair.

The chart which follows compares the various terms used by the larger society, the Hispano ingroup, and individual Hispanos referring to themselves.

References of Outgroup	References of Ingroup	References of Individuals Describing Self
White	White	White
	Trigueño Hispano	Hispano
	Grifo	Trigueño
	INTERMEDIATES [a]	
Puerto Rican or	Negro	De Color (of color)
"Mixed"	Trigueño	Trigueño
	Indio	Hispano
	Grifo	Indio
	Hispano	
Negro	Negro	De Color (of color)
	Trigueño	Trigueño
	Indio	Hispano
	Grifo	Indio
	Hispano	

[a] A category to include the numerous racial terms used by Puerto Ricans, introduced by C. Wright Mills, Clarence Senior, and R. Kolsen, in *The Puerto Rican Journey* (New York, Harper, 1950).

Hispanos can be grouped with reference to how they regard race and with reference to the social race they are assigned by the larger society in New York. There are those individuals considered Negro in Puerto Rico, "Puerto Rican," or "Spanish," by the outgroup in New York, and Negro by the Hispano ingroup; those considered white in Puerto Rico, white by the ingroup and the outgroup in New York; those considered to be in intermediate categories in Puerto Rico and by the Hispano ingroup, Negro by the outgroup in New York; those considered white in Puerto Rico, white by the ingroup, and Negro by the outgroup; and those considered to be in intermediate categories or to be Negro in Puerto Rico and by the Hispano group, white by the outgroup in New York City.

Among recent migrants are found those who had some prior

awareness that race in New York is a different matter than in Puerto Rico, particularly with reference to Negroes. Through letters, conversations with returning migrants, and newspapers in the island, it has become common knowledge that there is prejudice here against Negroes and that Negroes are located in separate districts from whites. To many migrants these practices do not seem discriminatory, but rather are often justifiable when exercised against American Negroes, but not so when they are extended to Puerto Rican Negroes. Thus, being identified as Negroes is often a major threat for Hispanos.

In Eastville conflict resulting from the social racial situation arises primarily in those individuals considered intermediates by the Hispano group and Negroes by the outgroup, those considered intermediates by Hispanos and white by the outgroup, and those considered Negroes by the Hispano group and "Puerto Ricans" by the outgroup. Those who were Negroes in Puerto Rico and are still Negroes among Hispanos and Negroes according to the outgroup, and those who were white in Puerto Rico, are still white according to Hispanos, and are white in terms of the outgroup find straight bridges to social race adaptations that conform to the demands of the larger society. Intermediates, on the other hand, occupy ambiguous positions in New York, and though they may learn American orientations, they are likely to remain unassimilated for a longer time than those who are either white or Negro according to the Hispano group itself. In this way concepts of social race operate to halt or to foster assimilation, that process whereby individuals lose their identity as members of ethnic or social racial groups.

Yet social race does not deter Puerto Ricans from learning adaptations to American society. Intermediates have more difficulty finding a place for themselves in the larger society because it divides itself into only two parts, Negro and white, and intermediate Hispanos continue to emphasize the desirability of whiteness in a society where many are not considered white.

They do not want to be identified as Negroes, and this is where the larger society is likely to place them. One finds in Eastville individuals who were born in New York and educated in the city's public schools, who have no loyalties toward, knowledge of, or social relationships with Puerto Rico, and who express strong dislike for Puerto Ricans, but who have continued to live within the context of New York Hispano society. These are generally intermediates, and this is their adaptation to American society.

Ralph Santos, for example, an intermediate young man born and reared in New York, was sitting one day on a stoop when a fieldworker approached him and asked him in Spanish if he were Puerto Rican. Ralph laughed and replied that he was, adding, "You thought I was a Negro, didn't you? Yes, because I look like a Negro." Trapped in his desire not to be identified as a Negro, Ralph speaks of the "colored people" and the "Spanish" as different groups. Describing his feelings about the Puerto Rican migration to New York, however, he says:

"It reflects on me this way . . . the majority of people coming from there are illiterate and, well, the various things that people have to say about them, such as they are coming from Puerto Rico and not wanting to work, they work for such wages as thirty dollars a week, making it hard for guys like me who have been brought up and raised in this country to obtain work at the wages we are used to getting."

Ralph's ambivalences concerning group identification are not atypical of others in his position. Being classified as "Puerto Rican" by the outgroup is preferred to being classified as Negro, even if the term "Puerto Rican" carries undesirable connotations in the larger society which have been adopted by Hispanos themselves. Angela Elias who was a Negro in Puerto Rico, and is a Negro among Hispanos, but a Puerto Rican according to the outgroup, helps to explain this preference. She regards

being considered Puerto Rican by the outgroup as an outlet to
a better status. "If you are dark," she says, "you can't go near
[white society in Puerto Rico]. It is not like that here. There it
is all like that. . . . If you are light and you don't have the right
kind of hair, then you can't go [participate with the whites]
unless you rich." In Puerto Rico she was neither light nor rich.

Mr. Lenk, a teacher in an Eastville public school, informed
a fieldworker with surprise that he had asked Mary Ramos, a
nineteen-year-old girl, what she wanted most in the world. She
replied, "To be white." "But you are white," he told her. "No,
I am not," she insisted. Mary is a light brunette with curly hair
and thin facial features, yet she does not consider herself white
because of her hair. She told a fieldworker that once she had
been coming down the street when she met Jack Velez, a Negroid Hispano, who told her to straighten her hair because it
was "bad." This, she added, embarrassed her very much because "there were other people [not Hispanos] present who
heard it."

Mary Tomez, a Negroid woman born and reared in New
York, related that the first time she ever felt "racial prejudice"
was when she was eleven years old. She met a girl in the street,
recently arrived from Puerto Rico, who told her that she did not
speak to Negroes. And, said Mary, "She was only four shades
lighter than me!"

Sylvia Ornes, an old migrant woman who is defined as white
and considers herself as such, speaks about race in a somewhat
neutral vein. "My sister in Puerto Rico, she is very poor, but
such a clean woman. She is *prieta*, black like a piece of coal."
Nina Lugo, an old migrant who is white in New York, though
not among Hispanos because of her kinky hair, once volunteered
to a fieldworker that she came from a good white family, but
that her neighbor, Angela Solon, had done a "work" (used
witchcraft) on her and made her hair "bad." Alicia Olmeca, a

white woman who has lived in Eastville for over fifteen years, called her son's fiancée and told her that she wanted them to break up because the girl had bad hair.

Consciousness of race is an important element in the appraisals Hispanos make of themselves and others. When people are being gossiped about or even just mentioned casually, their color and whether they are white or Negro may be brought up spontaneously. Individuals are often characterized by their color, and associations about their character and their looks. approval or disapproval are likely to involve racial affiliations. Close personal relationships with persons considered Negroes are discouraged, particularly by those defined as white by the outgroup but not by the ingroup.

Isidro Velez, a distinctly Negroid man, had lived for twenty years in Eastville when he discovered that a childhood chum, Damian Toro, was also living in the neighborhood. Damian and his family are considered white in New York. Isidro went to visit Damian, and they sat in the living room to reminisce about their home town and their childhood. Isidro continued to visit the Toro family and once came while Damian's daughters were alone in the house. Julia, Damian's wife, told a fieldworker that this made her angry, because she had told her daughters never to let anyone into the apartment when trusted adults were not present. After a while she claimed that her oldest daughter, Inez, was also very angry. "That daughter of mine," Julia said, "is so proud, she does not like to see Negroes here upstairs in the living room." Isidro, then, gradually discontinued his informal visits with Damian, and he was not mentioned again. He did not even attend parties at the Toros' any more. However, when Charlie, the youngest child of the Toros, was baptized, about a year after this incident, a number of distinctly Negroid persons were at the house party that followed the baptism. One of them was introduced to the fieldworker as a sister of the host. Her husband, who was darker, was also introduced, but his identity was not revealed. A teen-aged American Negro boy, a classmate of one of the Toro children, came to the party accompanied by a Sunday school teacher. He was referred to by the hostess and her daughters as "that Negro," or "the Negro," yet no reference was made to the race of the cousin who looked just as Negroid. Mrs. Toro, on another occasion, was telling a fieldworker about her past life and mentioned how at thirteen she fell in love with a very handsome man. "He adored me," she remarked, "and used to tell me he would never marry anybody else but me. I had to break up with him because my family did not want him. Imagine, just because he was a colored man."

In New York whiteness continues to be regarded as an important social attribute, a more important one here than it was in Puerto Rico. Among recent migrants who were of intermediate racial categories in Puerto Rico, the fear of being associated with Negroes generally seems stronger than among those who have lived in New York for a number of years. Children, adolescents, and adults who have had their homes in the neighborhood for most of their lives associate with each other regardless of color or social race. The barriers of race, however, operate to separate recent migrants from the older groups of Hispanos in the city and from those who are born and reared in New York. Nonetheless, there is a tendency for white girls of recent migrant parents to marry intermediates who were born and reared in New York, particularly those who have well-paying jobs.

Prejudice on the part of Hispanos and core tensions related to race center in those considered Negroes and those "mixed." Prejudice works in terms of affecting close interpersonal relations, but it is not extended to justify discrimination in employment, housing, or casual friendships.

Living with others in the neighborhood

THOUGH Eastville is a "mixed" neighborhood, to a visitor it is likely to seem overridden by Puerto Ricans. While numerically Puerto Ricans constitute only the neighborhood's second-largest ethnic group, they stand out more prominently than members of other ethnic groups, because their group has the greatest number of individuals who do not conform to the ideal standards of American culture. Since there is a tendency in the larger society to regard individuals and groups who do not conform to the ideal of the assimilated American as automatically having social problems, Puerto Ricans are assumed to have such problems indiscriminately, regardless of whatever real problems they may have of their own. This expectation adds extraneous content to the perception that visitors have of Puerto Ricans. In the context of modern America, Puerto Ricans in Eastville do share real common problems with their neighbors: all are subject to substandard levels of living, to inadequate housing, and to the cultural and social conflicts inherent in slum life. They cannot, however, be said to share as an ethnic group common problems of cultural conflict stemming from their cultural background and a lack of adjustment to American society. The picture is more complex and cognizance must be taken of the characteristics of the Puerto Rican sociocultural group, as much as of the particular segment of the society in which they live, in order to determine whatever adjustments it may be possible for them to make.

In many ways the Puerto Rican migration to New York is a reminder of the European immigrations and settlements of the past. But should one probe into the reminiscences about earlier waves of foreigners and also look carefully at both through the systematic research of today, significant differences would be discovered between the Puerto Rican migration and the immigrations of the Europeans of years gone by.

For one thing, American life has changed profoundly during the past three or four decades of our century. The great immigrations from Europe took place at a time in American history of manpower shortages that would have hindered the coming mammoth economic developments without the influx of large numbers of people from abroad. The nation needed this human power to build up its economy and to expand its resources. To get it, America went all out to attract foreigners to its shores. These, in turn, were pushed out of their homelands by social, economic, psychological, and political pressures. Puerto Ricans, on the other hand, started to come to the States *en masse* well after American technology had reached a high level of development and after the European immigrations had been curtailed by law. So, instead of to build up the nation's labor force, Puerto Ricans started to come to fill a labor vacuum in the unskilled and semiskilled fields in marginal sectors of the economy not yet subjected to automation. Puerto Ricans, then, have come to a New York different in social and economic context than that of the days preceding the First World War. The Puerto Rican labor force, although primarily an unskilled one, as the European was, has a tradition of labor unionism in its background in the island. In this sense it differs from some of the immigrant groups that came from Europe in the past. It comprises a low-income class of wage earners, but it has come to the United States in an era in which minimum wages are guaranteed by law and in which both state and Federal government agencies exist for the laws' enforcement. These are times when unemployment compensation and social insurance are taken for granted. Moreover, today there are more private and public social agencies to protect citizens from hunger, ill housing, and sickness than in the past. It is a time, too, of greater awareness of civil rights and greater human understandings. At the same time, the large-scale migration from Puerto Rico has coincided with a philosophical climate that conceives of immigration as an evil to American life and equates it with hardships and increasing social problems. The migrants of today, then, are assigned a position in the social hierarchy of New York comparable to that of the many newcomers who preceded them. Thus low-income Puerto Ricans face multiple problems in living in the United States, but these problems are not necessarily inherent and unique in them. They are like those of any other lower-income group in this society as they are a product of the American social system. Puerto Ricans in middle- and upper-income groups have no social problems that come to the attention of social and welfare agencies. Yet Puerto Ricans are perceived by many sectors of the population indiscriminately as a "problem." This is a social attitude that has developed in the society as a result of the evaluation of previous experiences and attitudes toward other culturally foreign minority groups in the past when being culturally foreign became identified with poverty. However, the physical and social picture of New York has undeniably changed since the days of the old immigrations. More liberal attitudes have developed in the society and greater recognition of civil rights has worked against the less tolerant older views on foreigners. Physically and socially Puerto Ricans have contributed to change the picture of the city.

Most of the city's old enclaves of European settlers have dwindled, and many have disappeared altogether. The Italian, Greek, or German districts have lost their exclusiveness and their distinctive appearance. Today only in the poorer neighborhoods of the city is there any significant evidence of imprints of the past. Many other ethnic districts are nothing more now than thriving commercial sectors that add to the cosmopolitan atmosphere of the city. Into what used to be large districts occupied by members of a single ethnic group, Puerto Ricans, among other underprivileged groups, have started to move, and with them have come the bodega, the Spanish Pentecostal church, the shops featuring *alcapurrias* (plaintain meat pie) and *pastelillos* (fried meat pie), the herb stores, and airplane agencies and retail businesses with bilingual employees. Concentrating in small neighborhoods, except for the larger settlements in east Manhattan and the Bronx, Puerto Ricans live all over the city. The increasing arrivals from Puerto Rico, the shuttling back and forth between New York and the island, and the cleavages among Puerto Ricans wrought by differences in socioeconomic class, color, and assimilation into other segments of American society, all continually affect the composition and social characteristics of New York neighborhoods where Puerto Ricans live. Today, perhaps with the exception of American Negroes, Puerto Ricans are the most "visible" minority in the city. Language and social behavior are the main clues in this kind of "visibility," although physical traits many times are a factor in the social identification of Puerto Rican persons, since it is assumed that all Puerto Ricans "look alike," are short and dark. In this sense it is "easier" to identify a Puerto Rican migrant, particularly a recent arrival, than a second-generation Italian or German or a Southern American Negro.

Culturally, too, Puerto Rican migrants differ from the old European immigrants. Even those coming from rural areas in the island have been exposed to the electoral process, public education, wage systems, large hospitals, and other institutions, as well as to mass communication services that have given them a broader outlook on the world beyond their communities and the island itself. In addition, throughout their lives, they have been exposed to many things and institutions that are "American." They know of the value of voting in political elections, they talk of freedom of speech and the rights of man as warranties of the United States Constitution, and they regard American citizenship as guaranteeing human freedom. These social and political ideas were not available to the European immigrants in their homelands. Furthermore, in the island itself, Puerto Ricans have unavoidably become familiar with a variety of imported American products, in foods, appliances, apparel, and household items. These American imports, both the tangible and the intangible, have become adapted and are now part of Puerto Rican culture. Thus Puerto Rican migrants are closer to home in New York City than were the immigrants who preceded them. Yet Puerto Ricans are regarded as strangers in New York, and New York is strange to them.

Even in a small neighborhood like Eastville, where people rely on neighbors for friendship and sociability, Puerto Ricans find that they are not liked and approved. Hostility is frequently displaced upon the recently arrived ones because of their being different, and these, in turn, retaliate with hostile dislike of strangers, particularly American Negroes. Migrants are resented and disliked by members of all other ethnic groups and old Hispano migrants and New York-reared adults of Puerto Rican parents as well. To other Puerto Ricans who have made their homes in New York these newcomers to the city represent a threat to their own acceptance in New York. The migrants are regarded as a source of problems for them partly because of a recognition that the outgroup will react to the newcomers in an unfavorable way, and will extend its attitudes to all Puerto

Ricans regardless of how long they have lived in New York. In other words, Puerto Ricans who are established in the city also accept the dictum that newcomers are undesirable. Living with others in the neighborhood, hence, hinges upon strong conflicts in intergroup and intragroup relationships, in the vortex of which are recent Puerto Rican migrants.

In Eastville there is a level on which neighborhood solidarity operates, crosscutting all ethnic groups. It appears sporadically, expressed by individuals, when the neighborhood is considered under attack by the press or some other organ of public opinion. Discrimination against minorities in general may evoke words of anger and protest against those who proffer it or are suspected of doing so. Descriptions of living conditions in the neighborhood or information publicizing the work conducted by social agencies there are interpreted as insults and signs of discrimination against its people.

On another level solidarity is expressed in terms of loyalty to one's ethnic group. The instances when these were recorded had to do with incidents affecting members of an ethnic group accused of antisocial behavior, regardless of whether they were from Eastville or not. In such cases the whole ethnic group was defended against the accusation made toward an individual. Voices of protest would also be raised when discrimination or unfavorable treatment of one's ethnic group in relationship to another was recognized. For instance, American Negroes would complain that social agencies were showing favoritism to Puerto Ricans. This was claimed to be a disadvantage for Negroes. These broad levels of social solidarity, however, did not have the same basis as the interpersonal networks of human relationships that appear in the small groups of the neighborhood. In the latter informal groups solidarity based on close interpersonal relations kindled through the years of living as neighbors operated to break down the barriers of prejudice and discrimination among members of different ethnic groups. The greater the

number of tasks or interests that neighbors shared with each
other, the closer their relations and the stronger the networks
binding them in social intercourse. People living in the same
building for many years, or patronizing the same shops, or attending the same church, or those who grew up in the neighborhood and went to school together formed the core of the small
groups of individuals of different ethnic groups. For example,
American Negroes who have been in the neighborhood for a
number of years and Hispanos who have also lived there for
years often participate in churches together, become close
friends, visit each other, and do not seem to be subject to frictions related to race.

Most people living in Eastville, however, are really newcomers to the city and to the neighborhood and are left out of
these groups. They are either American Negro migrants from
the South or Puerto Ricans. The newcomers find that they are
not welcome in the neighborhood and that they cannot circulate
socially within the circle of longtime residents there, so they
tend to participate in small groups with people of their own ethnic group, newcomers like themselves.

Living in the midst of people who still acknowledge membership in nationality or racial groups, Hispanos have continued
this tradition of vesting individuals with an ethnic group. The
principal ethnic groups recognized by recent Hispano migrants
are Cubans, Americans, American Negroes, Italians, and Jews.
Of these, Americans and Italians are the most highly rated.
Jews, Cubans, and American Negroes are, as a rule, less fa-
vored, particularly the two latter groups.

The evaluation of different ethnic groups by Hispanos, as well
as their social attitudes toward the members of the various
groups, reflect the cultural cleavages and the stages of acculturation of the Hispano group. Data on this subject obtained
from Eastville Hispanos can be represented graphically as
follows.

	Americans (white) and Italians	Jews and Other European Immigrants	Cubans	American Negroes (including West Indians)	Puerto Ricans
Recent migrants	H	L	L	L	H
Old migrants	H	M	M	L	M
Second-generation and migrants raised in New York	H	H	H	M	L

In turn, members of other groups evaluate Puerto Ricans thus:

	Recent Migrants	Old Migrants	Second-Generation and Migrants Raised in New York
Italians	L	L	M
Americans (white)	L	M	L
American Negroes	L	M	H
Jews and other European immigrants	L	L	L
West Indians	L	M	H
Cubans	M	H	H

H = high   M = medium   L = low   *Source:* Field materials.

Besides assigning individuals a status within an ethnic group, recent Hispano migrants also recognize a broader category called "American." In Puerto Rico they had formed stereotyped conceptions of Americans based on the movies and on other information about the United States and its people that they acquired without having experienced personal friendship and social equality with Americans. It is likely that if they had any personal relation with Americans there, it was either in the armed forces or with clergymen, teachers, employers, physicians, or other officials with whom they had little personal contact aside from the one specifically connected with their jobs. In New York the picture of what an American is changes, for here not everyone who is not a Puerto Rican is an American. An individual may be an Italian, a Hungarian, or a Puerto Rican, even if he and his parents were born here. So the idea that an individual's nationality is determined by the place where he was born is not borne out by the facts about nationality in the United States as it is in Puerto Rico.

In trying to make sense out of the new concepts of nationality identification found in New York, Hispanos go through a period of social learning. The lesson is that only a few people are to be considered Americans. In one sense, however, Hispano migrants consider themselves so. That is, they acknowledge their American citizenship and boast of it defensively when anticipating that others may regard them as foreigners. As stated before, their children born in this country are said to be *americanos,* and are told so by their parents, friends, brothers, and sisters. From early childhood they are taught that their nationality is American. At the same time, they are also considered Hispanos and are so taught. Yet, as adults, those born in this country do not look forward to Puerto Rico as their homeland, nor forward to it as their future. Their orientation is toward America, and toward things and values they consider American.

Americans are also descendants of Italians, Jews, Irish, and other immigrants. But these descendants are also and primarily Italians, Jews, and Irish, rather than Americans. Their names may be used as a guidepost to identify them as members of an ethnic group, and when describing or identifying them, it is likely that reference will be made to their ethnic group. An undisputed American, or someone who is an American and nothing else, is conceived as having a name that cannot be identified with or traced to a foreign origin; as being reddish and white in complexion, tall, blond, and blue-eyed; as doing professional work; and as not knowing Spanish, or as having an accent when speaking it. He does not understand the Hispano people. Americans are nice, honest, beautiful, and funny. Should one or more of these traits be missing, the individual is suspected of not being a "real American," but something else instead.

Americans are considered the most highly desirable people. The men make the best husbands for one's daughters. The closer an individual comes to being an American, the more highly is he judged. It is to one's credit to count Americans as friends and to have them in one's family. They are wonderful people, and they have a good system to live by. They are all kinds of people, and are "just like anybody else." But still, Americans are not like Puerto Ricans, even though they resemble somewhat the Puerto Rican children reared in this country. "Americans are different." As an informant told a fieldworker of a man who lives in the neighborhood: "He is not from Puerto Rico. He says he is Canadian. Or if he is from Puerto Rico, as many people say, he came as a little boy. He is no American." A Puerto Rican man, who, during the Second World War, worked as a timekeeper at an American military base in the island, said he knew the Americans because he had worked for them at the base. "Here they say we are bastards [he used the Spanish word *bastardo,* meaning illegitimate], and we are not. They are. An American sergeant told me that."

Regardless of how inaccurate these concepts about Americans may be, they are used as guides in intergroup relationships of Puerto Ricans with others. The concepts that members of other ethnic groups hold about Puerto Ricans in turn guide their relationships. Hispanos born and reared in the neighborhood, for instance, are highly appreciated and evaluated, and are accepted as friends and in other close personal relationships by other longtime residents of Eastville. The aged Italian immigrants, however, are deprecatory of Hispanos, particularly recent migrants and old migrants who retain a high degree of ethnic visibility—either by their mannerisms, or by being dark-skinned, or by talking in Spanish. These Hispanos, in their turn, are highly resentful of old Italian immigrants.

Among the aging European residents, as well as among Hispanos who grew up in this country, resentment against recent Puerto Rican migrants was commonly expressed. But both recent migrants from Puerto Rico and the old European immigrants expressed great resentment toward American Negroes. For the aging Europeans, it was the coming of the Negroes and the Puerto Ricans that destroyed their community life and caused their children and grandchildren to move away. Actually the old Europeans who have stayed in Eastville are people who came from a peasant background on the Continent, who have quite restricted their lives to their own ethnic groups, and who still have only a limited knowledge of conversational English. Most of their children and grandchildren reared in this country were able to make the grade out of the neighborhood and out of the ethnic subculture. The second- and third-generation Europeans who still remain in the neighborhood are, like Hispanos of this group, also oriented toward American society, but they have remained attached to the place where they were raised, either on account of their occupations (many run small neighborhood businesses), or because of their strong ties to their families.

Social relationships in the neighborhood also vary according to age groups and length of residence there. As a whole, the aged in each group maintain more restricted social relationships than middle-aged or young people. Mrs. Reed, a seventy-five-year-old woman who came from the Virgin Islands, expressed this in a way similar to that heard from other old folks in Eastville.

"I don't like the system here. It is so different from the way I was raised. You could be poor but yet decent, and you didn't have to mix—to meet a lot of people. The social life is different from what I want." When I asked her to explain further, she said, "For instance, the conversation is rough. It don't suit me. All my days I'm raised in the church and religion. When these church members visit me often, I'm satisfied with that."

When asked about other friends, she said she knows others from the Virgin Islands here, but "we don't meet. I was raised in St. Thomas, just with the family. I never went around. I had just acquaintances, not social friends. I keep them like that. My husband is the same. He has friends but he don't go to dances either. If one friend is sick, we go to visit."

The aged Puerto Ricans are perhaps the least restricted of the old people, as they tend to live with their married children and mingle with many of the visitors who come to see the younger people.

Counter to the social isolation of the aged in Eastville are the multiple groups in which young and middle-aged people can participate. Between these groups center many interactions of social conflict. Interpersonal frictions generally involve individuals with members of other small groups or with individuals who do not belong to any small group. A clique or group is expected to side with its members and to protect their interests against those who threaten them by criticism of the enemy and those who protect him. Being active in Eastville society places the individual in the midst of many warm friendships, but also directly in the midst of the many conflicts tinging ethnic group relations.

The mainsprings of intergroup tensions in the neighborhood lie between recent Puerto Rican migrants and American Negroes. One can also say that one of the strongest forces binding peoples and groups in Eastville are those that group people against each other. The attitudes and definitions of recent migrants and American Negroes about social race are important aspects of these tensions on one hand and of the strengths of groupings on the other. On a verbal level these are expressed by American Negroes through criticism of the views of Puerto Ricans on race, claiming that many of them who are really Negroes are not considered to be so and are accorded the same privileges as if they were white. Puerto Ricans, in turn, speak of Negroes as "bad," dangerous, and capable of violence against them. An unexpressed fear of being identified and associated with Negroes in the public eye is also found among Puerto Rican migrants. This can be inferred from the hostile remarks of dis-

approval and the claims of antisocial behavior made by recent
Puerto Rican migrants against American Negroes. But, as has
been mentioned, American Negroes who have been in the neighborhood for many years, like Hispanos who have also lived there
for a comparable length of time, have learned to associate with
each other in small groups, become close friends, visit each
other, and share in real comradeship, without having their relationships subjected to the interethnic group tensions of the
neighborhood. So it is found that close friendships and other
intimate relationships may develop between New York-raised
Negroes and Hispanos. New York American Negroes are given
a fairly high evaluation by Hispanos who have grown up in the
city, and, like, this Hispano subgroup, the New York Negroes
express disapproval of recent migrants from Puerto Rico on
such grounds as that they accept low-paying jobs and that they
pay landlords large sums to secure apartments.

When recent Puerto Rican migrants and American Negroes
are brought together to cooperate in some civic or formal social
activity without due recognition of the social system and tensions of the neighborhood, it is likely that these tensions will be
expressed overtly when any situation of conflict—even an unre-
lated one—appears. The Reverend Jones, who is minister of an
Eastville church, had to face a problem of this kind. Explaining
to a fieldworker why there are not many Puerto Ricans in his
church now when in the past this was not so, he said, "One of
the reasons we have few Puerto Ricans in the church has been
the Negroes. Puerto Rican parents do not want their children
mixing and dancing with Negro children. There was one Puerto
Rican group some time ago, but the Puerto Rican and Negro
women had a fight for leadership. The Negroes made cracks at
the Puerto Ricans. One of the Puerto Rican women got insulted
and took all the Puerto Rican women away with her. Since then,
we have never made too much inroads."

Yet, despite the social and cultural barriers that separate

recently arrived Puerto Rican migrants from their neighbors, a crisis may bring forth mutual sympathy and help. The case of Gilberto Gontan illustrates this point.

When Gilberto, a nine-year-old Puerto Rican boy, ran away from home—an event that occurred quite often—his father and mother, both recent migrants who could only manage a few scattered words in English, sought information about their son even from non-Spanish-speaking neighbors. Mr. Gontan would go through buildings in the neighborhood, knock at the door of a non-Spanish speaker, pronounce the name of his son, and gesture the size of the boy with his hand. The person questioned would reply in sign language or with the word "no" that the boy was not there. On the sidewalks neighbors of different ethnic groups would be informed of Gilberto's disappearance, and the general concern of all was indicated by the questions people asked about it. One night a fieldworker met Gilberto after one of his disappearances at Avenue D with an Italian woman who had found him near Avenue B after he had been missing for several hours.

There was no common language among some of the East-villers trying to help the anxious parents whose son was missing, but there was communication. The neighbors had learned that the frequent disappearances of the boy threw his parents into despair, and they had started to cooperate in locating the boy. The parents had learned that they could rely on their neighbors, regardless of their background, to assist them in these moments of crisis.

In a neighborhood or other complex form of social organization where interpersonal relations are highly valued, schisms within the large groups can be mended when individuals representing the factions enter into face-to-face interpersonal relations of mutual understanding and concern. This situation creates new meanings and sets of relationships that diminish the emotional need to rely upon the schism group for support. A church leader told a fieldworker a story of such a reconciliation in a building occupied exclusively by American Negroes until recently when Puerto Ricans started to move in.

"[This] is the case of a twelve-year-old girl from Puerto Rico. All the families in the building were Negroes who didn't bother with them. The little girl annoyed a Negro woman and she became very angry. I asked her to tell the woman, 'I am sorry.' The girl told me, 'I did not do anything, but I'll say it.' The woman knew the girl did not mean it, but enjoyed her saying it, and invited the girl for refreshments. Now in that building the Puerto Ricans and the Negroes are friends."

One of the characteristics which heighten distrust of recent Puerto Rican migrants and strengthen the barriers of separation is language. Knowing English, speaking it without a foreign accent, and using it in social situations where both Hispanos and persons who do not understand Spanish are present is a requirement made of Hispanos by the outgroup. This requirement runs from the neighborhood itself, through casual contacts Hispanos make outside the neighborhood with professionals and businessmen, to less personalized situations, such as riding in a subway or on a bus. Although Hispanos value learning to speak English and see as desirable the ability to "dominate" (*dominar*) this language, for them knowing and speaking Spanish still has value too; it serves as part of their identification and self-definition. Knowledge of English among Hispanos ranges from a few words to familiarity with the language as a native speaker, but Spanish is still the language in which old migrants speak to their children, in which recent migrants speak to theirs, and in which small children speak to each other. Spanish is the language of the home, of intimate relationships, and it is symbolic of the Hispano group. It is the language in which one can express oneself better, especially when talking to other Hispanos. There are also other advantages. Even if one does know English, he can use Spanish as a private language that others will not understand, and furthermore, it comes in handy if one wants to ignore something unpleasant that is being said in English. There is also another aspect of the language issue: a person may feel incompetent speaking in English, even if he understands what is being said, or he may not know how to say more than a few words in English and not understand anything of what he is being told. But in New York, Spanish changes too. It is not the same as in Puerto Rico. A whole new vocabulary has developed, drawn largely from English words and phrases which have been smoothly accommodated into the patterns of Spanish. Examples of this variety of Spanish are, "Ven a comer el porcho" (Come eat the pork chop), or "Ponte el couh" (Put on your coat). Anglicisms in words and phrases are freely used in "speaking Spanish" and conversely Spanish is frequently intermingled when friends are speaking English to each other.

Not knowing English in New York is for Hispanos cause for embarrassment. It is regarded as a characteristic of ignorance. In time, both men and women pick up English enough to "defend themselves," that is to understand, to get along around the neighborhood, and in other routine situations. Often, however, they refuse to admit knowledge of English because it is "not good English," and prefer to be accompanied by an interpreter when they have to deal with professionals or other persons in higher socioeconomic groups. There is a cultural justification for recent migrant women, especially housewives, to pretend they know less English than they may actually do. This is partly connected with the idea that a good woman is helpless, that she does not know how to cope with the outside world because her job is in the home—and English is learned in the street. Men are usually less embarrassed about daring to speak in English even if they do not consider their English "good." Women who desire employment and men of all ages may attend night school to learn English and even continue their grammar or junior high school training in New York.

Second-generation Hispanos, as well as non-Hispanos, express dislike of the use of Spanish, particularly when non-Hispanos are present. One said: "Yes, they talk with Americans, Spanish, and that's why a lot of people gets to hate them, because they don't know what they're talking about. But they're talking harmless, they're talking about everyday life, what happens to them. But they be laughing so much that people, they might be riding a subway, and people might think they be laughing so much that people, they might think they be talking about them.

"That's why it's no good to talk some other language, unless you're talking real business, and you don't be laughing. They'd be carrying on something awful, and there's many a time when I didn't know what a guy was saying when I was riding the subway, well, I think I would jump up and hit him, because he keeps looking my way and laughing, and if I didn't know what he was talking about, I'd figure he was talking about me."

There are certain occasions, however, on which Spanish is utilized to express hostility against members of non-Hispano groups. For instance, two conversations, one in English and another in very fast Spanish, may be carried on simultaneously. In the one carried on in English, the outsider is allowed to participate, but he is left out of the second, which may be charged with biting remarks about him. This is one of the ways in which is handled the embarrassment caused by English-speaking persons of higher socioeconomic rank whose actions and behavior are regarded as derogatory or patronizing toward Hispanos.

When Mr. Frank Carson, a young social service worker, visited the Carle family in an effort to get the family to participate in a neighborhood social center, he tried to befriend family members. Mr. Carson looked at Mr. Carle and told him he looked like José Ferrer. Mr. Carle and his family took this as a joke that transgressed the respect Mr. Carson owed the father. He blushed and indicated his displeasure by frowning. Mr.

Carson then asked the daughter, Rosa, directly to attend a social function at the neighborhood center. He did not seek permission from either her father or her mother, as is expected of a polite and respectable person such as Mr. Carson was supposed to be. In a further effort toward breaking the ice, Mr. Carson, who was unaware of the "mistakes" in etiquette he had committed, started to speak in Spanish. His knowledge of the language was very limited, and now the members of the Carle family started to laugh at him because of his inadequate use of Spanish. Mrs. Carle, addressing her husband, daughter, and son, and the fieldworker present, said very fast, "Míralo, que carapones," a pun referring to Mr. Carson's puzzled face. The fieldworker asked, "And what are 'carapones'?" and the members of the household continued laughing.

Though the Spanish-speaking persons were making fun of Mr. Carson, he was unaware of it and laughed with the rest, while asking the meaning of the conversation and complaining that he could not follow it because Puerto Ricans speak too fast.

Individuals who speak and understand English resent being spoken to in Spanish. Hispanos who grew up in New York particularly avoid speaking in Spanish in public situations, such as when they are on buses or with Americans. They may often act as if they knew less Spanish than they actually do when Americans try to speak to them in Spanish on the assumption that they will not understand English. In recent years a few second-generation Hispanos from Eastville have found that they did not qualify for jobs because of not knowing Spanish, and at least one made a trip to Puerto Rico to learn it.

Other people in the neighborhood do not have the emotional conflicts that Puerto Ricans have regarding the use or knowledge of English or Spanish. Their feelings of identity and approval or disapproval are not located in that area. Some of the American Negroes, West Indians, and other adults in the neighborhood boast of their knowledge of Spanish and want their children to learn it. For example, Julia, an American Negro woman who is outspokenly anti-Puerto Rican, says with pride that her son Jack is taking Spanish in school, and Joe, who is four, is picking it up from the Spanish kids next door. Jack who stood by said "agua." "See," said his mother laughingly, "he speaks Spanish."

Marva, a sixteen-year-old American Negro girl whose parents came from the South, said in discussing her older brother: "He is a pretty good old brother. He helps me in fights. . . . He gets really good grades and doesn't study. He is learning Spanish. I want to learn Spanish. . . . Yes, I want to learn, because you get more money when you know Spanish, in secretarial work."

In school such children may attempt to exchange words in Spanish with Hispano children. Those recently arrived are likely to avoid them out of fear of being hurt by other children from the neighborhood, in particular by American Negroes, while those born in New York or those who have been in school here for a number of years refuse to speak Spanish and even act as if they did not understand it. To many Puerto Ricans, especially those reared in New York, knowledge of Spanish conveys no particular sense of accomplishment, nor is it something to boast about. Like non-Puerto Ricans, they regard the constant use of Spanish, as well as any other form of behavior that distinguishes Puerto Ricans from Americans, as detrimental to Puerto Ricans in New York. Yet, while culturally they have become Americans, they find themselves having constantly to strive toward maintaining that identification, for in the terms of the larger community, they are not Americans.

Family and kinship

THE ideal Hispano family consists of a father, a mother, and their unmarried children who all live together in the same household. This is the basic unit, the immediate or nuclear family. The father is supposed to impart respect to the children and to provide for the family; the mother, to care for the children and her husband and to maintain the standards of respect and good behavior set up by the father. Ideally, their home will be near those of close relatives, members of the "great family," including uncles, aunts, sisters, married children, grandchildren, and so on, and they will get along well with each other. All these relatives are supposed to help one another and to share in many common activities as members of the extended family.

Family Organization in Eastville

The parents in the immediate family may have been married by a judge or a clergyman, but they also may have been living out of wedlock in what they consider a perfectly respectable relationship. Their friends, relatives, and neighbors may regard it in that way too and consider them to be the same as if they were legally married. Two types of marriage are recognized among Eastville Puerto Ricans, the legal and the consensual (*que viven*). A legal marriage is considered more desirable than a consensual one, but in the practice of everyday life, in the proper conduct of family business, and in the expectations of behavior between a man and his wife, between parents and their children such a marriage may not be any different from a legal one. A consensual marriage that meets the standards of a good marriage gains as much social approval as a legal one, and those involved in such a relationship are not considered to be "living in sin." A legal marriage is in principle preferred to a consensual one, particularly among young adults and by older adults for their children. There is social pressure on young women to marry legally, but after a woman has lost her virginity it is good enough if she can settle with the intent to carry on a permanent relation with a consensual mate. There is no social pressure on men to marry legally except that of the women and their parents who prefer a legal tie. The larger society through its laws and agencies frowns upon consensual marriages. Hispano professionals, as well as other middle-class professional people, exert pressure against consensual marriages and in behalf of legalized ones. The clergy advises parents to marry legally. Schoolchildren are said to be ashamed of their unwed parents and of their being illegitimate because "the teachers know and so do their classmates." Pressures from the larger society, furthermore, may involve direct sanctions. Lack of proof of legal marriage may disqualify a low-income person from obtaining an apartment in city-owned low-rental buildings. Professionals, in addition, may take it upon themselves to deny a service unless parents marry legally, as when Carlos Rondon's crippled child was not considered as a candidate for a special school on grounds that his parents were not married. Despite the social and economic disadvantages of nonlegalized marital unions in New York and the growing disapproval of them, these unions are common in Eastville among Puerto Ricans and non-Puerto Ricans as well. While they are subjected to disapprobation in the light of the values, norms, and attitudes of the larger society toward marriage, they are not particularly disapproved of in the context of the slum subculture itself. Hence, in the context of the slum the Puerto Rican family based on a consensual relationship is protected from some of the stresses placed upon it by the larger society.

Among Puerto Rican migrants, a man or woman who married legally in Puerto Rico may enter into a consensual union in New York with someone else without taking legal action to end his marriage. While this is a commonly accepted way of entering into a second marital relationship, there are instances, because the social pressures for a legal marriage are so strong, in which a legally married individual may re-marry in City Hall or in a church without benefit of divorce. On one hand, obtaining a divorce in New York is considered to be extremely difficult, and on the other, public pressure may compel an individual to enter into a legal marriage in order to become eligible for certain social privileges that accompany that status in New York society.

Jose Duval tried to get a divorce in New York, and not being able to do so, re-married anyway. He advised his friend Charlie Montes, who has a legal wife in Puerto Rico from whom he has been separated over fifteen years, to do likewise, because "there is no divorce in New York"—his interpretation of the limited divorce laws of New York State. Charlie migrated to New York ten years ago with his consensual wife, Juana, who bore him four children. He and his consensual wife have repeatedly expressed their desire to marry legally. Living in one room, Charlie and his family have been refused public housing on the grounds that they are not legally married. His wife told a member of the field team that she would leave him, if necessary, to get an apartment in a city housing development for herself and the children.

Other marriages are terminated by divorce, and ordinarily a man or woman desiring a divorce takes a trip to Puerto Rico and obtains it after claiming legal residence there. Among migrants, it is considered easier to obtain a divorce in the island than in New York. Seeking a divorce in Puerto Rico is also an occasion for visiting friends and relatives, which eases the anxieties connected with a marital breakup. After a couple with children is separated or divorced, the father, even if he has deserted his wife for another, may come and visit his former home "to see the children" several times a week. His former wife serves him and acts toward him as if he were a guest, claiming that this befits his status as the father of her children. On these visits he is expected to exercise his authority over the children, correcting, advising, and punishing them as a good father does.

For many Eastville migrants the information that in this country "it is important" to be married legally reached them before they left the island. After deciding to migrate, they may have legalized a consensual union there. Zenon and Betina Pozo had had several children in Puerto Rico in a consensual union that had lasted over twelve years. Shortly before Zenon was to fly to New York, he and Betina were married in the Catholic church of their home town.

There are also other types of nonlegalized sexual unions among Eastville Hispanos, but these are not considered respectable. Casual sexual intercourse, prostitution, and affairs (*bretes*) fall within this category of unpreferred unions. Adultery on the part of a woman is strongly disapproved of. A husband may be warned by his neighbors of his wife's misbehavior, and he is expected "to do something about it." There is more tolerance for a married man who has extramarital affairs both from his partner and his friends because "he is a man." Wives, nonetheless, are not supposed to know of their husbands' adventures. Should they find out, they and other women will discuss his conduct and that of his mistress or girl friend as being "fresh." A jealous wife may send one of her children, particularly a son, to follow his father and find out for her whether he went to see another woman. She may try to surprise them and announce that she is leaving him and taking her children with her. A married man may brag to his male friends of his sexual conquests, but he is expected to protect his wife and children from learning of his escapades. It is on this basis, and on the basis of the strong love expected of a father for his children, that a woman has bargaining power with her adulterous husband.

Among recent migrants it is said that extramarital affairs and other disapproved kinds of sexual relations occur more frequently in New York than in Puerto Rico. This is seen as resulting from the influence of New York on men and women. It is said that in New York women become loose and lost by developing an interest in married men and fathers with family responsibilities and by entering into affairs with them. It is also said that males (*machos*) must respond to the allures of these women lest they doubt their own masculinity, and that many times they leave their own wives and children to start housekeeping with such women. Wives, particularly young ones, often speak of being jealous and state their disapproval of husbands who have girl friends, mistresses, or affairs, or who dress up and go out to dances or movies by themselves. If the behavior of children is "bad," older women blame it on their husbands' running around with other women and on their drinking. In the women's words, "The children's father did not set a good example for them." Younger women predict difficulties with their children in the future if their husbands do not stop running around.

Hispanos reared in this country criticize recent migrants for not having enough concern about legal marriage. For them, this is an added factor that is damaging to the reputation and good name of Puerto Ricans in New York, and hence reflects upon their own prestige. They also speak of having different ideas about marriage and the family than the "Spanish people" do.

Women reared in New York expressly state their wish that husband and wife share and discuss their problems with each other, that they go out together for recreation, and that the husband help the wife with household chores, particularly with the care of the children. Husbands reared in New York do not, as a rule, object to their wives being employed and contributing to the support of their household, nor to helping their wives in the household, nor to going out with them for fun. Men who have migrated as youths or as adults, however, are likely not to accept these roles for men in relation to their wives. For them, a good wife is still a "woman of her home"—one who takes care of the children and keeps herself busy day and night by cooking and doing all her household chores; by seeing that the family's clothes are washed and pressed properly, the house clean and in order, the children bathed and dressed, and dinner ready by the time her husband comes home from work. By women from this group the husband, in turn, is defined as a good one if he provides for his family's needs and exercises his authority to maintain order and good behavior in his children. But he should also be considerate, and when his wife is sick, he is supposed to help her do the heavy work in the home.

Hispanos expect adults to get married or to show definite interest in the opposite sex before they are "too old." Susana told a fieldworker that she was very worried about her son Lipo, because at twenty-two he had never had a girl friend nor shown much of an interest in any girl. Marriage of boys and girls in their early teens does occur in Eastville, but this is usually "forced" marriage, the product of a girl's pregnancy. Yet a man has to have girl friends or women—and in this he is encouraged by his father or mother—at least from his mid-teens onward, or else he will be suspected of unmanliness. The preferred age for a first marriage for both men and women is in the early or mid-twenties. They should be about the same age, although preferably the man is the older of the two. He should be able to support his wife by the time he enters marriage, and marriage should help both to develop more maturity (*capacidad*).

There are, however, liaisons of a marital nature in Eastville between middle-aged mothers and young adult men. In these arrangements the men are supported by the women, who, like those who enter into legal marriage for a second or third time, claim that they live with these men because their children need a man to respect, a father. Such liaisons are often sneered at and criticized by others, who say that what the woman really wants is a "male" (*macho*), and not a "man" (*hombre*), who, by definition, would support her and teach her children respect. These unions are not considered equivalent to stable consensual marriages but are defined as affairs (*bretes*).

In Puerto Rico, even a woman who is legally married may properly call herself by her maiden name and not by her husband's name. On migrating to New York, however, she will probably take her husband's name for official purposes. This she may do regardless of whether her marriage is legal or consensual, for "in this country a woman takes her husband's name." In one case, a man took his consensual wife's name, explaining that "in this country the husband and wife have the same name and she cannot take mine because we are not married." Friends and relatives may continue to refer to a married woman by her maiden name or as So-and-So's wife, however.

As for children, they are expected to use both their father's and their mother's last names, in that order. This is a common usage among peoples of Spanish traditions throughout the world. In New York the children may find out that non-Hispanos identify them by their mother's surname because that comes at the end of their full names. In terms of the naming traditions of the United States, it is construed that the father's name is the middle name and the mother's the last name. Hispanos may continue to use their mother's name as surname, assuming that "that's how one does in this country." Hispano children may be given first names in English by their parents even if they are born in Puerto Rico. Or in New York their names may be translated or even changed by the schools, by employers, or in other settings of the larger society. A member of the field team witnessed such an incident while visiting an Eastville public school. A Hispano woman walked shyly into the principal's office, handed a note to a clerk, and said that she was looking for her son, Albert Cruz. The clerk looked at the note and went to the files. He searched through the cards, and then returned to Mrs. Cruz, saying, "Oh, you mean Louie. We call him Louie. See," he continued, "here's his card and his name is Louie." Mrs. Cruz commented, "At home we call him Albert." The clerk asked her, "What is your name?" She replied, "Maria." "And your husband is Albert, right?" The mother nodded. "No," said the clerk, "your boy's name is Louie. It says right here that your name is Maria and his father's is Albert and he is called Louie." The clerk claimed that the name Louie had been taken from the birth certificate of the child, to which the mother replied, "But at home I have a certificate that says his name is Albert." At that the clerk said flatly, "You had better start calling him Louie because we do."

While in Puerto Rico it is understood that a child who bears his mother's last name instead of his father's is illegitimate, in New York the surname a Hispano uses is no index of legitimacy, for even adult Hispanos find many times that their names are changed here, are informed that this is their correct name in this country, that they should not use any other. To avoid difficulties and in compliance with the demands of the larger society, an individual may use one name when involved with agencies of the larger American society while continuing to use his native legal name with his friends and relatives. The assumption that an individual who uses his mother's name is illegitimate also need not be correct in New York, given the tendency for non-Hispanos to refer to Hispanos by their mother's name rather than by their father's. In Puerto Rico the father whose marriage is consensual may legally recognize his children whether he is single or also has a legal wife if the latter does not oppose it. Legal recognition of a child makes him legitimate, both socially and legally, regardless of whether the parents are legally married. (Under Puerto Rican law, children born out of wedlock before 1942 to parents intending marriage are automatically legitimate and entitled to use their father's name and to inherit from him, just as are the children of legally married parents.) Having the right to use one's father's name—this being the sign of legitimacy—is considered much more desirable than "not having the name," for illegitimacy is a social stigma and is sometimes used as an argument to devaluate a person's worth. Some migrants who in Puerto Rico were not recognized by their father have, on their own initiative, taken his name in New York. To be able to do this and thus escape the undesirable social position which was theirs in the island might in fact have been a reason for their migration.

Whether the children are legitimate or not is, however, not an important factor in shaping the attitudes and feelings of the mother and father toward their offspring. Children, either legitimate or illegitimate, may live with one of their own parents and a stepparent who have established a marital union. They share in whatever wealth or poverty there may be with the children of the new marital arrangement and whichever of their stepparent's children are living under the same roof. Essentially, all the children are treated alike, except that the real parent is expected to show greater favor and kindness to his own children. Large numbers of children are not approved, and a woman left alone without a spouse who has more than one or two children will have difficulty in setting up a stable marriage in the future, although she may be courted and propositioned by younger men who will not assume economic or social responsibilities for her. Small families are considered desirable, particularly by wives, who see it as producing too much work for them and too many troubles to have a lot of children.

When Mrs. Perea told an anthropologist that "five boys are too much for a poor family," she was referring specifically to her daughter Maya, the mother of five. Mrs. Perea is a recent migrant who came from Puerto Rico to live with another of her daughters but moved to Maya's home when Maya started to have children. Her statement on family size in terms of there being "too many children for a poor family" is not an unusual one in Eastville, where, particularly among recent migrant women, one often hears such comments. They will frequently speak about a family's having become too large to be supported adequately and for the children to be brought up properly. Many voice pleas for smaller families, even those who already have passed what they consider the limits of "good" family size.

While there is no concept of family planning and no standard number of children that can be said to be "the ideal" for a family, two or three children are generally not objectionable. Ordinarily, the economic circumstances and the levels of aspirations of the parents and older children seem to play a major role in determining the number desired, as witnessed by an adage frequently heard: "While God sends children, a poor man should try to avoid having too many." As soon as parents have reached a point beyond which they cannot support the family properly because of another child, they consider that having another will mean they have had "too many" already.

As the source of support for their children, recent migrant men also speak in favor of smaller families, and may blame their wives "for not knowing how to take care of themselves." The wives, in turn, may blame their husbands for too many children by saying, for example, "He wanted me to become pregnant so I would not go back to Puerto Rico," or "so that I could not go to work in a factory."

Migrants know about birth-control techniques, but one is

likely to find ideas among them concerning birth control that may play an important part in the development of large families. Among wives preferred techniques are usually abstinence or withdrawal, even though the latter is considered "bad" for a man. Men, as a rule, avoid using contraceptives with their own wives, though some men, particularly those who spent several years in the armed forces, do not seem to hold strong objections to this practice. Women's mechanical means of contraception, such as diaphragms, are known to exist, yet they are not considered desirable forms of prevention. Among other reasons for this, diaphragms—and also men's prophylactics—are regarded as "dangerous" to the woman; it is said that pieces of rubber may become detached and stay in the womb, causing cancer. From the point of view of both men and women migrants, the safest, most desirable, and most convenient form of birth control is sterilization for the woman. Sterilization for men is considered undesirable on grounds that it may jeopardize their masculinity. A woman may try to secure surgical sterilization in New York, but if she fails to obtain it, she may then go to Puerto Rico while she is pregnant. After bearing her child, she will try to seek *la operación* there on medical grounds.

Religious objections to sterilization and birth control are strongly pronounced and communicated in Eastville by members of the Church of the Pentecostal God sect (referred to in Eastville as the "Aleluya" church). The Catholic church also condemns birth control and sterilization, but while Catholic women who have undergone sterilization may acknowledge this to be "sinful," they say they saw no other choice but to have it done. The growth of the ideal of small families and the selection of sterilization of women as the most effective and desirable means of birth control are directly connected with the rising practice of medical sterilization in Puerto Rico. In Eastville these two phenomena are associated predominantly with recent adult migrants. Among adults reared in New York, while the tendency is also toward desiring small families, sterilization is not regarded in such a favorable light. Nor is it sought after as intently as among recent migrants, unless one of the partners in a marital union is a recent migrant who presses in that direction.

In Eastville women who are not sterilized and do not become pregnant are characterized as "lucky," while about one who has frequent pregnancies, it is said, "I pity her" (*pena le tengo*). So desirous to avoid adding to an already large family are the women that abortions and other forms of discontinuing pregnancies may be attempted. A woman may take homeopathic remedies, patent medicines, castor oil, quinine pills, strong purgatives and teas—referred to in Spanish as *tomando porquerias* or "drinking waste"—in addition to very hot baths to induce a miscarriage, or "throw it out," even after the fifth or sixth month. Either a natural miscarriage or one ostensibly induced by these techniques is called "an abortion" by recent migrants from Puerto Rico. Illegal abortions, although carried out in Eastville by women (*comadronas*) who do them for small fees, are closely guarded secrets, for, reported one informant, "a woman who has an abortion can be sentenced to death in the electric chair."

Children nevertheless are regarded as essential to married life. Through marriage and children the bonds between individual nuclear families and their numerous relatives by blood and in law will, ideally, continue to be important throughout the life span of an individual and remain sources on which he can draw for companionship, help, and emotional support.

The "Familia Unida"

In practice, not all the relatives one knows of, nor even all those one knows personally, are involved in or considered part of the "great family" group. There are certain circumstances that call for ignoring particular blood and in-law relatives—even those living in New York. For example, if one has kin he considers hopelessly poor, to whom he has never "owed anything," or to whom he is not to be grateful for any favor, these may well be disregarded. Conversely, those considered too rich will not be acknowledged either as members of the "united family."

Individuals who may ignore poorer relatives in New York, however, might have been helpful to this same kin had they stayed in Puerto Rico. In fact, many Eastville migrants buy used clothing, or accept gifts of various essentials from others, and send them to close relatives or friends in need in the island. A relative in New York who is in dire, but temporary, need of money may be helped financially, but he is expected to demonstrate his gratitude by repaying what was given him as soon as he can afford it. If, in addition, he tells other people in the social group important to the donor how good this person is and of the help he received from him, makes gifts to his benefactor, and pays him visits, he is considered *muy agradecido,* or very grateful. To demonstrate gratefulness is an attribute of a good person, and by his expressions of gratitude he gains in stature and approval even if he is poor.

Relatives in need likely to receive financial aid are those who are close biologically—sisters or brothers, mothers or fathers. Cousins, aunts, and uncles probably will not be the recipients of loans or gifts of money. If they live in New York, they may be assisted in obtaining welfare aid or a job, but after a short while in the city, an individual is not bound to his kin in as strong a network of obligations as he would have been in a small community in Puerto Rico. Thus here one is not necessarily obliged to give his relatives any sort of aid, nor does he necessarily expect any from them. In New York an individual's primary and almost exclusive duties as an adult are to his own children and his spouse, and he may "cry about his situation" (*llorar su situación*), or complain of his being in debt or not being able to meet his "obligations" on his income, to a cousin or aunt who expects his economic assistance. It is not unusual to meet an angry person who claims his cousin or sister told him of his economic misfortunes "as if I had gone to ask him for something."

Among migrants, relatives and ancestors are traced through three or four generations in direct line of descent. Cousins and aunts and uncles, two or three times removed, are also traced, their names mentioned and salient events of their lives talked about even if one has never met these ancestors or collateral kin personally. This knowledge about kin and interest in discussing them, however, is notably absent among adults who have grown up in this country. They may even refer to their aunts, for instance, as "sisters of my mother," or to cousins as "cousins of my mother or father," rather than in terms of the direct relationship to themselves, as is more often the case among recent migrant children or adults.

The use of different terms of reference for relatives is not a casual one; rather, it provides an important clue as to the nature of kin relationships and family definitions found among the various subgroups of Hispanos. While adult migrants, particularly recent ones, look backward toward past generations in Puerto Rico as the basis of family cohesion and identification, younger adults who have grown up in New York orient and emphasize their family definitions toward life situations in New York. Their emphasis is on their own parents and their own nuclear families instead of on an extended group that includes a large number of relatives living either in New York or in Puerto Rico. An exception to this occurs when one's relatives in Puerto Rico are considered rich or socially important. Then the names of these relatives are mentioned among Hispanos and non-Hispanos alike to display one's own social importance. One may hear both migrants and adults brought up in New York speak about their kinship with well-to-do or prominent individuals in Puerto Rico, regardless of whether such relationships are real or fictitious. They are claimed as a means of self-enhancement, one recognized as valid among Eastville Puerto Ricans.

Members of an extended family that acknowledge belonging to a "great family" and act toward each other in the ways that are expected of this group are referred to as a "united family" or *familia unida*. A family group of this type usually consists of a number of biologically related nuclear families which recognize mutual obligations toward each other in case of need. These are relatives who can be relied upon. They are included in activities related to important events in the lives of individual family members, such as sharing in the celebration of happy occasions and in the grief of pain, illness, disgrace, or death as well. Thus a birthday party, a wedding, a christening, and Christmas or New Year's Eve parties are occasions on which members of the extended family get together and express their feelings of joy and mutual affection by exchanging presents, cards, and other souvenirs. When there are crises, family members meet in the home of the one who has trouble and give him comfort, offering to help "in whatever way we can." They overtly demonstrate their emotional identification and concern by such physical expressions of sadness as remaining quiet and distraught for a while or crying. Women especially may express their grief with an "attack" (*ataque*). The pattern involves loud screaming, falling to the floor while keeping the arms rigidly extended and the hands clenched, and occasionally shaking. *Ataques* produced in this kind of situation are regarded as a demonstration of intense grief and as an expression of great affection and consternation for the person who is in danger. The woman who has an *ataque* in turn receives the attention of other relatives and friends, who rub her arms with a perfumed, mentholated rubbing alcohol (*alcoholado*) and carry her to a bed where she remains until she is able to relax enough to sob and burst into tears.

Men are expected to show their sorrow without tears. Their grief is "inside." Yet a man is not criticized for crying or having an *ataque,* particularly when the person in crisis is his child or his mother. Family members who do not conform to these expectations about grief and who continue to go about their daily routine without overtly showing their discomfort over the situation are said to "lack sentiments." Resentment over this behavior on the part of these persons may lead to extending disapproval to other areas of their lives. It is considered an essential quality of a good and worth-while person that he "have sentiment."

In a major crisis several related nuclear families, or members of the united family, may gather for whole days at a time, and perhaps even stay overnight together, until the uncertainty has passed. On such occasions the women share in the cooking and housekeeping of the apartment where they all stay. Sleep, if there is any at all, is for a few short hours. It is often interrupted by those who cannot sleep on account of their worrying. While news about the resolution of a crisis is awaited, snacks are served frequently, the women gossip and tell stories, and the men occasionally participate in these conversations or play cards or dominoes quietly.

When Dolores Mangual, a member of a *familia unida,* was taken to a hospital for sudden surgery, her brothers and sisters and their children came from different boroughs of the city to the home of one of her sisters in Eastville. Over thirty persons —men, women, and children—spent several days and nights there waiting for reports of her condition, in readiness to do what they could in her behalf.

This kind of interfamilial cooperation is part of what can be expected of a united family, that is, a family in which satisfactory relations among its members are maintained throughout their lives. Other types of cooperation within such a united family can occur in several other situations. A sister, brother, or nephew may be invited to use one's home as his own, to receive mail there, and to obtain services through it that legally are restricted to people who are residents of certain districts in the city. For example, when Natacha, who lives in the Bronx, was ill, she complained to her sister Marva about it. Marva asked her to come down to Eastville for treatment in a near-by clinic. To obtain treatment, Marva told Natacha she should say that she lived in Eastville with her and not in the Bronx. Natacha kept appointments at the clinic and benefited for a while from the medical treatment she received.

One is also expected to protect one's kin, their honor, and their interests, and to protect oneself from their rejection by, for instance, denying that one has relatives when being investigated by the Welfare Department. Such was the case when Lola claimed that her brothers and sisters were dead, because then they would not be questioned by social investigators nor be asked to help support her in place of her receiving welfare aid.

The Eastville united family is a two- or three-generation group, consisting of a number of brothers and sisters, their children, and their grandchildren. They will claim to have gotten along well with one another, recognizing and exchanging obligations and maintaining close personal contacts with each other all through their lives. Such a group can be said to be permanently established in New York City, although some of its members may go back to Puerto Rico occasionally, staying there for years sometimes before returning to New York "to the family."

From the point of view of those who uphold their united family, it may at a given time include relatives living either in Puerto Rico, in New York, or in some other part of the States. The bonds with brothers and sisters and their families who are too far away for frequent visiting are kept strong by the frequent exchange of letters and gifts. Among Eastville Hispano migrants there is a greater emphasis on maintaining closer relations with maternal relatives than with those on the father's side. This phenomenon is consistent with the emphasis placed on the importance of the mother as the reliable and loving figure who is devoted to her children and to whom they can turn for help. She herself is justified in turning to her own mother, brother, or sister for help because by definition a woman is expected to be dependent on her family. Her husband, however, is expected to be self-reliant and to be a protector of his own family and kin rather than a dependent or a supplicant for help in the solution of his problems. Psychological and social factors of migration and life conditions in Eastville have contributed to accentuating the individual's feelings of need and reliance upon his mother and kin. This help may be denied and such a course justified to others either on grounds that "things have changed" or on grounds that one "cannot afford it." Nonetheless, kinship ties, particularly those of persons related through the mother's line, are very strong. This alliance of kin based on relationship to the mother is characteristic of those families headed by mothers who brought up their children alone without much contact with the father or his family.

Though the ideal of the *familia unida* is spoken about in Eastville as a desirable kind of relationship among kin, in practice, it is warded off. The trend is for large numbers of acknowledged relatives to gradually disperse and concentrate into smaller units of kin and friends who are considered to be as if they were members of the family. The preference for the *familia unida* type of family in which an individual can rely upon kin near or far for emotional support and assistance is particularly expressed by recent migrants. These, nonetheless, are likely to suffer disappointments and conflicts when facing the reality that while the ideal favors the *familia unida,* actual living works against it. Under the stress of migration, recently arrived Puerto

Ricans are likely to try to rely more on their kin than they did in their home towns in Puerto Rico.

Unlike less ambitious individuals, those who are consciously motivated toward achieving a higher standard of living and comfort, as well as approval from the Hispano and the larger society, are likely to react against taking responsibility for recently arrived kin, particularly those who are under duress. Years of separation from the island, and of consequent discontinuity of relationships with kin, reduce the sense of obligation and emotional ties between them. Since the migration is a continuum, on the other hand, many families have been moving from Puerto Rico into Eastville and other parts of New York within short intervals of each other with a consequent continuity of the norms and ideals of a functioning united family.

In the practice of family living, in the economy of the household, and in the organization of family life, the basic group recognized among Eastville Puerto Ricans is the nuclear family. In New York the nuclear family is more sharply delineated and has greater importance than in Puerto Rico. The extended family group as defined here in terms of a united family is still linked in many important ways to the nuclear family, but in the context of New York the concept of the united family has been and is changing. The independent life careers of nuclear families, the social differentiation in status and achievements, social race, and the different types of life outlooks and values which migrants and their children have developed in New York City have all contributed to the modification of the united family, restricting and changing many of the activities and obligations delegated to it in the context of life in Puerto Rico.

In Eastville some individuals who considered themselves a part of a united family while their parents were alive now complain about the indifference of their relatives, particularly that of their nephews and nieces. Complaints are also heard about "how much the family members quarrel with each other when

they are together." Both of these complaints are characteristic
of those individuals whose brothers and sisters migrated years
apart from each other and whose children have grown up in
New York without much social contact or interaction with their
aunts and uncles. Often these children will have felt no ties of
affection and no obligations toward their relatives on meeting
them in New York. It is not uncommon to hear among adults
who have lived in New York all or most of their lives expressions of disapproval of their uncles, aunts, and cousins who have
migrated recently. They do not see much mutual ground on
which to meet, given their understandings versus those of these
relatives, and they refuse to be bound in family obligations or
ties or friendship with them. Young adults who have grown up
in New York do, however, seem to be friendlier and more accepting of the uncles, aunts, and cousins whom they have known
since early childhood. With these they maintain sustained interpersonal relationships, and may continue to do so throughout
most of their lives.

Although several relatives may live near one another and be
neighbors, the united family in Eastville, whatever its extent,
does not occupy a single apartment or household unit. Selected
relatives or friends may, however, live indefinitely in the household of a nuclear family. Individuals who do not operate as
members of a united family will not visit or maintain close
personal relations with relatives, simply because they are relatives, even if they live in the vicinity. The ignored relatives
acknowledge such persons as kin but not as members of the
united family, for they act "as if they were not of the family."
On the other hand, there are certain individuals who, although
not related biologically, are regarded "as if they were members
of the family." Frequently terms applied to real relatives, such
as cousin, or aunt, are used to refer to these special friends, because they are "like a sister of my mother," and her child is
"my cousin." Such friends are expected to visit each other

frequently, to participate in activities "of the family," and to demonstrate their sense of reciprocal obligation and affection as evidence of the enduring nature of their bond. Usually the members of the extended family and the friends that are considered "as family" are neighbors, although some of the individuals—kin or nonkin—in this category may still be in Puerto Rico, or they may have moved away from the immediate neighborhood.

Special friends may be even more strongly incorporated into the family group through coparenthood. The institution of coparenthood serves to strengthen the sentiments and bonds of affection and obligation between individuals. When one individual becomes a coparent to another, he knows that from that moment on he is expected to give and can also expect to receive much greater loyalty, affection, respect, cooperation, and services from the person who has become his coparent. Coparents are chosen from among one's special friends, favorite relatives, and immediate family members. An individual may have many coparents, and proof of his wide acceptance as a friend and a person "of trust" is the number of coparents he has. Men are cofathers (*compadres*) while women are comothers (*comadres*). These are the terms by which coparents address and refer to one another.

One individual may become a coparent to another by promising that when he has a child he will allow the other to become the child's godparent. He may never have a child, yet the two individuals will continue to consider each other coparents. When an individual does have a child, the baptismal and confirmation godparents of his child automatically become his coparents. The focus of the coparenthood relationship is between a child's own parents and his godparents, rather than between a child and his godparents. A church baptism or confirmation may never be held for a child, yet, since he has been assigned godparents, he has them, and his parents have acquired co-

parents. It is the lay social relation of special friendship or
favorite kinship, rather than the religious sacrament of baptism or confirmation, that coparenthood enhances.

Parents may either seek godfathers and godmothers for their
child, or men and women, friends and relatives, may offer to
become his godparents. The parents tell their child that he has
a godfather (*padrino*) and a godmother (*madrina*), or more
than one of each, since children may have several godparents,
and he is expected to address them thus and to ask their blessing when greeting them.

Padrinos and *madrinas* are said to be like parents to the child,
and if a parent dies, godparents are said to assume the role of
the deceased for their *ahijado* (godchild). In practice, it is the
padrino or *madrina* who is also a grandparent, a sister, or a
brother of one of the parents who usually will bring up his
grandchild, niece, or nephew in case both parents die. An
uncle-*padrino,* an aunt-*madrina,* or a grandparent-godparent
who does not give birthday and Christmas presents or "does not
even send a card" to a godchild will probably be disparaged by
both the parents and the child. Such an individual may be described as stingy and criticized for not fulfilling his obligations.

With migration to New York, the practice of having children live with their close-kin godparents in Puerto Rico, or of
sending them to stay with their kin-godparents in New York,
has become quite common. The former is particularly true
among husbandless mothers who have come here in search of
employment. These women, who usually bring one or two of
their children with them, leaving others either with their own
mothers or with their sister-coparents, are sometimes separated
from some of their children for a number of years. A special
friend, regardless of whether he is a godparent or close kin,
may ask a parent to "give" him a child, and a child may be sent
to live with such a person to be reared. This is most often done
when the parent cannot provide for the child.

In Eastville comothers who are neighbors may be asked to keep a child for a few hours without recompense while the mother goes out on an important errand, but a woman who takes care of children in her home in order to earn money will expect to be paid for taking regular daily care of even her comother's child. When Carmen went to the hospital to have her fifth baby, she asked her comother Naby who lives in the same building to take care of her older children, one of whom was Naby's godchild. As Carmen's family was receiving supplementary assistance from the city, she consulted her investigator from the Department of Welfare about Naby's being paid for this service. According to both Naby and Carmen, the worker agreed that Naby should be paid, but afterward changed his mind, "because Puerto Ricans do things for each other." Naby informed one of the fieldworkers that she had had a fight with the worker who got very angry and said she was prejudiced because she told him, "You should not do that to my coparent because she is a Negro like you are." Although the parents did not pay Naby for the service either, she and Carmen continued their close personal relationship, both of them blaming the worker and feeling annoyed at him for Naby's failure to receive payment.

Ethics and the Family

The problems of family living and the decisions that affect family size, the training of children, and the behavior of family members are affected by the norms, ethical values, and religious ideas of the Hispano sociocultural group. These cannot be explained in terms of religious orthodoxies, nor in terms of the social ethics of either Puerto Rico or the United States. The norms and ethics and religion of Hispano migrants make sense only in terms of their specific Puerto Rican backgrounds and their specific life experiences in the United States.

In most families neither the father nor the mother is likely to have been a churchgoer in Puerto Rico, and many will have held only nominal church membership. But here, as there, they will probably send their children to attend church services regularly and to participate in other church-sponsored activities. Both parents, however, are likely to resent attempts to bring them into church activities with their children as a family group, even should they be religious and members of that church, since, according to their standards, adults and children are not to partake jointly in activities considered serious, such as worship. A child who is not allowed to go out of his home alone may be taken by his father or mother to a religious service, or a child may accompany an adult to church just "to keep him company," but the motive of going to church as a family group is rarely, if ever, present or the idea accepted.

In religion members of the same family may hold different views, and small children may be allowed to choose the church they wish to attend, regardless often of their parents' own church membership. So, it was not strange that the grammar school age children of a Pentecostal minister in Eastville were members of the Presbyterian church. In principle, "All religions are good, they all believe in God," and it really does not make much difference which particular church one follows. All that is necessary, it is said, is that "one must believe in something," and to religion appeals are made in crisis and desperation. Children, nonetheless, should go to some church as part of their growing up, for it helps them to be good.

Man's life is believed to be subject to fate, and luck plays an important part in the events that are to lead him to the fulfillment of his destiny. A man may not be able to achieve his life goals if bad luck plagues him. A man of character, a man who is good, may have bad luck with his children and his wife, and a bad man may have good luck with his family. This preoccupation brings forth the problem of disappointment and life struggles that may turn out to be useless. The attitude is that while a man may try very hard to "get ahead" and be proper and good, he may be trapped by his own destiny or by bad luck into not being able to realize his goals. He will have lost them. Illness, poor economic conditions, serious misbehavior of the children, and "getting into trouble" are due to causes beyond one's control, particularly when one knows he has been good and done everything right. In the face of such events a person may have to reach for supernatural explanations. "What have I done that I have been punished this way?" asked Leon Toro of a member of the field team after his wife and all his children had been hospitalized for tuberculosis. Those who have been bad are the ones who can expect to receive punishment, and one may have to assume he has been bad in some respect and paying for it in order to account for misfortune.

A person must also protect himself from the evil power of others, and must try to do something to change his fate and to control immediate situations that are annoying and disturbing. To protect one's small and beautiful child from the power of the evil eye one can buy a bead charm of coral or jet to be worn on a bracelet or on a chain around the neck. The charm is supposed to inhibit the evil power of the person who unknowingly desires and envies the beauty and health of the child. And if a child suddenly falls ill or dies, it is possible to trace the killer to the person who was looking at the child, commenting with envy on his beauty and health. One can protect one's home from the power of evil spirits by placing permanently a glass of water on the transom of the entrance door, and one may have to spray the house with water in which aromatic herbs have been boiled to cleanse it of "bad influences." This is good for improving one's luck, for helping one to cope with and solve certain problems, such as chronic illness, chronic unemployment, and chronic bad luck. Whether Catholic, Protestant, or atheist, one can appeal to the saints and the Virgin for help.

The images of saints are kept in many homes regardless of their church affiliation. Prayers are offered them for they can make grants to individuals in need.

Religion or ideas about the supernatural then are not circumscribed within the boundaries of any particular church, even by persons who are members of a given church. They transgress into a variety of ideologies, which are not seen as conflicting with each other, but rather, are connected under the premise that all religions are good and that religion plays an important part in the training of a good child, and for the purpose of understanding the nature of forces that are beyond the control of the individual man.

Household Organization in Eastville

To speak only of the Puerto Rican family in New York and ignore the important variations found in household organization, ways of life, and cultural orientation would be to oversimplify the picture of family life in Eastville. Hispano families here are certainly not replicas of Puerto Rican families in Puerto Rico, nor are Hispano families here carbon copies of one another. To be understood the family has to be examined in the social context of its social experience and history in both Puerto Rico and New York. Many changes in the characteristics of Eastville Hispano families have been adaptive responses to the social and cultural conditions they have encountered as a result of their settlement in a New York slum.

Among Eastville Hispanos "living" in a household means sleeping there regularly at night. One may spend every day at a daughter's, sister's, or friend's apartment, but one does not live there unless one sleeps in that house at night. To Hispanos the basic household unit is the home of the nuclear family, and while other persons may live with them, this is not "their home." The family may include children the parents are rais-

ing as if they were their own (*de crianza*), but married children (with or without their spouses), other relatives, or friends
do not belong to the immediate family. When they live with a
nuclear family in its household, they are simply staying in
someone else's home. Say Hispanos, "Those who get married
should live apart."

An unmarried child is said to live with his parents, while a
parent who shares a dwelling with a married child is likely to
say, "I live with my child." "When I lived in Puerto Rico, my
children lived with me. Now I live with them," an old woman
now living in Eastville informed a member of the field team.
These statements reflect the fact that the authority of the household rests in the marriage unit, centering on the husband, who,
as head of the household, is called "the owner of the house," and
in his absence, on the wife.

Those who live in someone else's home, or *casa ajena,* are
expected to be bound by the central authority of the household
and are not to defy it. In someone else's home one is not supposed to do "what one wants," but to be restricted by and subordinate to the family of the home, "not as in one's own home."
The good household owner, in turn, however, is expected to
demonstrate his appreciation for the respect a guest has shown
him and his home by telling the guest to make himself at home
"trustingly" (*de confianza*).

Among Eastville Puerto Ricans having relatives come to live
in one's home is not considered desirable. One may have
trouble with them. Disagreements may arise over money, the
relatives may hold views that conflict with those of the household, or they may gossip about the household with outsiders. Yet
after an individual has come to New York, found an apartment
of his own, and written his family or friends in Puerto Rico
about it, he may still offer them his hospitality. In fact, before
migrating he may have promised to send for a relative or a
friend and to help him secure employment in New York. It is

difficult to renege on such a promise or to turn away family or friends who arrive here jobless and with very limited savings, for it is important to show the people one knew in Puerto Rico not only that one is doing well, but also that one is generous, hospitable, and capable of feeling pity (*pena*) and sympathy for someone else who comes here and is in need. But those who stay in the home of a migrant are expected to quickly find a solution to their problems of housing and acquiring some source of income of their own. Looking back on their first experience in New York—living with relatives and friends— migrants may later comment, "En casa ajena se sufre" ("One suffers when living in somebody else's home").

Although new migrants who stay with a family in Eastville may not find themselves entirely welcome and may feel uncomfortable, visits, both temporary and permanent, are a widespread phenomenon among Eastville Hispanos. Individuals staying with a nuclear family may be visitors (*de temporada*) who have come for a temporary visit. Their visits may be of indefinite length, and in practice they may turn out to be permanent. Those who come for a temporary visit may have their own homes elsewhere—in Puerto Rico, in New York, or in other parts of the United States. Lina Garcia's home is in New York. Her brother made her a gift of an airplane ticket to go to Puerto Rico for a visit, but as Lina was receiving supplementary welfare aid, she did not want any of her neighbors to find out where she was going. So she instructed her family to say that she was going to stay in Brooklyn for two or three weeks on a visit to a coparent. This seemed a most reasonable and believable excuse in the context of seasonal visiting patterns familiar to Eastville Puerto Ricans.

A woman with her children may ask her mother to come to New York to live with her and help her to take care of and bring up the children. A grandmother may leave her own household and her husband in Puerto Rico and come to New York for this purpose. Yet she can also justify herself for not leaving home to help her daughter, as she is still responsible to her own household, and her duty to her husband comes first.

When Ana Polo was bedridden, Ana's mother, who lives in the Bronx, came to visit her for a few hours each afternoon. She always left early, however, because she had "to cook for her husband." One day she said that she wished she could do more for her daughter and grandchildren, but since she had a husband, she could not take the time. Ana acknowledged that "a woman with a husband cannot." Meanwhile, the cooking, housekeeping, and care of Ana and the children, who were also sick, including an infant, devolved primarily on her six-year-old daughter, who was sick too.

If a mother who has a husband does come to New York to help her daughter in a crisis, she probably will return to her own home in Puerto Rico after the crisis is over. A husbandless mother, however, may live temporarily with her different children, particularly with her daughters, helping in their households, being supported by the "owners of the households," and perhaps receiving occasional gifts from her other children. But her married children, particularly her sons, who do not contribute will be justified by her. She will say, "They have a family to support."

An individual may live in New York and go to Puerto Rico temporarily on a visit to his friends and relatives, either for a vacation or to see if he can stay there permanently, and an individual from Puerto Rico may come to New York for similar reasons. This implies the dual residence patterns which are intimately related to patterns of migration to and from New York. When an individual moves to New York, more likely than not he will leave his family in Puerto Rico until he can send for them. As a rule, all members of a nuclear family do not migrate at the same time. At least a child or two will probably be left in Puerto Rico in the care of a sister-coparent or a grandmother, and sometimes they stay there permanently.

Antonia Gado, a woman in her thirties, came to New York by herself and left her son Carlos, an infant, in the care of her sister-coparent. In New York, Antonia married Juan Gado, and they had a family. She has not been back to Puerto Rico, but through the years she has corresponded with her son, who is now a college student. Carlos, she says, "does not want to come to New York . . . except for a visit." "Can you imagine," she added, "how he loves my sister, he calls her 'mother' and her husband 'father.' "

Tinna Rivas, a woman in her late twenties, was married in Puerto Rico "with veil and crown," that is, she was a virgin. Her husband, she claims, used to beat her daily, so she left him and came to New York to a cousin's home. Her two children remained with her mother in Ponce. After she got a job in New York, Tinna had to pay for her keep at her cousin's and had no money left either for herself or to send to Puerto Rico. Then she met Juan, who was married and had three children. Juan left his wife and went to live with Tinna. Now they have three children of their own, but Tinna has sent her New York-born daughter Cassy to Puerto Rico, also to stay with her mother, claiming that she was unable to take care of her.

Eastville children are sent to Puerto Rico for other reasons too. For example, Jack, a seventeen-year-old Eastville youth, says that his mother sent him to Puerto Rico nine times, because he was such a bad boy that she could not manage him.

An Eastville child may also go with his mother or father or godparent to visit in Puerto Rico. Perhaps he will attend school there and then return to his old school in New York when the visit is over. Children make other types of visits too. They may be sent to stay for a while with relatives or friends elsewhere in New York, sometimes just "to keep them company." A child from Brooklyn, the Bronx, or somewhere else in the city may come to stay indefinitely with his aunt or grandmother in Eastville, transferring from his regular school to one near his relatives while he is with them.

Children who are not with their own parents may be considered either to be living in their own home, even though it is not the home of their real parents, or to be staying in someone else's home. The distinction is meaningful to the child with reference to his position in the family he is growing up with. The child who grows up away from his parents but in "his own home" from a very early age is a "child by rearing" (*hijo de crianza*), treated by his "parents" as if he were their own, to such an extent that only intimate friends or close kin may know he was not born to the "parents." Such children are not considered to be adopted, nor may their "parents" ever undertake legal proceedings to adopt them. Rather, the status of these children is like that of children brought up by their own parents. They are referred to as "my children" by their "parents," who are "father" and "mother" to the children, and consequently, this becomes their family and their home is their own.

The children who live in someone else's home, rather than with their real parents or "their parents by rearing," are not fully integrated in the family as are those of parents by rearing. These children are placed with a relative or friend for a time which may be of indefinite length. The child in this position knows that where he is living is not his household, that his own home is elsewhere. He knows that he can be returned to his own home either at the will of his parents or at that of the persons with whom he is staying. Presumably such children will be sent back to their parents eventually, but a child may stay in somebody else's household for years. He is not referred to as "my child" by the head of the family with whom he stays, nor does he refer to that person as "my father," or "my mother"

Mary, a twelve-year-old girl whose parents and brothers and sisters live near the city of Caguas in Puerto Rico, is an example of a child who is staying in someone else's home. Mary's father is a carpenter who does not make very much money. Her aunt, who is also her godmother, asked Mary's parents to let her come to New York, promising she would send her to school and care for her in her Eastville apartment. When Mary's parents consented, the aunt sent Mary an airplane ticket and clothes. But Mary says, "I don't live in my house here in New York. I live in my godmother's house." In this house she is expected to help with chores, take care of her godmother's children after school hours, and baby-sit evenings until eleven, as both her aunt and uncle work late. Mary does attend one of Eastville's public schools, and her relatives provide for her, but her status is not that of a daughter of the family. While "a daughter of the home" would be expected to help in the house as Mary does, she is aware that this is not really her position in her aunt's home, but instead, that she is just a person staying there.

In Eastville some friends and relatives are considered to be in so close a relationship of obligation and "trust" (*de confianza*) that, although they are not residents of a household, they may act in the same familiar fashion around the house as if they were in their own homes. For example, they may be seen cooking or washing the dishes. They are usually neighbors—a coparent, a sister, a brother, or an in-law. Such a person is made to feel that he is trusted in the household and that he can behave in it as if it were his own home.

One day one of the fieldworkers met Linda Roman on the sidewalk as she was saying to her children, "Come into Tata's home, I am going to fix lunch." The fieldworker accompanied them into the apartment and saw Linda search through the icebox and cupboards, prepare sandwiches of tomatoes and tuna fish, and serve herself and her children. Tata passed by the table where they were eating and unconcernedly went on out of the apartment. The two women, Tata and Linda, are coparents, and are godmother to each other's children. Linda, in addition, is the coparent of one of Tata's own children. The kind of behavior this incident illustrates is not generally common to neighbors or coparents in Eastville. It is also considered undesirable. In the case of Linda and Tata, however, the intimacy had been made admissible and validated by their multiple relationships as coparents and godparents.

Ordinarily, trusted persons may drop in casually with their families at a neighbor's home at any time of the day or evening, and sometimes even a family's dog "visits" the neighbors by himself. Such persons may occasionally eat at their neighbors on spur-of-the-moment invitations, but these arrangements cannot be said to constitute joint households, for there is no common budget, nor does the planning of family activities include the neighbors. In practice, one is expected not to take literally the expression "Make yourself at home," for no matter how much trust one is accorded in somebody else's home, one is supposed to observe certain restraints.

Classified according to patterns of household organization and living, there are two main types of families among Eastville Puerto Ricans: the nuclear family and the joint family. The nuclear family takes several forms. These are stable couple with no children; stable couple and their children (their own, theirs "by rearing," and those who are "staying" with them); stable couple and their children, plus children of prior relationships; one parent and his or her children; and one parent, his or her children, and a temporary spouse. Joint families consist of two nuclear families under a single authority, who share living together on a common budget under the same roof as a single family unit.

Among adults who have grown up in New York, the emphasis on the nuclear family as an independent unit is very strong.

Although they may resort to their migrant parents for occasional help and may visit them frequently, particularly if they live near by, the most desirable form of residence for them is away from their parents' household and, ideally, in their own household. Recent migrants and old migrants emphasize the nuclear family, too, as the primary unit for coresidence. In contrast to Hispanos who have been raised here, however, for migrants the patterns of close interpersonal relations and the recognition of obligations toward kin, although usually weakened by residence in New York, operate to a great extent as special bonds that strengthen both relations with other Puerto Ricans in New York and relations with kin and friends still in Puerto Rico. The recognition of such bonds often modify household arrangements.

It is clear, nonetheless, that the fundamental unit in family living in Eastville is the nuclear family. If the father is living in the household, he is its head, and in his absence his wife substitutes for him. He has bought their apartment for her, and nominally it is her apartment. She and the children are expected to obey and respect his decisions, although informally and without boasting about it, she is likely to hold the real power. Within the nuclear family there are mutually adjusted expectations, duties, and obligations to be performed by its various members. Other persons who live in the household are under the authority of the head of the household, but what is expected of them is different from what is expected of the members of the nuclear family. To illustrate how a migrant nuclear family lives in Eastville, the story of the Rios family, a fairly typical one in terms of its organization and norms for living, is presented here.

In 1950, Tomas Rios received his terminal leave pay from the United States military base at Arecibo, where he had been steadily employed from 1946 to 1948. In the two years from

1948 to 1950 he moved from job to job, trying small businesses and odd jobs, all of which ended in unemployment for him. His efforts to find steady work were expended in vain, and he managed to earn only enough money to provide the most meager support for his wife, Paz, and his five children, who then ranged in age from four to twelve years. In a flashback of his life story he speaks of the many kinds of jobs he had in Puerto Rico, and says, "I started to work when I was twelve years old. . . . I have worked all my life." He had been out of Puerto Rico before his migration to New York in 1950, traveling as a sailor to South America and also to New York. He had worked and earned substantially in Puerto Rico during the war years in the construction of airports and bases, yet after the jobs created by the war had dwindled away, he could not find any job in Puerto Rico that would satisfy the needs of his family. Tomas had a brother in New York, and his wife had two sisters here; he also had nephews and nieces, cousins, coparents, and friends from his home town of Arecibo who had migrated to New York. When he received his terminal pay from the military base—two years after his job there had ended—he decided he would come to New York by himself, get a job, and later send for his family.

He flew to New York, and after his arrival rented a room with a family living near his brother in El Barrio. At the Migration Division office, operated by the Department of Labor of the Government of Puerto Rico in New York, where he had gone in search of a job, he accepted an offer of agricultural work on a New England farm. For three months he was employed as a farm laborer—Tomas's first experience with this type of work. Catching a cold that he "could not get rid of," he left this job and returned to New York. Then, through a private employment agency, he "bought" a job as bus boy in a Bronx restaurant, a job which eventually paid him fifty-five dollars a week, including double pay for overtime. He sent money regularly to his wife and occasionally sent gifts and clothing to her and the children.

A year afterward his wife sold their home in Arecibo, a bungalow they had bought seven years before near the homes of some of her brothers and sisters. Paz used the money she realized on the sale of the house to come to New York with the children. Dalia, her comother living in the Bronx, had written her that the whole family could stay in her home until they found an apartment. Paz and the children arrived in 1951, and with Tomas they moved into Dalia's apartment. The Rios family bought their own food and tried to contribute toward the gas and electric bills. This, their host refused. With the help of one of Paz's sisters who had lived in Staten Island for over fifteen years, Tomas found a four-room apartment in Eastville, which had some furniture in it—an old and dilapidated club chair, a love seat, and a bed. They "bought" this apartment from the tenant for $600 cash. Paz's sister lent her $300 to complete payment on the apartment as she and Tomas had but $300 themselves, and the family moved in. The rent was fourteen dollars a month.

Paz says she did not want to come to New York, but she thought her husband might start going out with other women: "On account of my damned jealousy I came. After he left Puerto Rico he never turned his back to look at it," she adds. The children were placed in public schools, and with Tomas's fifty-five dollars a week, the family managed. "We had no debts, we bought with cash in the hand, and I could always save some money," says Paz.

In 1953, Tomas had a work accident. He was hospitalized and released after a few days. Six months afterward a major orthopedic operation—recommended some months previously by his physician—was agreed upon by the New York State Compensation Board and performed. Since Tomas had been bedridden and suffering pain, the family had run out of income.

The payments for accident compensation had been discontinued, and they had used up all of their savings. Paz occasionally received small sums of money from her sisters and brothers in Arecibo and from her sisters here. This assistance was used for food and other essentials.

While the family was suffering this economic hardship, Paz became pregnant again. A visiting nurse informed the Rioses that they "should go on welfare" because they could not continue meeting the exigencies of life in this country without a steady income. The children were passing the winter in tropical clothing, and Paz could not step out of the apartment because she lacked a coat. There was no money to pay the rent, nor any for transportation and lunch for the son attending a commercial high school uptown. The visiting nurse convinced them that they should apply for aid, and she herself contacted the Department of Welfare, recommending the Rioses as clients in emergency need.

Paz was listed to receive supplementary aid for herself and the children. By this time Tomas's case had been reopened and the New York State Compensation Board had reinstated an assignment of eighteen dollars a week for him. As required by law the Rios family transferred their life insurance to the Department of Welfare, which became beneficiary in case of death of any of the insured members of the family.

Today, Paz Rios is a forty-year-old woman. Her husband is forty-five. They have been married twenty years. Tomas was always the main provider until his arm was injured in the work accident. Since his surgery he has continued to suffer from illness and has been unemployed. Meanwhile, he has been attending night school, and already has completed grammar school and started junior high. He still receives erratic, though frequent, medical attention, both privately and in clinics, and has continued to appear at hearings before the Compensation Board. Gradually, they have reduced his assignment of funds.

Trying to obtain an indemnification settlement for the injuries sustained at work, he frequently consults lawyers and friends. While Tomas has been losing his compensation, the Welfare Department has been increasing their aid to match the funds lost so that the family's income has remained constant. The children, as well as the parents, object to having to receive welfare aid.

The three older boys, aged thirteen, fourteen, and eighteen, have been working Saturdays for the past two years, delivering parcels for shoppers in the local grocery stores and earning from two to five dollars a week, which they give to their mother. Out of this income Paz provides the boys with a small allowance, pays for their haircuts, and manages other miscellaneous small expenses of the family. Paz herself has been supplementing the family income by taking children into her home for day care, and by occasionally cooking Puerto Rican delicacies, which she sells to neighbors who order them in advance. She spends three or four dollars at a time on this project to make a profit of about the same amount.

During this period, also, the family's rent has been doubled, and they have been shopping on credit at a bodega, as they have no cash available until the bimonthly Welfare Department checks are received. The children have been attending school regularly and have obtained special certificates for their good conduct and scholastic performance. They have learned to speak English fluently, while at home they continue to speak Spanish. Paz and Tomas promote the use of "correct" Spanish in the home, at times worrying that their children may "forget their language" and correcting their pronunciation. Tomas has also learned to speak English, and he can use it in conversation with relative ease, though he retains a strong foreign accent. Paz, who spends most of her time in the home, and who in New York for the first time has had to learn to go shopping for clothes and food for the family, understands conversations in English, as well as prices and other related information, but uses only a few scattered words and phrases in this language.

The Rios children now include a preschool-age boy, two children in grammar school, two in junior high, and the oldest son, who simultaneously completed both high school and training as a bookkeeper. His special training as a bookkeeper was made possible by rearranging the family budget and through the subsidiary economic activities of the mother, himself, and two of his younger brothers. Since the completion of his education, he has been employed "obtaining experience" in Hispano-owned enterprises, and expects to find a better-paying job so that the family "can get out of Welfare."

Not allowed to play in the neighborhood streets, the Rios children are growing up "in the home," although the boys are "given permission" to go to the park or to the back alley to play by themselves for a while. The girls are not allowed in the street by themselves, except to go to school or church, but go out visiting or to a home party or community center dance accompanied by their father. The children are active in church work and are members of one of Eastville's store-front churches. Through the church they attend parties, movies, and play groups. The boys are also "given permission" by their father to go to camp during the summer months, also through the church, but a daughter, now aged twelve, is not allowed to go any more. She went until she became *señorita* (menstruated for the first time), when her parents decided that she should not be away from home unless she was chaperoned. Tomas is a member of the same church as his children, and he and his wife insist that the children attend Sunday services. Tomas himself, however, does not go to religious services regularly, and Paz professes that she is an atheist and has never attended any church.

In the Rios family, authority as well as labor is divided

among family members. The children are supposed to ask permission of their father and mother before going out of the
house. They are expected to comply with parental decisions,
and disobedience is punished by either Tomas or Paz. Paz and
the children acknowledge Tomas as the head of the family
and its main authority. On one occasion when he was hospitalized, Paz gathered the children together and warned them
to be "good and obedient" with her for their father was sick
and "may leave us." Paz, a woman who claims never to have
been ill in her life, does most of the household chores and decides which housework is necessary to keep the house clean and
operating. She does all the cooking, assisted occasionally by
her twelve-year-old daughter, who also does the dishes because
"she must learn." Her daughter also helps with the small children, sews and repairs clothing, and in her mother's absence,
takes over the cooking and assignment of household duties.
The boys and Tomas are sent to the stores to do errands. Tomas
is also expected to perform such duties as taking the children
to the hospital, going to the schools to find out how they are
getting along, and doing some of the shopping for the personal
needs of his wife and children.

The Rios family receives frequent visitors who drop in to
chat day and evening. These include recent migrants from their
home town who live in the neighborhood, cousins, nephews,
brothers, and sisters of both Paz and Tomas, and non-Hispano
friends whom the children have met at school, church groups,
and summer camps.

Frequent contact is also maintained with relatives in Puerto
Rico. Paz writes her brothers and sisters three times a week.
The children have expressed a desire to go to Puerto Rico and
speak of their having been able to play more and have more
fun there than in New York. Paz says that she would like to
return, even if only for a visit, and that when she thinks of the
difficulties they have encountered in New York, she would like

to return to her family in the island for good. Yet she has not done so because her husband wants to remain in New York, and New York has been good for the children and for their education.

A migrant family like the Rioses may thus run into difficulties in New York. Yet their cultural adaptation provides them with resources that buffer the disintegrating elements of stress and reinforce the emotional ties of the members of the family. Having to rely on the community for financial aid is a source of pain to the Rioses, notwithstanding the fact that they supplement this with their own self-help and the occasionally accepted but not requested aid coming from their relatives. The Rioses, nonetheless, are a nuclear family household, and, as it is preferred by Eastville Hispanos, getting along with each other and with their kin without imposing on them.

Other household set-ups and nuclear family arrangements are also found in Eastville, however. Some people stay or live in the same apartment with a nuclear family. Their relationship to the members of the nuclear group is of different kinds and degrees, but they are appendages to the family, not integral parts of it. Such is the case with the grandmothers who come from Puerto Rico to live with one of their married children. Though they help around the house and with bringing up their grandchildren, they have no voice in making decisions for the household. These individuals—grandmothers, friends, coparents, and relatives—are subordinate to the authority of the head of the household, for they are living in *casa ajena*. They are living in the household that belongs to a nuclear family, rather than in their own home.

Another type of household arrangement is that of the joint family. This kind of family unit differs from the nuclear family that has other relatives or even another nuclear family living with it under a common authority and administration, for in the joint family there is recognition that all are family members and belong in this household, which is their own home. With this type of family unit members of three generations share the same household under the direction and authority of a grandparent who is "owner" of the house. The married children and grandchildren of this grandparent are subordinate to him. The grandparent in this position is, as a rule, a grandmother who is better off financially than her children and who has maintained her own household. There, her married children can find economic and social security after they have experienced difficulties in keeping up their own independent households, while her unmarried grown children do not have to seek to establish a home of their own because they can live with their mother. In their ways of living joint families promote the ideals of the united family. Family sentiment and obligations are encouraged to such an extent that the individual can always believe and even feel that he can rely to the fullest on his own family, that he will never have to turn instead to those who are not related to him. The joint family is nonetheless an expression of a type of family structure which leaves its members particularly open to the diverse conflicts which may beset Hispanos in the context of New York. In this sort of family structure grandchild, parent, and grandmother form a continuous unit. The conflicts of the young with the old, of the individual who has grown up in New York with his Puerto Rican-oriented parents, and the conflicts which are generated by the constellation of authority versus the various roles of subordination may be exacerbated for those who live within such a unit. The Junco-Chel joint family is an example of this type of family arrangement. Its story follows here.

On the fifth floor of a walk-up, in a four-room flat, lives the Junco-Chel family. The apartment is antiseptically clean; the cushioned furniture in the small living room is covered with plastic protectors; and wax shines on the linoleum which covers the floors. All the furniture looks new, including the table-model television set in the living room corner, which is also kept covered. The dinette set was a gift from the children to their mother. There are curtains at the windows, and no dust or dirt can be detected on the white window shades. The head of the household, Rosa Chel, is a "clean woman," who spends a large part of her time in the flat cleaning it.

With Rosa live her divorced twenty-seven-year-old daughter, Celia, Celia's two daughters, and Jack, Rosa's thirty-year-old unmarried son. Rosa is now fifty. Her skin color is light olive and she has kinky hair. Her father, she says, was a "white man," while her mother was dark brown. As a young girl in Puerto Rico she had a boy friend who was also a "white man." Rosa's mother did not like her boy friend because, she predicted, since he was white, he would leave her on account of her color. Rosa's own children regard themselves as Spanish and colored.

In New York, Rosa has learned to speak English fluently and with as much ease as she speaks Spanish. Her children speak English without any foreign accent, as do her grandchildren, but they all can speak Spanish, and continue to do so when they speak to each other and to Hispano migrants.

Rosa has lived in Eastville for twenty-seven years. Born in a small town in Puerto Rico, she was still a child when her family migrated to Santurce, a suburb a few minutes from the center of San Juan. Her father, a laborer, died when she, the youngest, was five. The family consisted of thirteen children, the oldest being eighteen at Rosa's birth. After her father's death her mother supported the children by running a small vegetable business. Marya, Rosa's oldest sister, migrated to New York in the early 1920s. Rosa grew up in Santurce and attended school through the ninth grade, quitting at sixteen, though she had wanted to become a nurse, because her mother could no longer afford to keep her in school. While she was still a child, one of her brothers, Juan, who was married and the father of three children, was killed in a street brawl, an incident she recalls with sadness. Her mother, she says, was not strict with the children and Rosa was allowed to go dancing and have boy friends. After she left school she helped her mother in the vegetable business. At seventeen, she eloped with Jaime Chel, an electrician, who was twenty years her senior. When she became pregnant with Jack, she returned to her mother's home. At first, her mother would not take Rosa back, and though she did so in due course, she would not admit Jaime Chel into her home until years later.

While Jack was still an infant, Rosa came to New York. Her sister Marya had sent for her and had found her a job as a maid in Westchester. Meanwhile, Jack stayed with Rosa's mother in Puerto Rico. Then Jaime came to New York and Rosa went to live with him in Eastville. They never married legally, yet Rosa took his name, describes herself as his widow, and still uses his name. "I didn't want to marry," she says. "I would have had too much trouble getting a divorce. In Puerto Rico I don't know how it is today. Before, people were living together for years and years better than married [legally]. I know people who were living together years and when they got married, they separated."

In 1930, two of Rosa's nieces came to New York and brought Jack with them. Jack stayed with his parents only a few months and then returned to his grandmother's home in Puerto Rico, accompanied by his aunt-godmother. Shortly afterward, Celia was born. The following year, Rosa had another daughter, Risa. A few months later Rosa was advised by a New York physician to have a cyst removed, and she went to Puerto Rico to have the operation performed. She took Celia and Risa with her, and while they were there, Risa, only nine months old, died. "They claim young children die if you take them there."

Rosa remained in Puerto Rico for three years, living with her mother and her two remaining children while her husband stayed in New York. In 1933 she returned to New York and to her husband, but left the children in Puerto Rico with her mother until 1934. In 1937, Rosa and Jaime separated "officially"—the years they had spent as a "married couple" were over. Rosa describes Jaime as being originally a good provider who later became a drunk, never buying her clothes or caring about the house or the children. Celia recalls one fight in which her father knocked her mother against the wall, which so frightened her that she took a baseball bat and hit him on the leg, throwing him to the floor. During the depression years, Jaime was frequently unemployed, working only occasionally on WPA projects, and Celia remembers how badly off they were, how often they lacked even food.

Jack and Celia stayed with their mother after their parents' separation, and Rosa received welfare aid for two years. Afterward she held several casual jobs as a cleaning woman. Then in 1942 she obtained a factory job that she has had ever since. In 1947, Jaime died of a brain hemorrhage.

When Jack was sixteen and in high school, he wanted to join the air force, and his mother "signed him up." Celia met a young man recently arrived from Puerto Rico in Eastville, and at seventeen, shortly before she finished high school, they were married. She and her husband lived with Rosa. Two children were born to this union that ended in divorce within a few years. When Jack returned to civilian life, he also returned to his mother's home. Both Jack and Celia are now employed and contribute to their mother's purse. Rosa is the head of the household: she makes decisions about food shopping and eating, she administers the finances, and she still exercises a rigid authority over both her children and her grandchildren.

Between the late 1920s and the mid-1940s, Rosa's mother, brothers, sisters, nephews, nieces, and their own families had

come to live in New York. Some of them occasionally returned
to Puerto Rico and then came back to New York again. Prior
to these trips to New York, Rosa's immediate family had maintained close bonds of affection and cooperation with her relatives on her mother's side, though apparently not on her father's.
"After we grew up and came here [to New York] we had more
arguments," says Rosa, pointing to the tensions that exist in
the relationships that she and her children have with their relatives in New York now. Still, in moments of crisis, Rosa is
called upon by a cousin or a sister to help, and she acknowl-
edges her obligations to them by doing things for her kin who
are in trouble. She, however, does not seem to be able to
reciprocate her relatives' reliance on her, for she complains
about how they depend on her and exploit her.

Rosa's relatives cannot be said to operate as a cohesive unit
—or as a united family—for their cooperation is sporadic, and
they seldom count on each other for recreation or visiting.
Spread throughout the different boroughs of New York, through
the years the families which formed a functioning "large family"
have become considerably independent of each other and less
bound to carry out mutual and reciprocal obligations. Yet the
"big family" still recognizes the norms or expectations that
guide preferred behavior among kin, though they fulfill them
only partially. Today, the Junco-Chel family is oriented toward
and relies primarily on social groups and institutions not connected with their kin. The family has friends in the neighborhood
and outside it—people they have met through their participation
in schools, jobs, churches, and so on. Rosa's closer friends in
the neighborhood include a number of "old migrants" from
Puerto Rico, but they also include old neighbors from non-
Puerto Rican groups. Her children's friends are primarily
English-speaking Hispanos and American Negroes, and so are
her grandchildren's friends, for her children grew up in Eastville, and her grandchildren are also being reared there.

Today, most of the Junco-Chel family's acknowledged relatives are living in New York, except for one sister of Rosa's who, after nineteen years' residence in the city, returned to Puerto Rico on medical orders. Rosa went to Puerto Rico for a visit with this sister in 1947. Her own children have not been back to the island since their childhood, but her grandchildren spent a year at their great-aunt's home and attended school there during that time.

Home Life

The home life of Eastville Hispanos is conditioned by their living in New York. Though recent migrants' home life contrasts at many points with that of Hispanos who have grown up in New York, the home life of both is different from that of Puerto Ricans in the island. Hispanos who have grown up here regard "American" home life as being different and as suiting them better than that of Puerto Ricans. They overtly try to be different from Puerto Ricans and to come closer to American ideals of family living.

For recent migrants, on the other hand, keeping the family functioning properly in New York is a new enterprise in living, requiring many adaptations. Young or old, the individual is oriented toward placing his family's interests before his own, and toward subordinating his own individual needs to the demands of family life. Recent migrants find that rules for family living are changing right before their eyes, and that new rules and codes for living are developing, regardless of whether they approve of them or live by them. These appear as part of the cultural adaptations taking place among Hispanos. Rules of behavior, authority patterns, decision-making channels, and the expectations of family members reflect the changes in the routine of everyday family life. This is an unavoidable aspect of the process of adaptation that migrants must undergo in order to live with minimal conflicts. The end-product may, however, prove to be maladaptive and hence destructive of the adequate functioning of the individual. Yet whatever happens to the Hispano family in New York is pivotal to what will happen to the personal and social development of the individual Hispano.

The Puerto Rican family in Eastville lives within the setting of a slum subculture, and is subjected to the stresses and difficulties, as well as to the social, cultural, and psychological potentials of positive adaptation that that style of life offers the underprivileged in this society. The family is also affected by the rules and standards set up by the larger society and its institutions. In addition, the cultural influences stemming from the adaptations of the Hispano subculture in New York present the Puerto Rican family with changed rules and norms to live by. What will happen to the family in New York is contingent, too, upon the degree of cohesiveness and adequate functioning it had in Puerto Rico. It is likely that a migrant family which did not function adequately in the island will disintegrate in New York in the light of the additional conflicts in norms that its members will meet here. The family that functioned adequately in Puerto Rico, providing basic emotional and social supports to its members, on the other hand, has greater resources to cope with the changing sociocultural environment, though it too here faces severe conflicts and stresses that may bring about its destruction. The process of adaptation of the family involves an emphasis on cultural traditionalism. As a means of counteracting social and cultural changes that seem incompatible with the adequate functioning of the family and its members, the uprooted family tends to reinforce the values of the past and to channel these socially by stressing the importance of parental authority as a source of control. That authority acts as a guide in the selection and acceptance of new influences, and the parent in whom it is vested is expected to use his power to halt undesirable changes. Should the authority fail, the migrant family is likely to be shattered. In the framework of the historical and environmental contexts of the Hispano migrant family, then, it is unrealistic to expect its smooth transition in the direction of middle-class core American values.

To insure its own survival, and to insure some kind of social and emotional balance for its growing children, the Hispano family will tend to seek adaptations that are compatible with its cultural ideology as well as with its subcultural settings in New York. In Eastville these adaptations are made in the direction of learning to cope with American life from the starting point of the slum subculture. There, while the father is the boss of the family, the mother holds the responsibility for managing family matters. This responsibility has been delegated to her by her husband, to whom she, in turn, is responsible. She can make rules for the children and other members of the household (except her husband) to follow, and while she can be overruled by her husband, there are areas, in which to please her, he will go along with her. This is particularly so in matters pertaining to disciplining the children and teaching them to behave properly.

A family in which "order" is maintained is considered necessary to the development of "good" children. Good parents must inculcate respect in their children, as respect is essential to the maintenance of order in the family and to the smooth conduct of family affairs. The lines of authority in a family are supposed to radiate from the father, as center, to the mother, and thence from the older to the younger children. When authority channels operate thus, a family is said to be one in which respect has been instilled and order is maintained. A good father expresses his love for his children by his control over their conduct and by presenting them with an example of a good man. In practice this means he is to support, guide, and discipline them.

Juan Ramon is considered by his wife a good man, except for three faults. The first is that he is weak with his children; they do not respect him and he does not do anything about it. Second, he is a jealous man. And third, he is "a man of color." However, he is a good father otherwise, because he supports his children, not only those of his present wife, but also those he had by his first wife.

Eastville Puerto Ricans also distinguish between "ancient" (*a la antigua*) and "modern" families. The family that is rigidly ruled by the father, or the mother, is called "ancient," and is different from the "families of today." The ideal of greater leeway and tolerance for the children is more distinct among young adults, whether they came from Puerto Rico recently or grew up in New York. As a rule, the younger parents are better educated than their own parents, have broader outlooks, and uphold the idea that there should be fewer restrictions placed on children by their parents. Especially among adults whose fathers were of the "ancient" kind and who made their mothers suffer either by infidelity, mistreatment, physical punishment, or desertion of the family, is there outspoken criticism of this type of family. It is said that these are different times, that one should bring up the children in a different manner, giving them more freedom and allowing them to play. Yet even among these individuals decisions about family affairs reside in a central authority, usually the father. The difference is that the authority is more flexible, less restrictive, and less formidable.

Good parents are always right, for what they do is for the good of their child, so new rules may be invoked and all rules changed at will by the parents in order to resolve problems between them and their child. The child has no voice in decisions made by his parents about himself or anything else. One day when twelve-year-old Joe, and his ten-year-old brother, Jim, were playing in an alley behind their home, Joe found a knife. His father who watched their play from a window, noticed the object in Joe's hand and called both boys upstairs. In an angry tone the father asked Joe, "Where did you get it?" to which the reply was, "In the yard." "What were you doing there?" Jim:

"Playing with a boy." The father took the knife out of Joe's hand and told both Jim and Joe that children should not play with knives. He warned them that "if the police see children playing with knives, they put them in jail." The father then said he was going to throw the knife out of the window. The mother, who had until then remained silent while watching the father scold the boys, noted that the knife belonged to some American Negroes who had lost it in the alley. The oldest son, a young man, said that the knife should not be thrown away but kept for stirring up the earth around the plants. The mother asked in astonishment, "What plants?" (there are no plants in the household), and continued, "I am going to use it in the kitchen; it is a good chopping knife." The father then went on with his scolding of Jim and Joe in the same angry tone: "If you find another knife, it must be brought immediately to your mother to see if she can use it in the kitchen." Then, looking at the fieldworker who had witnessed the scene, he added: "You see, they don't know how to play with knives, and did not know what to do with it." By this time the two boys were standing quietly beside the window in tears.

Thus the father switched his command arbitrarily in mid-stream, and whatever he might say or do could not be questioned by his children and at least not directly by his wife, for he holds the responsibility and authority. In most ways, the father is a "free agent." He can come and go as he pleases, but his wife is supposed to tell him or the children where she is going when leaving the household, or where she has been on returning.

At least once a week the father is likely to go out by himself, and seldom is he seen in the company of his wife. If they do go out together, he will probably walk in front while she lags behind with some of the children, as rarely does a woman go out at all without her children. Her husband, in fact, may be seen in the street more often with the children than with "the missus" (*la doña*). If he is invited to a party or some other recreational gathering, it may be specified that he "bring some of the children," which he will do. And even for other social occasions, unless he goes by himself, he will be much more inclined to take his older children than his wife. Hardly would both father and mother go out together socially leaving the children at home alone, for babysitters are not used. It is understood that the father is to spend part of his income on his own personal recreation and amusement, which includes buying beer for his friends, playing the numbers, and going to night clubs. Both at home and in the street he is likely to be better dressed than other members of his family. In a word, his own economic needs are recognized to be of greater importance than those of any other individual member of his family, although as a father he is supposed to acknowledge his obligation to support his wife and children.

To carry out his obligation of support, the father assigns his wife an allowance (*un diario*). She decides the family menus on a day-to-day basis, and on Saturday prepares a list of items for her husband to bring from a supermarket or the city market which is located within walking distance of Eastville. Although the heavy shopping (*la compra*) is done only once a week, not all that is needed for the week ahead is purchased then, nor is it planned in accordance with a weekly menu. Rather, the weekly shopping consists primarily of approximate quantities of the bulky staple items, such as rice, potatoes, beans, and other grains, which form the foundation of the family's diet, plus the particular food that is to be consumed over the weekend. In addition, it includes a number of special items not considered essential to the family's diet, but which have status value, or are indexes that the family is well off. These are beer, both with and without alcohol (black malt), soda pop—especially cream soda—cakes, and canned pear, apricot, or orange juice. The father also makes arrangements with a near-by bodega for the family to buy on credit some of the daily incidentals, such as meat, milk, and eggs. Not only does the father take care of the family's food shopping, but also he does most of the shopping for their clothes, medicines, and articles of personal use. If he is too busy or if his wife complains too much about the quality of his shopping, he may tell her to go and do it herself, but the children are likely to have little to say about what either parent selects for their personal use.

The family depends on both cash income and credit to supply its needs, which are to be met as soon as they are recognized. As a rule, no one plans a budget for expenses. Wages earned by the father are already consumed or owed by the time he gets paid. His pay probably will not exceed forty dollars a week, and his job will probably be unskilled and seasonal, with layoffs. He may have to hock his watch or borrow from professional money lenders, a finance company, or friends at high interest rates in order to meet such emergencies as illness or requests made by the schools for the children, or to make a partial payment on an old debt. A wife may exaggerate to her husband the nature of family needs and debts and in this way acquire some money herself. Other ways she manages to obtain money are by shopping for bargains and by telling her husband she has had to borrow cash for an emergency. Either she will save this money for a real emergency, hiding it some place in the house—in an old purse, a shoe, or underclothes—or else she will use it to meet immediate needs of the children, the house, or herself. Most wives who earn money at home, like those who take care of working women's children, administer their earnings themselves. The husband of such a woman may, however, cut down on her allowance because now she has her own money.

The housewife who conforms to the expectations for a good wife is a "busy" woman. She is not idle, she does not gossip or wonder what the neighbors are doing. She stays home and works almost constantly, because "the work of a woman never ends."

In the morning the wife gets up before her husband and children, usually between six and seven, depending on the time her husband must be at work and the children in school. If she has a baby, it is to be fed soon after it wakes up, but one of her first chores is to prepare breakfast for her husband. She boils fresh milk and makes coffee, preferably a brand said to be of "Latin flavor" (*al gusto latino*), such as Cafe Bustelo or Cafe Crema. The coffee considered best is the strong and flavorful one, and this is at its best when served with a lot of milk—"quite white" (*bien blanco*)—and flavored with sugar. The husband may have a piece of white bread spread with margarine or butter with his coffee. While he eats his breakfast, his wife prepares his lunch, which usually consists of a sandwich of white bread, filled with a slice of processed meat or cheese, and a thermos of coffee. The wife may take a cup of coffee while she stands to fix her husband's lunch or does other early morning chores around the house, but she does not sit down to eat with him. If she has school-age children, she will call them, and it is her job to see that they clean themselves up properly. Breakfast for the children is not standardized except that all are expected to drink coffee with milk and sugar. This is the basic breakfast for both young and old. A child may refuse to consume more than this, but if circumstances permit, the children may be offered a choice of corn flakes, fritters, or a piece of cake. If they are skinny (*flacos*) or have no appetite (*desganados*), they may have to take "medicine"—cod liver oil or a liquid or semiliquid patent tonic "with vitamins." After breakfast, on leaving for school, the children are expected to ask a blessing from their mother and also one from their father, if he is still home.

Breakfast over, if she does not have to walk the children to school, the mother may start to reorganize the household by making beds and folding up cots, love seats, sofas, and other furniture used as beds. After she does this and her apartment looks tidy, she may go back to bed herself for a nap until around ten, when she is to start her mopping and the daily washing of shirts, bedding, diapers, dresses, pants, and so on. By afternoon one sees lines of clothing extending from one end of the kitchen to the other, or out of the window on a clothesline through the yard. While performing these duties the mother may have a second cup of coffee, and afterward she may have to go down to the bodega to buy milk or sugar or some other food-stuff, to use during the day, before she undertakes her other daily chores of ironing and mending. Several such trips may be necessary, and even when the children come home from school, they may be asked to bring up still other items that she "forgot" she did not have in the house and that will be needed for dinner or snacks. When the mother is not going far, she may leave the small children sleeping in the apartment by themselves, asking a next-door neighbor to look in on them occasionally while she is gone. While shopping she is likely to meet her friends and neighbors and exchange information with them, making it something of a social expedition.

For business that will require more time or take her out of the neighborhood, the mother will ask one of her school-age children to stay home to look after the younger ones, while another of her older children may have to go along with her. This child acts both as a translator and as a protector of her virtue, because a good woman is not to be seen alone in the street: a woman alone in the street must of necessity be doing something bad or looking forward to doing something bad.

The children attending school in or near Eastville may come home after having had their lunch at school for a second lunch at home—usually bread and butter or a slice of processed meat and a cup of coffee with milk and sugar. Children who claim they do not like the school lunch do not eat at school at all. They come home for their meals, which may consist of canned food, such as spaghetti or soup, with or without a slice of bread, coffee with milk and sugar, or just soda pop. The mother may have a cup of coffee and a slice of white bread for lunch unless there are guests in the house. When guests are present, she may either forego eating lunch altogether, or she may prepare sandwiches or canned food. After the children come home from school at around three, they are expected to have coffee with milk, and even a baby may be fed a bottle of coffee with milk in it at this time.

In the morning the mother will put beans in water to soak, and around two in the afternoon she will probably start to boil them and to prepare the dinner that will not be ready until sometime after six. Rice and beans, or rice and some other grain, are essential to a real dinner. The rice may be "white" or "stewed" (*guisado*). White rice is cooked in boiling water, and after it is soft, one or two large spoonfuls of lard are added. A basic method of making stewed rice is to fry chopped pieces of salt pork and add to this small chunks of tomatoes, garlic, onion, and greens, which are pounded on a wooden mortar with a pestle. The rice, which is first fried and then boiled in additional water until the grains are soft but loose, is added to this mixture, and on top is placed either *achiote* (a tropical fruit pulp, annatto) or tomato sauce, "to add color to it." To cook beans or other grains a similar procedure is followed, namely, small chunks of pounded ham, salt pork, tomatoes, and so on are fried and added to the beans or grains after they have boiled, and then the whole is simmered together.

Rice and beans do not constitute a balanced meal, however, though a complete dinner that includes them is considered necessary to good health, for "it is fattening and makes a person strong." To be complete a meal must include a side dish, called a "mixture" (*mixtura*). This can be fried eggs, fried potatoes, slices of fried plantains, or fritters of meal flour and dried codfish, meat, or chicken. After dinner, coffee is served again. Salads, green vegetables, fresh fish, and fresh fruits are seldom, if ever, part of the daily diet. Sunday meals, particularly the dinner in the middle of the day, usually consist of rice with chicken and beans; or rice and beans and pork chops; or filet of beef; or fried chicken as *mixtura*. Meats and poultry are cooked until well done.

As a rule, meals are not eaten by all the family together. Usually the father is served alone so that he will not be disturbed, unless a "person of importance" (*persona de cumplido*) or a close male friend of his has dropped in at dinnertime. For a person of importance a special meal must be prepared, or else he may be asked politely and without insistence, "Would you join us?" and he, according to convention, is to reply, "No, thanks. I already ate." A close friend, on the other hand, will be urged to stay for dinner, and such extras as canned soup, canned spaghetti, or more fritters prepared. That is, the wife improves on the *mixtura,* insisting that "there is enough for all."

On Sundays and holidays, it is expected that friends and relatives will drop in unexpectedly to "spend the day." They are invited to eat and are to be impressed with the good living the family is enjoying, as can be estimated by the quantity and quality of the food they are served. Such visiting at home, by one whole family with another whole family, or going to the parks or beaches in the summer, represents almost the only recreation indulged in by the members of a family as a group. Otherwise, leisure-hour activities are contingent upon the age, sex, and position in the household of individual family members.

Children are not to eat with adults. The mother calls and serves them separately, and she may have to prepare something special for those who say they do not like rice and beans and for those who say they will eat later. Mothers often claim that their children do not like Puerto Rican food: "They eat only American [food]." And this kind of food may be prepared for them. When asked what American foods the children like, mashed potatoes, spaghetti, fried chicken, and canned foods are mentioned. Mothers also often claim that they have to cook rice and beans daily on account of their husbands, because they themselves will "eat anything." Mothers may also say, "I hate milk," or, "I hate eggs," or, "I don't like meat." These remarks reflect, on a latent level, an aspect of "good" motherhood conditioned by circumstances of scarcity, namely, that a mother is to keep secret from her husband and children her liking for "expensive foods." She justifies her rejection of them by saying she does not like them. When she buys these products, it is understood that she is not to consume them herself but to leave them for her husband and children.

A mother will also cook special food for those children who are considered to be underweight or to have a delicate taste that does not permit them to eat "regular food," because they might get sick. These children are termed *delicado* or *mañoso.* In Spanish the auxiliary verb *ser* is used with *delicado* to connote "delicate." *Estar delicado,* on the other hand, means to have pulmonary tuberculosis. A *delicado* child in the former sense is actually a spoiled child, and psychologically he can be characterized as a child with strong dependency needs for his parents, particularly his mother, which he satisfies through special food demands. This is also a culturally acceptable way of dealing with sibling rivalry. The father or mother may punish a child who does not eat, though not if he is *delicado,* but rather if he was eating candy or bread before the meal (eating *vicios*), which spoiled his appetite.

The mother will probably have her own dinner after everybody else has been served. No doubt she will be so tired by that time that she will have a few spoonfuls of food from the kettles and pans rather than serve herself on a dish. As she takes her few bites standing by the stove, she may remark, if visitors are present, that she never has enough time to sit down and eat. Afterward, perhaps she will ask one of her daughters to help her with the dishes and with cleaning up the kitchen, but she is not likely to ask her husband or sons to help her with these tasks because they are considered "womanly."

While the mother cleans up, the father and the children may move into the living room where several activities will probably take place simultaneously. One child may study, another watch "The Lone Ranger" on TV, the father listen to the "Spanish Hour" on the radio, and visitors come in to chat. Watching TV, listening to the radio, and engaging in conversation are the chief pleasure-time pursuits in the home, and talking is usually reserved to adults, especially men, as children are not allowed, or at least not supposed, to move around too much, to play, or to make noise at home. While the father and the after-dinner visitors are talking, he may offer the guests coffee, hot chocolate, soda pop, canned juices, or nonalcoholic beer, which he will call upon his wife to serve. Then, after she has finished the kitchen work, she may come and sit in the living room for a time, until around ten when the children are to take their baths. At that point she will bathe those "who do not know how to." In the meanwhile, the father may have gone out "to the corner." On his return he will probably retire. There are many nights when the mother is not likely to go to bed until after midnight, however, or whenever it is that she finishes her household chores.

A good woman is expected to attend to her household duties regardless of whether she must seek employment outside of her home. She may call on her mother in Puerto Rico to come to New York and help her or else send for her niece or godchild to help her maintain the order and cleanliness that bespeaks a good family. Should she fail on this score, she is considered dirty and can only be socially justified on account of illness. Seldom are the condition of the buildings, the dirt and garbage in the surroundings of her home considered justifiable explanations for not having a spic-and-span household, for in terms of standards of recent migrants, the condition of the household is solely a woman's responsibility. By the same token, the condition of neglect of the neighborhood buildings, streets, and alleys is seen as being solely the responsibility of the government.

Among women brought up in this country the ideal of a good woman as one who is responsible only to her home, husband, and children is considered old-fashioned. Rather, among them prevails the concept of womanhood as associated with equivalent responsibilities between husband and wife, the availability of time for recreation and enjoyment away from household chores, both for the family as a group and for the couple as husband and wife. These ideals of behavior call for a different kind of organization of daily activities for women reared in this country than that of recent migrant women. Caught between these sets of standards, many Eastville Hispano women fail to achieve their goals, even if they pay lip service to the cultural ideals of good womanhood.

Growing up
in Eastville

ALL societies train their young to become the conventional citizens of tomorrow, who, in turn, will have the task of training their children, and so on through succeeding generations. This training-chain is characteristic of all human beings, for humans do not share the refined equipment of instincts that other animals possess to adapt themselves and to maintain their lives in the face of changing conditions. Men, instead, are equipped with a superior intelligence that has made possible many transformations of the natural world itself through the creation of science and art and the social and political institutions which are necessary to these developments. All these human products serve men in their living; they are cultural experiences that can be put to the service of better living and happiness or used to deter and destroy human life. In the United States, where man has created prosperity and abundance to surpass those of any other land, large numbers of people still are not able to partake of these fruits because they are denied some of their share of the human equality and opportunity for all individuals that stand at the base of the spiritual values of this country. Despite the social counterforces which act against these practices, many Americans continue to have their chances for adequate housing, earning a living, and educating their children curtailed on account of their race, religion, language, or cultural background. In New York City today, the two most salient groups of American citizens in such circumstances are American Negroes and Puerto Ricans. Their position as minority groups in the society profoundly affects their ways of life, their potential social adaptations, and the personal development and life-chances of their members. Rather than racial or biological explanations, the social circumstances of their lives as members of minority groups account for the problems and difficulties they face.

Theoretically increased social acceptance and tolerance for minority groups would widen opportunities for their members and consequently allow for their increased contributions to the community at large. Social discrimination and prejudice basically deprive a society of sound human relations and hence of effecting a greater development and achievement of its human potential.

In the midst of a society where opportunities for better living are being sought and social discrimination operates to hinder social achievement, Puerto Rican migrants must find a formula for living. Regarded as a problem for New York City, Puerto Ricans have problems of their own and solutions to them that, while not always recognized or acceptable to the larger society, make their lives tick. As pointed out elsewhere in this volume, not all Puerto Ricans in New York are migrants, yet a large majority are so, and come to New York, in their own words, "to adventure," "to progress," or "for the children's sake." Within the migrant community itself Puerto Ricans in New York are far from conforming to a common culture or system of values and ideals. Their adaptations to living in New York have been conditioned by their socioeconomic status, their length of time in the city, their age at migration, and their racial status. Those living in a slum like Eastville are particularly underprivileged, like other people living there. Their acculturation moves in the direction of adapting themselves within the slum subculture, learning about American culture from that standpoint.

Puerto Rican children growing up in Eastville are not unlike other children of this land who grow up on the wrong side of the tracks. As a whole, the life experiences of these children are probably more different from those of Hispanos living in Eastville today who grew up in small towns and on the outskirts of cities in Puerto Rico than from those of other children born in this country in similar socioeconomic circumstances. But to understand the Puerto Rican children now growing up in Eastville it is necessary first to look into their homes, their schools, and the ideals of behavior held by their parents, peers, and teachers.

Most Hispano parents in Eastville were trained to be good parents and learned their basic philosophies and techniques of raising children properly in Puerto Rico, where they were born and lived to adulthood, when they migrated to New York. The ideas and conceptions that they learned as proper for bringing up children were oriented toward Puerto Rican society. Had the recent migrant adults of today been reared in New York instead, regardless of whether their own parents were recent Puerto Rican migrants at the time they were being formed into adults, they would have been quite unlike their own parents, and unlike other Puerto Ricans of similar backgrounds to their parents'. Hispano adults of today who were reared in New York are likely to be more similar to other New Yorkers of comparable socioeconomic groups who also grew up in the city, and hence share more with them than with recently arrived Puerto Rican migrants in their views on how to bring up children. In response to the cultural and social changes brought about by migration, the recent migrant family may adhere to more traditional and conservative practices in child-rearing matters than

they might have had to in Puerto Rico. Through time of residence in New York, however, child-rearing practices may be
modified in attempts to cope with the contingencies of living in
the city. And the Puerto Rican child who grows up in New York
is likely to be more of a New Yorker than a Puerto Rican, as
can be predicted from New York-reared Hispano adults of
today.

The converse of this might be illustrated with an example of
an American family from Boston or Des Moines or anywhere
else in the United States moving to Puerto Rico and rearing their
small children there. If the children played with Puerto Rican
children, attended school with them, and stayed in the island
until they became adults, they would be more amenable to
"picking up" Puerto Rican cultural standards and would do so
more rapidly than their parents who were born and grew up in
the United States. The children would also learn to feel at home
in Puerto Rico with greater ease than would their parents, to
the point that they might even feel more comfortable speaking
in Spanish and living among Puerto Ricans than speaking in
English and living among Americans. It is then likely that in
order to keep the family going in terms of what the American
parents themselves learned was proper, given their various subcultural backgrounds, they would overemphasize with their children the "ways of becoming good Americans." They would discourage their children from mixing with Puerto Rican children
and would center their own family life among American friends
and neighbors, while maintaining a social distance between
themselves and Puerto Ricans. Even so, their efforts toward
Americanizing their children would create more conflicts for the
children than if they had stayed in Des Moines, for in Puerto
Rico, to become healthy, functioning adults, the children could
not live isolated from the influences of Puerto Rican culture on
them.

This process has striking parallels in the situation of Puerto

Ricans in New York City. Hispanos who have migrated as adults face similar problems in this respect to their American counterparts in Puerto Rico. Behavior which is considered proper and normal in the society which they have entered here is not always so considered by them, and vice versa. On trying to bring up a family in New York, recent adult migrants face a host of new problems, dilemmas, and conflicts. Many of their conceptions about child rearing just do not work with the same results here as they would have had in Puerto Rico, for they are not always approved of either by the larger society or by the Hispano subculture. Hence, they cannot be effectively inculcated in the children unless the techniques to enforce them are altered. As the children start to make friends and attend school, they are increasingly influenced by ideas and beliefs that are often seen as threats by their parents. Although the parents themselves are changing their ways, they are less exposed to the new sources of behavior than are their children, and as already developed adults they are apprehensive and less acceptant of integrating new beliefs and ideas that seem incompatible with their own lives.

Although the home is not the only institution in modern society that cares for the child and trains him so that he can learn the roles he will play as an adult, it is basic in shaping his values, social attitudes, and techniques for dealing with the particular society in which he lives. Thus it has foremost consequence in the ways Hispano children—like any others—are brought up in New York. Nowadays, however, mass communication media, the school, friendship groups, and multiple other social activities in which the individual participates at the various stations of his life are also of great importance in influencing and prescribing his future as a member of his society. Radio, television, movies, books, newspapers, and other techniques of communication have brought into people's lives new traditions, values, and ways of behavior. Neither young nor old have escaped the impact of those "visits into their living rooms" made through their television sets by persuasive MC's and salesmen. While these proselytizers partly support the home as a symbol of the good life, the modern family finds itself involved with all sorts of agents whose advice, teaching, and admonitions are not always easily incorporated into people's lives. Still, it is the family on which the society ultimately fixes the responsibilities for its youth, and the home is expected to act as a clearinghouse for the cultural inventory the child is to learn and make part of his own self.

The second most important institution in the life of the individual is the school. It trains him formally and informally for a number of years, attempting to broaden and specialize his capacity for living by imparting to him the technical knowledge and skills that he can use to build his future and serve his community. While at times the school complements the home, at other times the home and the school conflict with each other, even as they try to supplement their respective tasks.[1]

The social contexts of their home life—the society in which individuals live—leave strong marks on the way of life and cultural behavior of the society's members. Hispanos who grow up in New York from early childhood, for example, reflect this in many a social attitude and belief, often quite different from those of Hispanos raised in Puerto Rico. Many have reacted strongly against the child-training practices and beliefs of their parents, and look forward to their own family life in terms that are more meaningful and acceptable to themselves as members of American society. Though they identify themselves as Hispanos, many characteristics of social behavior attached to Puerto Ricans have disappeared among them under the impact of their continuous life experience in New York.

Important though they are, however, family training and

[1] Robin Murphy Williams, *American Society: A Sociological Interpretation* (New York, Knopf, 1951).

home life, school curricula, preachers' sermons, television screen, comic books, and friends are by no means the only sources of knowledge available to children. They learn from multiple informal situations, and as a result they often baffle teachers, preachers, and parents. These then try to explain the behavior of children either in terms of the company they keep, the kind of home life they lead, or, in extreme cases of erroneous explanations, in terms of their instincts or their "cultural patterns."

In the process of growing up, as in adult life, approval of those who are important to the individual is considered a necessary ingredient to acceptance of oneself and personal happiness. Yet quite often a child does not accept the teachings of his parents, teachers, or preachers. Consciously or subconsciously he selects the social knowledge that he will incorporate as part of himself. This is all part of the process of growing up. Yet, right or wrong, parents and teachers, among others, keep trying to form out of the child a conventional adult who can play his social roles adequately.

In scientific language the process and the rules by which any society trains an individual to become one of its participating adult members is called socialization. This process starts at birth. The infant learns first from his mother, his father, and others who are close to him. Since life is not static and men are constantly entering new situations and dealing with problems, big or small, that affect their lives, the process continues throughout one's life. Broadly, socialization is the process by which men become equipped to deal with the world in which they live as social beings, that is, they learn how to live with others, they acquire cultural behavior.

Hispano children who grow up in Eastville get to know and experience firsthand crowded streets, garbage, noise, old tenement buildings, the terror of gang wars, the presence of drug peddlers and addicts, missionaries and clergymen, group work-

ers and police officers, who are all part of the picture of life in
the neighborhood. Their homes are poor and they are acquainted with scarcity. They chew bubble gum and collect pictures of baseball stars. They live in a tough neighborhood where
bullies flourish and intellectual stimulation finds little if any
impetus. Often, they see their own families breaking apart
under the strain of misery, isolation, and illness. Their struggles
to gain acceptance as "good cats" in the neighborhood not infrequently lead them into trouble with themselves, their families, and society. In school, a new dimension is added to their
world. Teachers and school authorities represent values and
ideals of the larger society. They stimulate dreams of high standards of living, formal education, fair play, self-adjustment, all
goals that do not seem to fit into the crude experiences of everyday life in Eastville. In the home, the street, and the school the
children are likely to find trouble, for though the slum has no
monopoly on human difficulties, they pile up there and become
part of the normal everyday life. Differences in ethnic background have little bearing on the kind of world Eastville children
get to know in New York. It is a world full of tensions and op-
posing forces that pull a child this way and that. There are
many troubles and discomforts in this world, but the child
must learn to manage in it, and not infrequently he finds in it
acceptance, love, and understanding.

One day a brick was heaved from a roof and struck a nine-
year-old boy who was playing marbles in the alley below. He
was wounded in the head. His three best friends took him to a
clinic for medical aid, and the doctor instructed the child to tell
his mother to keep his bandage clean. The following day Ted
showed up with his friends at the clinic again, his bandage gone.
Ted's friend Charlie, age ten, commented that if he had been
told to see that the bandage was to remain clean and on the
wound, he would have kept it so, but Ted's sister did not care
what happened to him.

Many Eastville children like Ted who receive no attention or warmth at home seek it in the streets. They find it in adults or other children who become their friends, protect them from the aggression of others, and supply them with warmth.

The Role of His Family in a Child's Life

For Hispano children family life, values, and orientations vary primarily according to whether their parents were brought up in New York or in Puerto Rico. The children themselves vary in their attitudes toward society, in their own values, and in their social behavior according to the length of time they have spent in New York and in proportion to their age at arrival in New York.

Among recent migrant families it is often found that the whole family is not living together, but that some of the children have been left in Puerto Rico in the care of a grandmother or an aunt. A child may remain in Puerto Rico separated from his parents in New York for years. When he does finally come to New York, he has to become acquainted all over again with his father, mother, brothers, and sisters, some of whom he may never have seen before. Nonetheless, the lives of parents are oriented toward their children. They claim their children are the primary interest in their lives with the words, "Nothing in the world is loved like the children." Parenthood attaches special duties and obligations to men and women. A man who has children expects to be given preference when looking for employment, for he must work to support his children, though in practice he will probably spend proportionately more on himself than on his family. This emphasis on the family as the center of an adult's obligations is cultivated from early childhood, while individuality and interest in doing things just for oneself are discouraged as being of no value. Success and achievement on the part of the individual are encouraged only as ways by which he can help his family. In turn, the individual who does not succeed can expect to receive help from his family. Doing things for oneself is just "not right," but to do things for others and to recognize this as an obligation are characteristics of a virtuous person. Individuality and self-assertiveness are not as highly prized socially as are dependency and reliance through mutual obligations.

An individual is to be molded throughout his childhood in such a manner that when he grows up he will be a "good" man or a "good" woman. In order for children to become "good" adults certain steps have to be followed by their parents in bringing them up. The basic ideals of behavior to be inculcated in the child by his family are respect and the fulfillment of duties appropriate to his sex and age. The end-product of a boy should be a man of character, who likes to work hard, has acquired an education that helps him get a good job, assumes responsibilities toward his parents by helping and protecting them in their old age, becomes a good parent and a person of respect, and does not get into trouble, although he has courage. A girl is to grow into a modest and virtuous woman. She is to acquire an education in case she has to go to work and earn a living for herself and her parents or her own children. She is to know how to cook and care for a home, how to be clean. She is to be tied to her home, busying herself with her duties, and not to be on the street, unless on "business," and she is to be quiet, obedient, and faithful to her husband. She is not to use dirty words, and she also has an obligation to her aged parents. She is to help them unless doing so would interfere with her marriage and her children's happiness.

But these ideals of the good man and the good woman are not prevalent among the Hispano adults who have grown up in New York, and even many recent Hispano migrants in their twenties are departing from them. They consider the whole complex old-fashioned and see it as placing too many demands on the women, making it too easy for the men and too hard for adult children, who under the traditional system are expected to support and take care of their parents at the expense of personal sacrifice of their own lives. Generally, however, these new ideas are not acceptable to most recent Hispano migrants, who continue today to try to raise their children in accordance with the ideals they themselves were brought up with, modified though these ideals must be by change of time and locale.

For recent migrants the question of whether or not to have children does not arise. The desire to have children and having them are what is expected of a couple and what they expect of themselves. When the wife is carrying their first or second child, there is usually a rather permissive and relaxed emotional and interpersonal tone about it between husband and wife. With the growing preference for smaller families among Hispanos, however, some later pregnancies may be unwanted, so that anger and tensions anticipate the birth of the baby. Yet an unwanted pregnancy does not necessarily lead to an unwanted child. Usually at the baby's birth the mother's feelings of rejection will no longer be expressed in her social behavior, and the baby will become the object of her attention, love, and warmth. Her sublimation may never cease, and the child may never be made to feel unwanted, even though he was an undesired fetus. It is also possible, though, that if the mother's feelings against having more children were strong enough, the rejection which cropped out during her pregnancy may reappear later on and be acted out on the child as he grows up. Older children in the family may, if they wish, express overt disapproval of the baby before he is born, but afterward they, too, are expected to change their feelings to joy and acceptance. If they do not make the conversion by themselves, the parents will use punishment to force them to it, for a baby is to be accepted and loved. Generally, however, the older children find their situation eased after the arrival of their new brother or sister as a result of the cessation of stress created by their mother's pregnancy. No longer will one or all of them experience the beatings and scoldings their mother may have administered to them (*le da con ellos*), for actions which in other circumstances would have gone unpunished, in order to express her hostility toward her husband and the coming child.

Not only is the child's birth order in the family important; his sex, also, is significant. Eastville Hispano parents, particularly fathers, speak of preferring boys to girls on the grounds that boys can take care of themselves better than girls can. When Beno and Germa Simer were expecting a baby, Beno told a fieldworker that he preferred a boy "because if I had a daughter and any man around here abuses her, I go to jail, because I kill him. And I don't want to go to jail." Yet boys are considered more difficult because they are strong of character (*fuertes*) and harder to handle. While girls are said to be more docile by nature, parents find that girls in Eastville require too much surveillance and care to protect them from the excessive evil they are exposed to here. It is said that it is easier for a parent to bring up his children, boys or girls, in Puerto Rico than in New York, although there are advantages in rearing the children here that are not to be found in Puerto Rico. These include more medical services, greater opportunity to go to school and become educated, and the opportunity to become proficient in the English language.

Here, when a couple are expecting their first child, the woman may consult her own mother or some other experienced woman who is her friend as to what she should do if she is going to become a mother for the first time. She probably will be accompanied by a friend to a clinic for medical care, especially if she is legally married. If she is not married, and her family and friends believe her to be a virgin, she is likely to hide the pregnancy from them and even from her child's father as long as possible. A woman who has had her first child in Puerto Rico and without medical attention probably will not go to a clinic or a hospital for medical care here until quite late in her pregnancy, and perhaps will wait until labor pains start, unless the pregnancy is not developing normally or she comes in contact earlier with a friend, a physician, or a nurse who advises her otherwise.

For her first child the mother is expected to prepare a layette. She is likely to purchase it readymade in the stores, rather than sew it herself and do handwork on it as she would probably have done in Puerto Rico. For later children she will probably dispense with a layette, using the leftovers from her firstborn, and she may also then accept outgrown shirts and other clothing from the baby of a relative or a friend.

Pregnancy is regarded as a state in which a woman is not going to feel well and will tire very soon, but she is expected to carry out her routine household chores nevertheless. She is allowed food whims (*antojos*), however, as these are considered necessary to assure the birth of the baby. To give birth here the woman is more likely to go to a hospital than to try to arrange with a midwife or a physician to have the child at home. At the time she gives birth, if the woman has already had more than the number of children she wishes—one, two, three, or more—both she and her husband may desire that she be sterilized. She is not supposed to have sexual intercourse for forty days after the baby is born; rather, she is expected to keep *la cuarentena*. Postnatally, she is supposed to consume highly nourishing food, for she "has lost a lot of blood." On her return home from the hospital she will eat *caldo de gallina* (hen soup) and drink nonalcoholic beer (*malta*), which is also considered a highly nourishing, good blood-builder and weight-raiser. For a few days this may be her basic diet. Then when she feels "strong," she will shift back to her regular diet. Perhaps the expenditures for the special diet are a precipitating factor in her becoming "strong" again.

Since the older brothers and sisters of an infant are expected to express their love for him, a child who has not caught up with the acceptance the rest of the family is giving the baby will find himself punished. In the presence of visitors he will be exposed to the censure and disapproval of his family through slaps and verbal clichés, such as, "You do not have sentiments," "You love no one," or, "You are bad." The older children are expected to help their mother take care of the newly-born, and they "are not to make the baby cry." If he should cry while they are caring for him, they are likely to be punished, and the slap may be accompanied by a loud and angry, "Do not do that to the baby," or, "Bruto" (Stupid)!

Fathers expressed a preference that babies be breast-fed, while mothers said the condition of their health should determine whether a baby has a bottle or the breast. The matter may also be decided by the doctor. Sometimes the mother will start to breast feed the baby and in a few days change to a bottle because she feels weak and the baby *la seca* (dries her up). The baby's liquid diet, including water, is given warm, and boiled warm fresh or canned milk, with some sugar added, may early be substituted for the breast or for the milk formulae prescribed in the hospital. Milk may be supplemented with sugared orange juice, and pediatric vitamins may also be given the baby if they are medically advised. In Puerto Rico the baby's milk diet is supplemented with medicinal teas or *teses* made from fresh herbs such as *tuatúa* (Elaphrium simarubal 1.) and *almácigo* (Adenoropium gossypifolium 1.), which are said to be nourishing as well as curative for the stomach. Here, however, these herbs are used only for curing digestive disorders.

Weaning the baby may be either gradual or abrupt. When the change from mother's milk to canned or cow's milk is to be undertaken, the baby is first given a purgative in order to avoid indigestion due to "the mixing of foods in his stomach." To discourage the child from wanting the breast, the mother may coat it with the juice of a sour leaf called *sábila* (Aloe vulgaris, 1.), making it disagreeable to the child who will then reject it. This she can buy at any of the "botanical gardens" that flourish over most of the East and West sides of Manhattan, or she may send to a friend or family member in Puerto Rico for it.

Gradually, after the baby has acquired his first teeth, his diet is expanded to include mashed potatoes and plantains, mixed with milk and olive oil; fried foods (plantains, potatoes); rice cooked with lard; and sauces made from beans, grains, and meat. By the age of two, a child can eat regular *comida,* including coffee with milk, but, in practice, even children who are four, are fed baby food, plus a regular adult's diet, and several bottles of coffee with milk a day, in the hope that they will become overweight.

The good infant is the one who *no da que hacer* (does not bother adults), who sleeps all night and most of the day. An infant may be said to have a bad temper (be *bravo* or *rabioso*) if he cries when he wants to be fed, changed, or caressed, but, generally, a baby is to be pampered and pleased by adults and his older brothers and sisters. If, however, he cries too much at night because he is *engreído* (spoiled), he may be slapped on the buttocks. The baby who is *engreído* is one who wants to be held and who cries if he is not held by his mother or the person who has spoiled him. While his mother is ordinarily willing to gratify an infant in his demands to be carried around or held by her or some other adult (her mother usually), the mother who already has several children is seldom the one who makes the child *engreído*. The child spoiled by his mother will probably find with the birth of another child that his mother has discontinued responding positively to his whims and desires, but another person in the household may then take over this role by giving in to his demands. The older children may attempt it in order to gain the love of the baby, or a grandmother may be the object of the child's affection in this sort of relationship. The pampering of a child may continue for a number of years if there is a particular person in his family who will maintain this relationship with him. With migration some children who were pampered by a relative or friend while the family lived in Puerto Rico have been left with these persons until their families could send for them. Other children have been abruptly separated from the permissive adult who spoiled them when their parents decided to bring them to New York at the time of migration. Leaving their loved ones in Puerto Rico is a sad experience in the lives of these children.

In Eastville an infant is likely to have close contact with a number of adults—neighbors, relatives, and friends—besides his parents from birth onward. He is an object of their affections. They wander casually in and out of the apartment where the baby lives many times during the day and evening, and are sometimes so much a part of his life that he learns to call several of them "papa" and "mamma," as he learns to address his own parents. Among these adults are women who, as a matter of course, bathe or dress or put him to sleep, if that is what he needs when they are present.

As a baby, before he learns how to walk, a child is ordinarily not taken out of his home, except to see a doctor or except when his mother is going out to take care of some business, to pay a visit, attend a party, or a movie. She is likely to take the baby with her on such occasions unless her own mother is staying in her home and helping her to raise the children. If he has a baby buggy, however, his mother will also probably take him out for airings on warm days.

The child who walks, unlike the baby, is frequently taken into the street to play and to go walking. He is always to be accompanied by his older brothers or sisters, who may be only a little older than he, by one of his parents, or by a friend of theirs. He is to obey the person to whose care he is entrusted and is told that he must keep holding that person's hand and not run away from him.

When the child begins to walk, adults expect him to be ready to start learning and understanding new forms of behavior. Now he must commence to obey, to control his aggression, his body functions, and his hunger. Some aspects of babyhood, like letting the child suck a pacifier or nipple and take milk from a bottle regardless of whether he knows how to drink from a cup or glass, may be prolonged by the mother for two, three, or four years. But his demands for close physical contact with the object of his attachment, including sleeping in the same bed with that person, while earlier gratified or countenanced by his mother, will now commence to be thwarted. As his mother or the other adult who has made him *engreído* stops yielding to his constant demands to be held, he will be cranky, cry in front of strangers who try to come near him, and often act hostile toward them. Now he is said to be *malcriado,* or ill-bred. To terminate both the *engreído* and *malcriado* stages, the child will be slapped on the buttocks.

While the baby was crawling, if he hit an adult, he was not *malcriado;* his act was a joke. When he starts to walk, such hostility to an adult is no laughing matter, and he begins to hear about the respect he owes his elders. As he grows older, he hears more and more about respect, since this concept involves the limits and the freedom allowed the individual in his relationships with others. The concept of respect claims of a child that he not transgress the bounds of whatever adults expect of him, that he obey without question and accept with docility the decisions of authorities, namely his parents and elders. He will be taught that he cannot touch and take what belongs to others without their permission or that of his parents, that children are good if they are obedient and thus do not make their parents suffer embarrassment or shame. As a child who is poor, he will find that he is not entitled to respect from others, but as he grows older he is due the respect which age bestows upon him and which he must expect and claim from others. A person of respect is a person of dignity, and it is thus of the highest importance that the individual first learn what it means to respect so he can require whatever respect is due him, according to his age and station in life. The way the system works, an adult still owes respect to those in a higher social position or with greater social power than he and to those who are older than he, but if he is poor, younger folk who are more affluent will also expect deference from him.

By the time the child is starting to walk, his toilet training is also beginning. He is placed on a pot at certain regular hours, slapped on the buttocks and told he is to use the pot when he fails to do so. He is to forewarn his mother of his needs so that she can place him on his pot or on the toilet. A mother who is not concerned with toilet-training her child by the time he walks is considered *abandonada* and *puerca* (a negligent and dirty pig). A good mother is a clean woman, and such a one will get up several times in the night to clean her child and to instill in him the knowledge that he should not wet or defecate in bed. Doña Carmen, who boasts of being a very clean woman, speaks of having gotten up a number of times each night to take her grandchildren to the toilet from the time they were seven months old until they "learned."

A small child's interest in food in the presence of strangers is considered a discredit to his family—"People will think we don't feed him." He is not to ask strangers for food or candy, nor to stare at them while they eat. If he should look intently or extend his hand to someone not a member of his immediate family who is eating, his parents will apologize to the person with such formalities as, "He is just *mañoso* (ill-mannered and spoiled)"; "He just ate"; or, "He does not like that, I don't know why he asks for it." With arm outstretched, he may be slapped on the hand and told, "I am going to cut off that hand with a knife if you ask strangers for food."

Since he hears Spanish, mixed with words in English, the child learns to use words in both languages from the outset. He is taught the names of objects in the house, the names of persons in his world, such social amenities as greetings, and "dirty" words, which he is not to utter in front of strangers but which are considered cute for the family circle. He is allowed to dance and sing, and he can stay up until the adults go to bed. His running and jumping around the apartment are considered joyful notes in the routine of the day.

Between four and seven, the child enters another new stage in his life. Now he must stop relating to adult friends of his family as if they were his own playmates and friends. Conversely, these adults are expected to discontinue their permissive relationship with the child and to demand respect from him. The child may get into trouble by continuing to act as if he were the social equal of adults. His parents are to prevent this by warning him that he must become aware that So-and-So is an adult, not a child, and that the adult must be respected. The child is also not to get physically close to such persons, nor to ask them for money or candies as he was allowed to do earlier. An adult who plays with a child of this age, gives him money, and buys him candies is said to be risking the respect the child owes him, and is doing the child a disservice by not helping him to learn to respect.

At this age the child is also to stop running around the house. He is told to stay still, and that good children sit down and play quietly, without disturbing their father's rest or their mother's work. Children are now expected to leave whatever they are doing when their mother or father so commands. If a child does not respond immediately, his parent may become enraged, and if he has been playing with a toy, a pet, or some other object, the parent may destroy the plaything because of the child's disobedience.

Naro, an eleven-year-old boy, told of wanting to contribute to the support of his family, had been building a shoe-shine box on the fire escape, and was going to start a shoe-cleaning business. He disobeyed his mother while he was building the box, and she, in anger, destroyed it. A few days later Naro's stepfather threatened to kill his kitten on the grounds that Naro did not obey due to the fact that he was playing. Afraid, Naro moved his kitten to the roof, where he thenceforth cared for it secretly.

Children are given toys for Christmas by their parents and friends, but they are seldom allowed to play with them. The toys are placed on dresser tops or closet shelves, where visitors might glimpse them, as a display of family wealth and love for the children, but high above the reach of a child. If a child is granted permission to play with his toys, usually it is on the condition that he agree to handle them with utmost care and not to move or hit the furniture while he is playing. Accidental mishaps can cost him punishment.

The role of the child is sharply different from that of the adult, and while their statuses are complementary, they are always kept separate. The quality of the relationship between an adult and a child is different from that between two adults, for children are subordinate to adults, particularly their parents. The child has no voice in family matters, nor even in matters which pertain to him directly and exclusively. He has to be unfailingly obedient, for obedience is the hallmark of respect. Since the father is the dominant authority in the family, the greatest respect and obedience are owed to him, and he has the chief disciplinary power. While the mother also has power to punish the children, she often resorts to threats of invoking the paternal authority to control their behavior. The mother thus relies on the father's alliance with her to maintain her own authority over the children. She may punish a child, and she may be very harsh in her punishments, but menacing the children with, "I'll tell your father when he comes home," is considered a stronger means for controlling the child than the punishment she herself metes out. This technique also has a latent consequence: the mother displaces her role as disciplinarian onto the father, who becomes a frightening figure for the child. Often she only threatens and does not really tell the father, but when she does tell, she consoles the child after he has been punished. Thus she becomes his protector, strengthening further the affective bond between herself and her child while emotionally isolating the child from his father. This serves to instill a cultural ideal in the child, namely, that he is to be fonder and more protective of his mother than of his father.

While the father is alive, even if he is divorced or separated from his wife, he is endowed with the power to punish his children, and he is expected to carry out their punishment, both as a corrective and as a preventive measure. This is part of his duty as a father, for it is up to him to impose respect on his child. A child who grows without respect for his father is expected to become a bad adult, because a child, particularly a boy, needs his father's rule to tame him. Boys being "stronger of character" require stronger repressive authority than their mother can exercise. Independence and self-reliance are not to be encouraged in a child, and disobedience due to school, street, or community influences that work against family authority are considered threatening to the welfare of the child. Yet a child is to learn how to "defend" himself, that is, to protect his own interests, so that he can also help and protect his family.

As good children are defined as obedient, respectful, and docile, so bad children are the opposite: disobedient, disrespectful, and rebellious. Disobedience involves a wide range of actions of varying kinds and degrees which are all lumped together under the heading "misbehavior." The disobedient child may range from one who chronically rebels and does not acknowledge parental authority, claiming to have forgotten or not to have heard orders, to one who will respond submissively only to certain orders, obeying others when he is screamed at or slapped. With the first child neither scoldings, restrictions, nor beatings, however harsh, are effective. The parents of such children may reach a point at which they claim they are unable to handle them. They are seen as problems and considered to be on their own. In the case of the second, he will obey willingly when he is told to go shopping (his chance to spend some time in the street) or when he is not busy reading comic books, studying, or playing. Ignoring the parent's command when the child is "busy" calls forth screams and slaps from the parent for his disobedience, and the order will then be reissued. This type of child is said to obey only when slapped.

A child who does not obey his parents and cannot be dominated by his father or stepfather is seen as a threat to the ideal of a good child, and he may be sent to stay with relatives in Puerto Rico or reported to a social agency here. In the latter instance the parents want him placed in a school where "he will learn" and where he will be living away from the family. Parents seeking such schooling for their children tell authorities of the misbehavior of their children, stressing their own inability and helplessness in the situation, despite their efforts to correct the children. They regard these schools as equivalent to the boarding schools attended by upper-class children in Puerto Rico, and proudly report to their friends that they are sending their child to a *colegio,* or boarding school. They say it is a "place where one pays, not free," since "the government pays for the child's keep." After such children have been placed—either in a school for delinquents or one for emotionally disturbed children—the parents try to get them out, complaining of the bad company to which their children are subjected and of the treatment they are receiving. And they sadly comment on how much they miss

them. Those children who are sent to Puerto Rico for misbehavior are also recalled, then sent back again when the parents
feel they cannot handle them. On the other hand, legally defined
acts of delinquency or truancy on the part of the child may be
taken as affronts to the family, particularly if the child is being
brought up by the mother alone and she regards herself as
"living only for her children." In such cases she may protect her
child from the police, from teachers, and from other enforcement agencies, denying charges in public but harshly beating
the child at home afterward for what he has "done to his
mother."

While a disobedient boy may be reported by his parents to the
authorities for correction, the disobedient girl is likely to be
handled by the family alone, and assistance outside the family
group probably will not be sought. A girl's reputation must be
protected by the family, for should it become known to others
that she is "bad," her chances for marriage will deteriorate, although if she misbehaves very badly, she too may be taken to
the authorities. In addition, girls are thought to be more amenable to control by their parents than are boys, and a girl's disobedience is not considered as difficult for a parent to handle as
is a boy's.

To teach "right from wrong," to inculcate moral values,
parents employ warnings and advice, which are often accompanied by slaps and an authoritarian tone of voice. This is to
make the child understand that he is being given orders. Models
of conduct are set up for him through comparisons with the
behavior of other children, particularly brothers and sisters
when referring to good children, neighbors when referring to
bad ones.

In order to be good, children have to be punished. Beatings,
scoldings, and withdrawal of privileges, or combinations of
these, are used as disciplinary measures. Scoldings include a
summary of the act the child committed and an attempt at in-

stilling the notion that his misbehavior has flouted the respect he must hold for his parents. Occasionally, scoldings are accompanied by slapping and pushing the child around for additional emphasis. A child is punished when he has done something considered wrong by his parents, or when he is suspected by them of intending to do something wrong—a preventive measure. The kind of punishment he receives is contingent on the degree of anger and embarrassment his offense creates or may create for the parent. *Castigos,* cognate to chastisement, involve restriction of the child's activities. He may be forbidden for a while to do something he likes, such as playing downstairs or going to the movies, or he may be made to sit still on a chair for a number of hours. Some children of grammar school age speak of preferring a beating to a *castigo,* because the beating is soon over, but the *castigo* prevents them from doing things they enjoy. In certain cases, such as with children who stay away from home all night or with those who commit acts of delinquency, parents resort to extreme forms of *castigos,* such as tying them up, in addition to beating and scolding them.

While generally parents consider punishment necessary for the good of the child, some are afraid to administer it. It is quite widely held among recently arrived Hispanos that in New York children cannot be punished at all, because if they are the parents will be sent to jail. Parents who fear police authority and the legal system of New York claim that many children here turn "bad" because, since the "children belong to the government," they cannot be brought up properly by their parents. The heavy publicity given court decisions against parents who have used extreme punishment with their children has lent strength to the belief that any punishment of a child by a parent is a violation of the law. Mr. Ramos, a Puerto Rican schoolteacher in Eastville, said that he had seen children "defying their parents to beat them if they dared, because if they did, they were going to tell the police." This sort of behavior is found infrequently among recently arrived children, but it is not a rare phenomenon among children who have been in New York for a while or among those who have been born here.

A child who behaves properly, taking the responsibilities assigned him by his parents and executing them to the parents' satisfaction, is considered to have *capacidad,* or maturity. "Maturity" in this sense refers to the ability of the child to follow orders and to handle adequately the situations in which he is involved. It does not involve initiative, for a child who initiates something without the consent of his parents is considered daring, and this is not viewed as a good quality in a growing child. Growing up is looked at in one way as a process by which children develop *capacidad.* This is achieved through their ever-increasing respect for their parents and the growth of their general ability to handle life situations in approved ways.

Though the development of *capacidad* is an important socialization goal for the children of recent migrants, the ideals of behavior promoted for girls and boys differ in many respects. Since the good woman is expected to possess different qualities from the good man, the differences between boys and girls are stressed in every part of a child's life. This is consistent with the clear-cut double standards that obtain for men and women.

Since little girls are expected to grow into demure and virtuous women, they are also supposed to be innocent and ignorant of the physiological processes connected with sex and sexual behavior. They are supposed to be feminine in the sense of being coquettish, yet are to refrain from using their feminine charms to attract men, unless they are addressing themselves to a suitor who has parental approval. As she is supposed to be modest, a little girl is to have her body, and particularly her genitals, covered. Only women—her mother, sisters, or close friends of her mother—can bathe and change her. As an infant in her crib, the tiny girl is covered with a small sheet or other clothing when her diapers are removed. The genitals of the baby boy, on the other hand, are more likely to be displayed. His chest, like that of the baby girl, may be covered for protection against cold, but adults and older brothers and sisters are likely to tease and play with his genitals, kissing them and remarking on their size, commenting that he is a *machito* (real little male) or a *machote* (real he-man). A baby girl less than a year old may be slapped on the hands if she touches her genitals, but a boy can play with his until he is four or five. When the little girl starts to walk and to be toilet-trained, she is told that she should not take her panties off in front of others and that she is not to go around without them. But it is quite usual to see a boy of three or four going about the house pantless. After this age, however, boys are encouraged to cover up in front of strangers and the women of the house. They are called "fresh" and told they should be ashamed of letting women see them in order to train them to wear pants.

Well before a girl is five, she is taught that her chest is to be kept covered, for girls do not show their bodies. A girl is not to let men or boys touch her, nor is she to sit on their laps unless they are her father or her brothers. In turn, the men of her family are to stop caressing and fondling her as they did when she was a baby and starting to walk.

Boys are expected to develop a strong sense of maleness. This means they are to be aggressive toward their equals, although submissive to their parents. One of the duties which they must assume is the protection of the reputation and good name of their mother and sisters. Boys are considered strong and are allowed more freedom than girls, for girls are innocent and know less about the world. Girls are considered weak and in need of protection against the gossip of all, as well as against the advances of men. They are to be watched by their parents, brothers, and sisters, so that they will not become the subject of gossip and so that they will restrain themselves from behavior ill-becoming a girl. This means in practice that boys and girls are not to play together, unless they are brothers and sisters, and that even when they are, they should be supervised. From early childhood until they marry, this is the way girls are to be treated.

A girl is expected to walk to school, from grammar through high school, in the company of girl friends, who are supposed to be "good girls." If her parents think that no other girl in the neighborhood can be trusted, the daughter may have to go with her brothers or sisters, or in their absence by herself, if she is old enough. But a girl alone in the street is not desirable at any age. She will be warned not to speak to strangers—either men or women—and not to accept anything strangers might offer, particularly food, candy, or rides in automobiles.

Games vary with the age and sex of the individual. Adults are not supposed to play games, because by so doing they lose respect, as games are meant for children. The games of girls are different from those of boys, and this is another device used to keep boys and girls separated. Some games, like baseball, are for boys of all ages, but it is preferred that whatever the game, individuals attach themselves to persons their own age for recreation and play. Hispanos who have grown up in Eastville, however, do not generally follow these rules. Among them are those who openly maintain that there is nothing bad about girls and boys playing together, nor about people of different ages, particularly adults, engaging together in games in the street. "What is bad and dangerous," said Gloria Pima, a woman who grew up in Eastville, "is that children are not taught the facts of life at home." She was commenting on why she allows her daughters, ten and eleven, to count boys among their friends.

Doll games are considered ideal for girls, and they learn many of their future roles through playing with dolls. Children play "father and mother" at home, acting out parental roles with their dolls in which many times the dolls get beatings. The two- or three-year-old girl who imitates her mother doing household chores is considered very *graciosa* (cute). She receives hugs and kisses of approval from both her parents and from her brothers and sisters for this type of play, unless she plays at something dangerous, like trying to light the stove or cook, or unwittingly spoils the furniture or dirties the floor. Then she is scolded or spanked. By the time she starts attending school, she is expected to help her mother with the household work, and she may also be expected to start washing some of her own clothes. At this age, too, she is supposed to begin to learn how to take care of babies—how to stop them from crying, how to feed them and dress them. This she will probably learn by being assigned these duties with a younger child. Yet she is not supposed to know about sex or even about her own physiological development. Menstruation will take her by surprise, unless she has acquired some notions about it from friends in school or has overheard her father or mother or adult women at home speaking about sex. When she begins to menstruate, she becomes *señorita* (virgin), and the watch on her is intensified. While her brothers become more free as they grow up, more restrictions are placed on the girl (for example, she can no longer go to camp or Friendly Town once she is *señorita*), for she must protect her virginity. If she does not help in the house and her mother or father or whoever she lives with has to push her to do household chores, she is said to be *vaga* (lazy), and one who is *vaga* is not a good woman. The ideal is to develop into a hard-working woman who occupies her time from early till late with household chores. Though the *señorita* is not expected to devote all her time to the house, this is what she must prepare for, because it is expected of her when she becomes a wife.

Boys are not supposed to learn how to do certain household tasks, for instance, how to cook or take care of children. These are definitely woman's tasks, and boys are said to be unable to learn them. If a man's wife is sick, unless a kindly neighbor, a comother, his sister, or his mother drops in to cook for him and the children, his seven- or eight-year-old girl-child may have to struggle with the preparation of family meals. By the same token, a woman is not expected to know how to repair machines, drive a car, or do mechanical work, for these are the province of man. A good man, however, is to help his wife with some of the business of keeping the household running. He is supposed to be a handyman, to carry heavy objects, and to *hacer fuerzas* (use his strength), as these are not for women to do. Yet in practice men rely on their wives to perform all the work of the household, although this seems to be less usual where the wife is employed and *gana plata* (makes money). Thus women are often heard to grumble about the amount of work they have to do, about how they have to get up at six and are still working after midnight. Complaints of pains, head-aches, *mareos* (dizzy spells), and stomachaches are frequently voiced by the wives. While too much work is not considered very good for a woman because it will make her sick, there is such a high premium on hard work that she cannot afford to default. A woman who slackens her efforts endangers her repu-tation of being a good woman and a good mother, that is, one who labors ceaselessly for her children.

No transitional period between childhood and adulthood is recognized among recent migrants, although among migrants who have lived in New York for a number of years and among those who grew up here the concept of "teen-ager" is used to refer to adolescence. For recent migrants childhood is a period that starts at birth and continues throughout the years the child lives under his parents' roof, that is, until he marries and es-tablishes his own home. When Tono, a thirteen-year-old boy, borrowed a bicycle to take a ride, his mother scolded him be-cause, "I have forbidden you to ride a bike. You can ride a bike without permission when you are a man, when you are twenty-eight years old, not now."

Nonetheless, an individual is expected "not to act as a child" any more after he is twelve or thirteen. This means that though he is still under parental authority, he is to behave in such a way that his parents do not have to correct his behavior. He is expected to know the rules of the house, to live up to them, and not to defy his parents.

At about thirteen the children of recent migrants are likely to start courting. The steps leading up to marriage, however, are strictly defined among recent migrants and reflect strongly the sharp differentiation made between males and females and the rigid parental control maintained over the children.

A young woman does not go out on dates with boys unless she is accompanied by some sort of chaperon, even just a small child. Gloria, a fifteen-year-old girl, used to go dancing at youth canteens in Eastville chaperoned by her eight-year-old brother, Bob. When she and her partner danced close to each other, Bob, who watched his sister's movements carefully, would tap her arm and tell her to separate.

Though a girl is supposed to try to get a husband, she is expected to be circumspect about it, to be shy with men and initially refuse a suitor, who, if he is really interested, is supposed to persist. He may test to see if a girl is good, and girls are to protect themselves to show that they are. The man is expected to behave as if he had good intentions, and a man of good intentions is defined as one who respects a girl. The girl, in turn, should not be *ojí pelá* (literally, bare-eyed; figuratively, boldly flirtatious), and also should not show interest in more than one man at a time. If a girl goes out on unchaperoned dates with a boy friend to whom she is not engaged, or with different boy friends or pals, she is a *cabra* (goat), and it is expected that she will lose her virginity and thus her chances of getting married legally. Should a girl be deflowered, she is expected to feel ashamed of herself. Knowledge of the event will be kept within the family as long as possible because it involves shame for all of them. Meanwhile, though, the girl's mother or father is likely to try to force a marriage, and the girl herself may go to the police and describe the case as seduction in a desperate attempt to make the man marry her. Legally, in New York the man in such circumstances will be charged with statutory rape, which carries altogether different connotations than does seduction. This will not achieve the end the girl desires. The case of Maria and Juan was one of many such that we were confronted with in Eastville.

Juan (a young, second-generation Hispano) was Maria's (a recent migrant) boy friend, and one night he asked her to go up to the roof. She accompanied him and agreed to have sexual relations with him. The following day she told her best friend about it and confided that she thought she was going to have a baby. Her friend, a woman who had lived in New York for several years, told her she had to go to the police and inform them so that Juan would marry her. Maria went to precinct headquarters and told the desk sergeant that she had lost her virginity, having been dishonored by Juan. Later, she informed a fieldworker that the policeman had said, "This is rape," and that she argued with him that it was not. The police picked up Juan, his mother, his father, and his brothers, and brought them all to the station house. Juan told the fieldworker he did not know why the police had picked up his family or why Maria had accused him to the police, for she had said she loved him and had agreed to have intercourse with him. Maria explained that (as she understood it) if she accused him, he must then either marry her and honor her, or else he would have to go to prison. Further information from Maria revealed that she believed she had to accuse him to the police to make possible the marriage she desired.

Maria's idea was in line with the general notions of Hispanos that here the state has great power in family affairs and that the government protects women and children. In Puerto Rico

Maria or her parents might have appealed to a person of high position in their community to force Juan to marry her. Going to the police in New York was for her the equivalent.

The family of a girl who has lost her virginity and "cannot be honored" by the man who deflowered her is likely to go through a time of great emotional stress. So, of course, will the girl herself. They may discontinue many of their current associations with other people in the neighborhood, and may even leave it to live elsewhere. After a woman has lost her virginity she is considered a potentially lost woman, particularly if the man in point does not marry her, or if he continues to have an affair with her. If the man does not want to set up a marital relationship—legal or consensual—with her, she is suspected of being a loose woman, and a lost one, a woman who enters into casual sexual relations with any man. Even if such a woman wishes to refuse a man, he is still entitled to have her sexual favors because she is bad. It is considered quite unlikely, however, that girls who are good and have *capacidad* will either get into such situations or turn bad, because they will not be alone with their boy friends nor give them *confianza* (trust them too much).

A proper courtship is supposed to take place in the girl's home, where the suitor will visit and eventually inform the girl's father of his intentions, of his being in love with her, and thus of the reason for his visits. The suitor's declaration need not result in an immediate engagement, but may at this time be simply a request for formal acceptance of him in the status of *pretendiente* (potential husband). This visit (*la visita*), if it gains acceptance for the youth, presupposes that the girl will not receive other suitors, will not go out with other men, and will "wait" for him for his decision about marriage. The couple are now *novios* ("steadies"). By authorizing this status the girl's family both secludes her from other suitors and protects her *novio* from her betrayal. *Novios* may go out together unchaperoned, the *novio* having proclaimed to her parents that he will respect the girl, and he expects her to refuse his attempts to have any physical contact with him beyond, perhaps, holding hands. As the period of keeping company (*noviazgo*) lengthens, the couple may kiss each other, but necking parties or other intimacies between the girl and her *novio* are frowned upon. Their engagement commences when the man makes a specific request to marry the girl.

The story of Anna and Jack fits this parental ideal of courtship. Anna is seventeen, Jack sixteen. Anna is a high school senior and lives with her parents, brothers, and sisters in an Eastville apartment. She has been in New York for five years. A "girl of her home," Anna is not seen in Eastville streets unless she is on her way to school, church, or accompanying her mother shopping. She has no friends in the neighborhood. Jack, his mother, brothers, and sisters live in the same building as Anna's family. A high school student who has lived in Eastville from early childhood and who was "brought up upstairs," Jack noticed Anna and started to befriend her brothers, exchanging comic books with them. After a while, he began to visit the family regularly and informed his mother that he was in love with Anna. Jack told Anna's mother that he did not like girls who held hands or kissed. On his visits to Anna's family, he sat in the living room, speaking with her father and mother, playing with her baby sister, and occasionally addressing Anna. After six months of this sort of visiting, he asked Anna's mother to please take the baby for a walk and to leave the door open because he had decided to speak with Anna's father, telling him the truth about why he visited the house so often. He wanted Anna to wait for him until he finished his studies, when he would marry her and take her to live on the Coast. Anna's father said this was all right, and since that time Jack has been officially acknowledged as Anna's *novio*.

Anna typifies the ideal prospective wife and Jack the ideal

prospective husband. The girl a man is going to marry should be a good girl, virtuous, innocent, a virgin, and, preferably, a girl who has never had another *novio*. A good wife is *hacendosa* (knows how to do things in the house). A good man to have for a husband is hard-working, serious, capable, and one who makes decisions. He is expected to be protective and *complaciente* (he should please her) toward his wife; yet she is to respect and obey him.

The most desirable kind of marriage for a girl is the one in which she comes out of her parents' home a virgin to be legally married. Then she is "well married" and not wed by "obligation" because she has lost her honor, nor is she married consensually.

The Neighborhood and the School in the Child's Life

When a child is six or seven, he is considered capable of going out on errands, or perhaps for a little play, without being accompanied by someone older who would be responsible for him. As a baby he became acquainted with other people besides his own immediate family, and when he started to walk he was taken outdoors for relaxation and play. This experience under supervision presumably fitted him to take care of himself in the street. Even a child who is being brought up "upstairs" is at six or seven to know how and when to cross streets and how to avoid getting hurt "downstairs." The degree of freedom of behavior allowed children by their parents depends, of course, on the individual parents. Yet one can generalize that parents who have been raised in New York, and even many of those who grew up in Puerto Rico, have reacted against strong and rigid parental control over children and advocate giving them freedom to play. They consider this the "modern" way, the converse being "old-fashioned."

Young children of recent Hispano migrants will probably

not be sent to nursery school or to the play groups of community centers. For one thing, there they would have to be taken care of by strangers—teachers or group workers—who, according to recent migrants, might be critical of the way the children are being brought up and who might not take good care of them as they are neither their relatives nor their friends. It is only after years of residence in New York that parents start accepting the idea that the young child especially can go and play outside the home without becoming a "problem child."

"Modern" Hispano parents, on the other hand, consider it good to have their children of three or four attend nursery school, regardless of whether the mother is employed outside the home. By the time the children of recent, "old-fashioned" migrants are six or seven, however, they, too, are considered ready for grammar school, and the mothers or fathers of these children are frequently seen walking them to and from school. In Eastville many mothers, regardless of ethnic group, escort their daughters throughout their grammar school years, and one can observe any school day a number of women clustered in small groups near the school buildings waiting for their daughters to emerge.

Older children—and some younger, especially boys—walk to school with classmates and neighbors, ideally, those approved by their parents. In school they develop informal friendships that may not be known to their parents, particularly those who discourage, and even forbid, their children to become friendly with others. In the streets, in school, and afterward at play, children start to pick up conversational English and to use it among themselves. They learn to pronounce English with "the New York accent" that is so desirable to them and to their parents. And, as their parents point out, they may also find themselves in trouble. A child who is going to be good, therefore, has to be kept at home as much as possible, and making friends should not be encouraged. He ought not have friends of his own choosing, nor those disapproved by his parents, because he has to be protected from "bad company," which such sets of friends represent. Ideally, what he should do is return home directly from school and play there quietly with his brothers and sisters. In practice, however, it is acceptable to permit children to have some friends. Although girls "belong to the home," they may have a few girl friends— if their parents approve them as being good—with whom they can go to school and with whom they can visit occasionally. While less active control is exercised over the choice of friends for boys, good parents are expected to question and find out who their sons' friends are.

Eastville Hispano children whose parents enforce such norms seldom adhere to them strictly, however, especially after their first year of school in New York, when informal friendships with classmates start to emerge outside the boundaries of parental surveillance. Such children learn ways to circumvent parental rules while paying lip service to them. An older child, for example, may invite his younger brother or sister to join the play with his own friends after school hours, or may give his younger brother or sister a few pennies to keep secret from his parents the after-school play. Or he may strike a bargain with the younger child, telling him that he will keep quiet about some mischief the little brother or sister might have done, and of which their parents would disapprove, if the little one will not reveal the bigger one's playing with friends. Children eagerly seek opportunities for playing with other children and "having some fun," even if this means they have to pay for it. Parents who forbid their children to play in the streets or outside the home describe this practice with pride, secure in the assurance that if their children do not play away from home, they will turn out to be good. Children who have become bad are said to have learned in the street, from the candy store meetings, and from their "bad" companions. So widespread and pronounced among recent migrants is the fear that children may become "bad," because New York is a dangerous place where they learn to disobey and do not respect, that a great deal of the advice and punishment the children are given is due directly to such threats, often to the neglect of rewarding and recognizing the positive merits of their growth.

Speaking practically, it is not possible to carry out the ideal of keeping children upstairs in Eastville, because most of the playgrounds and centers of recreation are in the streets and backyards, where adults as well as children meet and socialize with each other. Good parents, nonetheless, should carefully keep track of their children and restrict their playmates, play, and time outside the home.

Between ten and fourteen, boys who have been in school in New York for longer than a year or two indulge in planning to go together to the same summer camps, to attend movies together, and to play competitive games, like marbles, tops, and baseball, together. The informal group of friends may have as a leader an older boy, who is more aggressive and has more money, or who dresses in such attire as a black leather jacket, tight blue jeans, bell bottom trousers, or black sun tans, which are considered symbolic of aggressiveness and courage.

When school terms end, boys of all ages, though only girls under ten or eleven, may be allowed to go to camp or Friendly Town. Many children join the nondenominational Eastville church and attend its services regularly because it will register them for the Herald Tribune Fresh Air Fund if they are members of the church. One hears from the children who have visited Friendly Towns that they would like to return to them. There they stay with American families for one or two weeks and establish bonds of friendship. They comment especially on how they are allowed to play without having to ask permission. Camp and Friendly Town visits do not seem too long for them, though their parents, brothers, and sisters at home in

Eastville bemoan their absence, and in the middle of the night leave their hot, though more quiet, apartments for a breath of fresh air on the sidewalk or in the park.

Going to school, then, is for children much more than attending a seat of knowledge; it is also being in a place where they learn new games, meet new friends, learn new ways, and play. Among parents, formal education for their children is regarded as having a very important role in their aspirations, whether they are to stay in New York for good or are hoping to return to Puerto Rico. As a matter of fact, education is highly valued by all Hispanos—recent migrants, old migrants, and New York-born alike. Ignorance is considered bad, and something one should be ashamed of. Knowledge is good, and it is an asset both for success and in terms of a person's own worth. Among recent migrants one of the foremost goals in their coming to New York is connected with educating their children to an extent they could not have achieved in Puerto Rico.

Parents view their children partly as vehicles through which they can achieve many of their own aspirations in life, particularly those of social and economic improvement. From a very early age a child is told by his mother, father, or grandmother that he will be a lawyer, a doctor, or an engineer. This is repeated in front of visitors, and six- or seven-year-olds themselves speak of having these vocational goals. If they mention one of lesser rank, such as wishing to become a fireman, they are quickly contradicted and corrected by their elders. A child is not going to be "like his father," or "like his mother," who could not continue with school; he is told he "will be *algo grande*," something great.

The ideals of a good education involve such long-range goals as having one's children become professionals, or at least tradesmen or skilled workers. They also involve the more immediate goals of having the children learn to speak English, do arithmetic, and write. School is good for a child, for there he is busy learning and is supervised and corrected by adults. He is also being protected from the streets and other sources of evil, for doing nothing (*estar de vago*) leads to evil.

Before starting school children are told about it informally. They play at learning how to read and write with their brothers and sisters or parents. By the time a child is two or three years old, he may already have been given a notebook and pencil for play. Yet when he gets to school he probably will not be able to follow instructions in either English or Spanish, but will understand and speak a mixture of both. He may, however, know some arithmetic, since it is probable that from about five on he will have been running errands to the store, and required to render accounts of expenses, prices, weights, and measurements to his mother or father.

A child who goes to school in New York is not likely to learn how to read Spanish unless his parents are literate and teach him at home. Hispano adults of today who have grown up in New York remember and speak the colloquial Spanish of Eastville, and some have even learned to read Spanish, although they are really at home only in English. Often they get lost when trying to maintain a conversation in Spanish and have to shift into English. While recent migrants desire that their children learn English, and bemoan not being able to speak it themselves, they also stress the importance of learning and not forgetting Spanish, complaining about those children who "have lost their language." Their Spanish should not be given up because, they point out, it may prove very useful, and in fact one may have to go to Puerto Rico to learn Spanish in order to hold certain jobs in New York.

There are few books in Eastville homes of recent migrants. Of those that are there, the most popular are paper-covered pulp novels in Spanish. Other popular reading matter includes such movie magazines as *Ecos*. Children of recent migrants buy comic books in both Spanish and English, which are read or

looked at only by the younger members of the family. Among
Hispanos reared in New York, however, comic books are read
by old as well as young. Recent Hispano migrants usually
listen to Spanish radio programs and watch Spanish television
programs in preference to those in English, although some of
their favorites—for example, "Tex and Jinx," cowboy films,
Arthur Godfrey, and "I Love Lucy"—are in English.

With a home background in which literacy is not high to
begin with and where what there is, is mostly in a foreign
tongue, where ways of living are different even from those of
neighbors, recent migrant children, particularly those who had
no previous schooling in Puerto Rico, are ill-prepared for what
they encounter at school in New York. There they are expected
to converse in grammatical English and to meet standards of
behavior that are not in agreement with those of their parents,
nor even those of their socioeconomic class. For all Hispano
children, attending school is the beginning of their intensive,
directed training in becoming American. Placed within this
institutional framework, they are exposed to new social situations for which neither the neighborhood nor their preschool
experiences at home have prepared them. The transition between home, neighborhood, and school is less drastic for
Hispano children who have been in New York long enough to
be familiar with the language and the ways of life of Eastville
children. Yet even these will experience difficulty, like other
slum children, for the schools are middle-class oriented, whereas
the neighborhood is not.

Among schoolchildren knowledge of colloquial English and
speaking it with the "right accent" are considered a sure
way of gaining the recognition and friendship of other children in the neighborhood and the approval of their teachers.
Many, in fact, achieve this goal in time and gain the acceptance
of their teachers and schoolmates.

Although school statistics lump as "Puerto Rican" children

born in New York to Puerto Rican migrants, as well as children
who have lived in the city for different lengths of time, the picture
of Hispano children is by no means a uniform one with respect to
their adaptations to life in New York, or to the extent and
quality of their knowledge of English and their familiarity with
American norms. For children who must go to school in New
York immediately after arriving from Puerto Rico, there is vir-
tually no transition provided. The jump is greatest for those who
have never before attended school, even in the island, especially
those who are no longer very young. Not only are they faced
with school itself, but with a strange city, a strange neighborhood,
a different language, and new ways of life. They find themselves
relatively isolated from other children, ridiculed as "Spics" and
"Marine Tigers," and the victims of pranks, because they are
"not in the know." Hispano children born in New York or
those who have lived some time in the city and can converse
in English have their own nuclei of friends from the school and
the neighborhood, even if their parents have forbidden them
to do so. Like them, their friends speak in English, play the
same games, and share interests and understandings. These
children do not want to play with or befriend the children
who have just arrived. Hispano children who have never been
to the island or who left in early childhood and have not been
back frequently object to speaking Spanish in school or in the
streets, although at home they may have to when speaking to
their parents.

To assist the children who do not understand English, the
schools may appoint bilinguals as "big brothers." Or they may
make the bilingual children monitors or place them in other
positions of leadership, because they can be helpful not only to
the non-English-speaking students, but also to non-Spanish-
speaking school personnel in communication between the two.
Eastville schools, like most of the schools in New York, have
been making adjustments and trying new methods to cope with

the educational needs of children from Puerto Rico who cannot
speak in English and who are at the beginning of the process of
adapting to living in New York. An intensive course in English,
for example, was being given at the two grammar schools of
Eastville for those children from Puerto Rico who had been in
New York less than a year and could not speak English. The
course, taught by a bilingual teacher, was designed to equip
these children with a sufficiently large vocabulary and understanding of English that they would be able to catch up with
the school program.

Eastville junior high schools with large numbers of Hispano
children also have coordinators of Puerto Rican affairs. This
position was explained by one of the coordinators as consisting of three parts: the training of teachers, guidance, and parent or community relations. She said, "In training teachers I
work not only with teachers but also with supervisors and ad-
ministrators. I work, however, primarily with teachers who are
teaching English as a second language. I make suggestions on
the methods to use and help develop materials to use in class. I
also have charge of organizing the classes for Spanish-speaking
boys and assign boys in and out of classes at will. I just tell
Miss Lawrence I am moving the child. I also take care of the
guidance of boys who do not speak English. This guidance is
both social and educational. If a teacher sends a boy to me
because she doesn't know what he is doing in her class, I talk
to him. I try to talk to him in English and if he doesn't understand I try Spanish. [Another time she said, "Sometimes I talk
in English when my Spanish is inadequate."] I also test these
boys—verbal and nonverbal. Sometimes I call in the parents to
talk to them about their child. Sometimes I also act as liaison
between home and welfare. A parent comes to me and I refer
her to welfare and write a letter for her. I also refer children
to one of the settlement houses for after-school activities. Some-

times I am called in by a teacher or the principal to act as interpreter or to write letters in Spanish."

Hispano children who had never been to school before, however, were assigned to grades with children of their own age group in Eastville grammar and junior high schools. Many recently arrived children, unable to communicate, found themselves with the additional disadvantage of having to compete with children who had undergone the training necessary to achieve their current school level and who were experienced in the process of attending school. Recent migrant children are identified by their tropical clothing, different hair styles, quiet withdrawal, and sadness in school. Yet, though they are so unfamiliar with neighborhood ways, they themselves speak only of "not knowing English" as the reason they cannot engage in activities they would like and as the reason for their loneliness and isolation. An interview which I conducted with four recently arrived children from seven to twelve years of age illustrates this point.

I: Here, in New York City, whom do you play with?

RAYMOND (*seven years old*): With nobody.

I: Do you know other boys?

RAYMOND: Yes, one whose name is Luis, one whose name is Juan.

ROSE (*twelve years old*): How awful it is not to know English, ah? (*looking at me*)

I: Why?

ROSE: Because if one has a friend, one cannot tell her what happens to one.

ANA (*seven years old*): I would like to learn a lot of English because if one has to go see a doctor, I don't dare to tell him what happens in Spanish.

CARMEN (*seven years old*): I don't know any English.

I: Do you want to learn it?

CARMEN: Yes!

I: Why?

CARMEN: Because yes. In school I don't understand.

ANA: My father came here two years ago. He knows a lot of English. He says he does not know much but that he was born under the American flag.

CARMEN: The one who takes care of the children next door is American. She knows Spanish and English too. I was stunned by this. Her boy friend, one of those "Italians," also knows Spanish and English.

ROSE (*looking surprised*): Ave María! I have nowhere to go, in my house there is no *radiola* (radio-phonograph), no television.

ANA: In my house we have no *radiola,* no television, but they are going to buy one.

CARMEN: At home there is a car and television.

ROSE: In your house, your godmother and your godfather work.

CARMEN: They are still paying for the sewing machine, the car, and the television.

Having no conversational knowledge of English, children like those interviewed keep very much to themselves and their homes. Though they are shunned by many because of their strange ways, some American Negro children, among others, do try to befriend them. Parents who have migrated recently, however, and who are still "green," are suspicious of dark brown American and West Indian Negroes. They claim they are afraid of them because Negroes are mean. Mr. John Hetch, a teacher in an Eastville grammar school, talked about the fear Puerto Rican children in his school have of American Negro children, who, in turn, feeling "curious" about the Spanish ones, try to get near them. He added that Puerto Rican parents encourage such fears, and according to personal observations and mothers interviewed in this study, his statement had a basis in reality.

Many teachers who look at teaching from the point of view of a middle-class neighborhood or suburb find it a very different experience to teach in a place like Eastville, because the parents and the children, regardless of whether they are Puerto Ricans or not, are not like "middle-class people." To others, simply having Puerto Rican children in class was automatically a problem, even if these children knew English well enough to understand instructions and speak the language and even if they had been in New York long enough to have made an adjustment to living here and to functioning in school and in the neighborhood. From observations carried out in schools and interviews conducted with teachers, attendance officers, principals, and other personnel in the schools of Eastville, the net inference gained was that the main problems presented to the schools there by Puerto Rican children were those of language. Problems in personal behavior and delinquency were found to cut across ethnic groups and were not the special province of any one particular group. Mr. Johnson, principal of the boys' junior high school, reported, "This is no blackboard jungle," and while inquiring among teachers and other authorities about problems of delinquency at the grammar school level, members of the research team were informed that delinquency was no problem for them. But, they said, it was widespread at the junior high school level. Then, the principal of the boys' high school, when asked specifically what the main problems were that his school faced with its children in general, replied, "Those of a reading nature. This school has had for many years the lowest reading ability in the city." His explanation was that a second language, namely, English, was being taught and that for this remedial reading was not enough. Over 50 percent Puerto Rican, his school population did in fact include many boys who were recent migrants and who had had less than three years of schooling before starting junior high in New York. As for attendance, the principal said that his school had "a very high attendance record. . . . We have truants, but our average attendance is among the first ten [schools] in the city."

In the formal atmosphere of the classroom the child is expected by his parents not to speak unless he is spoken to by his teacher, not to move around, and not to play; in other words, he is not to disturb the teacher. He is to respect his teacher in terms of the definitions of respect he has been taught at home. As a token of this respect he will address his teacher as "Teacher," instead of by name. The expectations of the teacher are quite different, however. Teachers expect children to volunteer to speak as a way of demonstrating their interest in the class, and schools encourage play and games. Parents look askance on these procedures. They say with reference to the latter that in Puerto Rico children learn more in school than here because here there is too much play at school.

Parents expect teachers to take full responsibility as their surrogates for the child and his actions both while he is in school and while he is participating in activities connected with the school. Thus the school field trip programs to acquaint the children with the city may encounter parental disapproval. The school sends home a written note for the parent to sign if he approves of his child's going on the trip, but the note stipulates that the child goes under the responsibility of his parents. A father noted in this connection that here the schoolteacher asks permission and then says that he is not responsible if anything happens to the child. To his child he said, "I am not allowing you to go on those trips again." He explained further that last week the teacher asked permission for one of the children to go to a museum and then left him with some other boys on 86th Street, telling them to take the subway home. "That is so complicated, he can get lost," and "even bigger boys get lost in the subway and have to go to the police so they be sent to their homes." School authorities also require the children to bring in

*Up
from
Puerto
Rico*

Commonwealth of Puerto Rico

Photos by
Michael Ciavolino

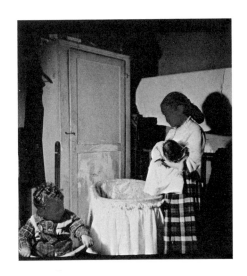

exact addresses and telephone numbers where the parents can be reached in "case of emergency." This was interpreted by one father as dangerous for his children. Said he, "The school should be in a better position to get a doctor or an ambulance for the children than we are."

For the parents, the school personnel and teachers represent not only a higher social class and persons of prestige, but also powerful authorities. The relationships between them are limited to matters concerning the children. Teachers expect parents to demonstrate their interest in their children by visiting the school and by responding to official invitations of the school to participate in school activities, such as parent-teacher association meetings and recreational programs planned by the teachers and involving the children. Invitations to visit the school may be a source of embarrassment or discomfort to the parents, who either expect that the teacher is going to complain about their child, or else assume that they do not have the proper attire for such an occasion or that they cannot speak English. And any of these is shameful. Whatever the situation, the parent who does not appear may simply ignore the invitation after he has directed his child to tell the teacher that he will come, or he may say that illness does not permit him to come. Either way, the parent may still be deeply interested in his child.

The schools learn about the home life conditions of the children only indirectly. As a rule, the teachers do not visit their students, are not residents of the neighborhood, and do not participate in other activities of the neighborhood than those that are connected with the school and officially required of them as teachers. Knowledge of the home life and extracurricular activities of the children is obtained by school personnel through information given by the parents, reports of the visiting nurse, the attendance officers, and the police, or from information provided by the children themselves. Teachers communicate with the parents by sending them notes and letters, many of which are written in both Spanish and English. Small children are seen with messages addressed to their parents pinned on their shirts by the teachers.

Though to parents the school is a symbol of authority, it is not, however, expected to encourage behavior or beliefs that conflict with those of the family. That it often does is not surprising, since parents and school work from such different premises. Protests by parents are not ordinarily registered with the teachers or other school officials, however, but are likely to be made to the child. A woman told one of the fieldworkers that she was angry because the teacher told her children not to drink coffee. "Also in school they teach them to eat bread, and bread waters the blood." The children were scolded for trying to follow the teacher's advice, and the teacher was criticized in their presence.

In the eyes of recently arrived Hispano parents, the privileges and obligations of teachers and school authorities are similar to those expected of all adult persons—whether friends, kin, or *personas particulares* (acquaintances and strangers)—who are in charge of children outside their homes. They are expected to ask permission of the parents to take the children out and are expected to report to the parent on the child's behavior. Should this report contain complaints (*quejas*) about a child, however, these are considered to be an imputation of censure of the parents' method of rearing their child, and a parent may enter into a defense of his child and his rearing techniques if a teacher or some other adult of respect complains to him. Afterward the parent may punish the child for having cast a reflection on his capacity as a parent.

While the parents expect the children to respect their teachers, they do not expect the teacher to punish the children physically, even if they tell the teachers they may do so if their child disobeys and does not respect. This permission is to be taken by the teacher as an expression of the trust the parent has in his abilities as a teacher and as a parental surrogate while the child is under his care. Teachers who beat up children are criticized by both parents and children, although complaints are not made to school authorities when parents are doubtful as to whether their children really deserved the beatings since they are afraid of becoming implicated in the possible misbehavior of the children. While children do not voice complaints about their parents' beating them and inflicting other harsh punishments on them, they do criticize teachers or other school authorities who give them the same treatment. Not only do children have to contend with beatings from parents and sometimes school authorities, but they may also be the victims of their classmates' aggression. The latter is just as frightening for some children as is the former. Nevertheless, parents expect their children to attend school regularly, except when they are ill or when family obligations have to be met.

Family business is placed ahead of school duties. If a parent needs a child to do errands, take care of the other children, accompany him when he has to go somewhere, or act as interpreter, the child must then miss school. While a child is doing his homework he will perhaps be asked to run errands, or a parent or some other adult may speak to him intermittently, expecting him to obediently reply. This, despite the fact that outside reading or assignments are desirable from the parents' point of view, since they keep the children busy and quiet in the home and are considered evidence that they are learning. (On the other hand, however, it is held that too much studying or reading is detrimental to the child's health, because too much weakens the brain and a person may go crazy from overstudying.) In the same room where a child is doing his homework, a television show or a radio program may be playing, and friends and relatives may have dropped in for a casual chat. Living conditions thus combine with the low evaluation given whatever a child does (even that which involves the highly prized education) to make for interruptions and lack of privacy in studying. Hence a child may be trying to complete his assignments till late at night, while he participates simultaneously in his family's social life. Children who sleep in the living room or in the kitchen must wait for visitors to go home and for their parents to retire before they can go to bed.

If a child does not have shoes, clothing parents consider adequate, a coat, or lacks money requested by the teacher for some purpose, it is preferable from his parents' viewpoint that he not attend school and thus avoid the "shame" of his family's poverty. A child who is not "properly dressed" is regarded as a criticism of his parents. Still, many parents weight the importance of attending school so highly that they take a chance and send their children to school without "proper" attire, even though they recognize that being well treated and accepted require that one be "well presented." "You are treated by the way you look," it is said. The standards of the family as to what is "well presented" also enter into this matter, for while a child may be "acceptably dressed" according to his school, he may not be by parental standards and for this reason restrained from going to school. Conversely, a child may be improperly dressed according to the school authorities and properly dressed according to family standards. What constitutes being well or properly dressed among recent migrants differs from the standards held by both middle-class Americans and middle-class Hispanos, as well as those of longer-time, lower-class residents of New York City. One sees, for example, recent migrant junior and senior high school girls in Eastville on their way to class in tight black satin sleeveless dresses. These are considered to be the attire of well-dressed girls.

A large number of children of migrants quit school as soon as they can get working papers or as soon as they have passed the required age for compulsory schooling. This is what usually happens with those in the neighborhood when they turn sixteen.

While numerous factors enter into making a decision to leave school, beatings by teachers and attacks on the part of other students push many out of school and into job-hunting. Others are pressured by their parents to leave school and go to work to help the rest of the family. There are parents, however, who, though they talk of desiring their children to reach the age when they can go to work, withstand personal and financial sacrifice to see their children over sixteen through high school. While the senior high school diploma is highly prized, a college education may be encouraged by the parents of children who have completed their secondary school training. But college is to be undertaken in the future at the children's own expense. Graduation from high school is considered to terminate the parents' obligation to their children, after what is viewed as a long hard stretch to prepare them to earn a living, and thus, in part, to assume the responsibilities of adulthood and marriage.

While in many ways the ideals of family life and the methods of rearing children of recent Hispano migrants contrast with those acceptable in American middle-class circles, they also contrast in many ways with those of Hispanos and other people who have grown up in Eastville. Hispano families in New York change in response to their social environment and to the culture of the society in which they are living. They develop new traditions, ideals, and manners of life, which are conditioned by their life circumstances in the city. In Eastville, therefore, the changes that Hispano families undergo are in the direction of the culture of the American slum, which, although different from the culture of the middle classes, is still American. Hispanos born in this country and those who migrated in early childhood acquire a kind of social heritage different, not only from that of their cousins in Puerto Rico, but also from that of their parents, who migrated as adults and who grew up to conform to Puerto Rican traditions and ways of life.

Cliques and the
social grapevine

ALL human beings belong to social groups other than their nuclear family as a necessary condition to their survival. An individual belongs to many such groups, depending on the structural complexity of his society. Never does he belong to and participate in all, for in every society the positions or statuses that any particular individual can occupy are limited. In modern society a person has multiple statuses, and must learn to take roles accordingly. Through role-taking he participates in social groups that range from informal, face-to-face small groups to highly complex and large ones, where he remains largely anonymous. Examples of the first type are the groups of friends who get together regularly to play cards or swim. Examples of the large and complex groups are business corporations, armies, schools, or ethnic groups. Within the large and complex groups the quality of social relationships is different from that of such relationships in the small groups, and we describe the relationships in the former as "impersonal," because in them the individual is relatively unimportant in relation to other individuals within the groups. While an individual may be loyal to and proud of his large group and feel rewarded by what this group does for him, he does not establish intimate and warm personal relations with all its members. In large groups, even the most highly complex ones, only small numbers of individuals enter into firsthand, face-to-face relationships with other individuals in bonds of common interests and understandings, such as those of office workers who get together regularly for bowling or lunch, or those of youngsters who listen together to their favorite records, go dancing, or play with each other. These small groups act in many ways as if they were independent of other groups in the society, as those who belong to them have relationships with one another that are distinct from other relationships. They also share in some pursuit or other that carries forward their interests as members of such groups. In everyday language we speak of "circles of friends," implying that there is an exclusive group of people with whom we meet in preference to others for certain purposes of common interest. But small groups are formed for other purposes than recreation, and in fact, these have been found to be of great importance in the development of teamwork in industry, government, and sports, for example, and in the pursuit of crime as well.

In modern society small groups generally consist of people who belong to the same social class, for socioeconomic factors separate people not only by income, but also by neighborhood, educational level, occupation, and so forth. The chances are that those who can come together and enter into face-to-face interpersonal relationships forming a common-interest group will have the same socioeconomic status. Those who get together in circles of friends (or cliques) share, in addition to some common interest, a sense of belonging, or solidarity, and feelings of trust cemented by interpersonal adjustments and emotional ties. Often, they are not aware of the feelings that bind them to others like themselves who belong, or even that they belong to such groups. Yet analysis of their social behavior will indicate that they do participate in such groups. With other groups that are more formalized or structured the members are aware of the groups' existence and even formulate by-laws making explicitly clear who may or may not belong and what rules they are to follow if admitted, as happens in clubs.

Sociologically, Eastville, like any other urban neighborhood, is characterized by a vast and intricate network of small groups. Some of these are segments of larger groups which are woven into the social fabric of the city and even of the nation. Local street clubs of city gangs, Boy Scout troops, labor union locals, and chapters of the American Legion are examples of these types of small groups. They are expressions of the fact that the neighborhood itself is a part of the larger society. Other small groups are restricted to the neighborhood and are not directly tied into the larger society. Within the neighborhood the small groups form a "social grapevine," which through communication and association enmeshes large numbers of people—Hispanos and non-Hispanos alike—in the web of the social life of Eastville. In this sense those who remain outside the grapevine are outsiders or strangers, as against those who participate within it who are said "to be from the neighborhood." The social grapevine is not characterized by smoothly operating patterns of human relationships, for social and cultural conflicts are aspects of the push and pull that drive toward separation of groups as well as toward their internal cohesiveness. Some groups operate to express socially the members' resentment and dislike for others, but they are nonetheless part of the Eastville social system. Anonymity and social isolation are rare in Eastville. A trained observer of social behavior soon becomes aware of this. When Puerto Rican migrants arrive in Eastville, they find an already established set of social channels through which they can build their adaptations. Some of these channels are confined to the neighborhood, others are part of the broader adaptations already opened up for Puerto Ricans in New York

City, and are not restricted to the locality of Eastville, nor exclusively to Puerto Ricans.

The most important small groups or cliques in which Eastville Hispanos can participate are those of people who came originally from the same home town in Puerto Rico. While some of these include individuals from all over the city, others are restricted to Eastville residents. There are also other types of cliques which depend primarily on residence in Eastville. People who have lived in the neighborhood for a number of years, for example, may participate in cliques regardless of ethnic background, and old Hispano migrants who live there may operate in these or in exclusive cliques of old Hispano settlers.

Cliques tend to consist of people of the same sex and of similar age groups. Recent migrants are excluded from most Eastville cliques, but there are exceptions for people from the same home towns, for Puerto Ricans living in the building, or for people who shop in the same bodegas. Old migrants and Hispanos reared in New York, on the other hand, have access to and participate in a wider variety of cliques and other social groups in the neighborhood.

Often recently arrived Hispanos will claim among the advantages of living in New York that here one does not know anybody, not even his next-door neighbors. Friendship is defined as "a dollar in one's pocket," and friends are said to "get you in trouble." These verbal clichés about friendship are also used in Puerto Rico and with similar meaning, implying that there, as here, one cannot really expect the cooperation and loyalty from friends that one was taught should be possible. These phrases are not to be taken literally, however. They are expressions of disappointment, a cynical indictment of what for migrants is a painful reality.

Migrants rely upon close interpersonal relations, friends, relatives, and neighbors, for aid and cooperation, and are often disappointed because they do not find reciprocal attitudes in those they rely on. As a result of migration into a new sociocultural environment, the psychological and social needs of migrants increase, as their personal and cultural resources here and now are not as effective as they were in Puerto Rico. Hence, they lean more and more on their available cultural resources to deal with the new life situations and make explicit norms of behavior that in the island were taken for granted. In other words, as a response to the new situation of New York, recently arrived Puerto Ricans tend to rely heavily on an exaggerated version of their Puerto Rican cultural orientation. Recent migrants find out in New York that even if their relatives and friends try to assist them, this help is never enough, and furthermore, that those who have been in New York for a while often refuse to acknowledge such obligations willingly, and require or accept payment of a fee for even a small service.

One of the reactions of recent migrants to this kind of behavior on the part of those who are expected to come cheerfully to help in case of need is to retaliate by not undertaking obligations to them, in turn, either. Resentment of people who as next-door neighbors might be friendlier and more accessible in times of need leads to the assumption that these, too, should be ignored, because they cannot be trusted. And many times the genuine concern and altruistic motives which impel an individual to be friendly with his neighbor are distrusted, questioned, and interpreted as prying and violating one's privacy.

It takes time living in Eastville for recent migrants to start to learn other modes of relating to individuals as friends in terms different from those they had learned in Puerto Rico and in their recent stay in New York for interpreting what friendship is. Acquiring new adaptations, they acquire chances to enter into cliques with other recent migrants, with old migrants, and eventually with non-Hispanos, as gradually other personal relationships than those based on an exchange of mutual obligations can be found acceptable and rewarding.

Cliques are of particular importance in the formation of inter-personal adjustments and in the carrying out of cultural adaptations, for they provide media for social living. They are part of the social gears that bind Hispanos to the rest of New York society. They also reduce and prevent personal loneliness by providing the individual with a sense of belonging and by giving him the feeling that there are others upon whom he can rely to realize many of his social needs.

Puerto Ricans have settled throughout the boroughs of New York City, concentrating in certain districts, blocks, or buildings in each. One important part of the social relationships among recent migrants is that the continuity they can find of their social life from Puerto Rico right in the city reduces the emotional impact of uprootedness. This takes place through the initiation and revival of ties of friendship and sentiment with people who came originally from the same home town in Puerto Rico and who exchange visits and other expressions of interest in each other regardless of how far apart they live from each other in the city.

An Eastville woman who does not speak or understand English and may not know such New York landmarks as Macy's at Herald Square may, however, know how to get with ease to obscure addresses in Brooklyn, Queens, and the Bronx. It may take her hours to make such trips and require the use of several subway and bus lines, but she soon learns to do this in order to visit a sister, cousin, or childhood friend. To her, the 1,500-mile trip from New York to San Juan is also a simple and feasible undertaking. She may decide to go almost on the spur of the moment to visit family and friends in the island. Physical distance itself or the use of complex and modern means of transportation do not cause her much concern. Rather, she takes them for granted as part of her life activities. The distance that concerns her most is the social one, and social proximity beats down any geographical distance. This same woman who travels so far physically may be frightened and bewildered at going to a hospital, a school, a social agency, or an American restaurant just a few blocks from Eastville. The social distance here is much greater for her than the long physical distances that her own social world covers—the world of those in which she finds herself at home and at ease, the world of people with whom she identifies as having a common social heritage, common ways of life and understandings. She is likely to be ambivalent or feel lost with a Puerto Rican of a higher socioeconomic status than hers in much the same way she would feel lost with an "American."

Through the home town cliques whole families may be bound in reciprocal relationships; or the men or the women alone may form separate cliques. Whether the whole families are included, or the men or the women form separate small groups of their own, the home town cliques share a common basis of interpersonal relationships of long standing, their participants have a common knowledge of each other's backgrounds, they serve to cope with problems of homesickness and confusion about New York, they strengthen the values of interpersonal relationships and mutual exchange of obligations, and both manifestly and latently they also serve to help new migrants find their way into the larger society. Psychologically they work to reduce the traumas of loneliness and cultural conflicts. These groups are important in recreation, in mutual assistance, and in setting up standards and goals for living in New York. The cliques themselves are not imported from Puerto Rico; they take shape and function in the New York milieu. Actually while those who belong may have known each other and been acquaintances in the island, their ties are reinforced in New York as a response to the strange social environment, and previous acquaintanceship in Puerto Rico is not a requirement for acceptance. This is not unlike what Americans do when they live abroad. While here it is not enough just to be a New Yorker to build ties of friendship with someone else, this may be a strong enough factor to pull together into friendship two New Yorkers in Singapore, Buenos Aires, or Paris.

Members of a home town clique engage in both formal and informal "raincheck" visits, dropping in on one another unexpectedly. On Sundays and holidays it is not strange to see a whole family getting ready to drop in to spend the day with some other family in Brooklyn or the Bronx. Appointments or warnings are not necessary, and a promise to come does not have to be kept, for it is a privilege of the relationship not to warn but rather to surprise the host with one's visit. People from the same home towns who also live in the neighborhood drop in casually at each other's apartments at any time of the day or night, as do other neighbors considered part of the neighborhood's cliques. Often neighborhood people arrive for a short visit through the fire escape window. Other occasions for visiting and recreation are more formal events, such as parties held at home, and called *paricitos,* to honor birthdays, weddings, and departures for Puerto Rico. A "demonstration party" may be used as an occasion to hold a party to entertain and feed people from one's home town. These parties are arranged between the head of a household and a door-to-door salesman who is interested in showing his product—usually household appliances—to a number of people all at once instead of canvassing households individually. The salesman purchases the food and other *obsequios* (trimmings), does the cooking, and sets up a display of his product in the living room or the kitchen. The hosts issue invitations, assuring their guests that they do not have to buy anything from the demonstrator but should just come in and have a *paricito,* eat, dance, and chat. In this way a Hispano can fulfill part of his social obligations without economic hardship.

Participation in home town cliques changes with the social fortunes of their members in New York, for the clique is a status-oriented group and social mobility and achievements in New York condition participation. One spring day in 1955, Vicky and I had been taking a walk on East Avenue. A car stopped and she walked toward it to greet the people in it. Introducing them to me, she referred to the various persons in the car as "my aunt," "my uncle," and "a friend." Then she asked them to come and visit her home. They replied that they would. After the car had driven off, Vicky commented, "They are rich now, that is why we never visit them." Yet Vicky's family maintains strong friendly relations with people from their home town, both in the neighborhood and outside it. Vicky's mother, however, would often comment on how badly off these persons were, like Maria who had to go to work in Long Island as a maid while she was ill in order to supplement her income from home relief.

The men's cliques, those formed by men from the same home town, have an age-range from the teens to the forties. They meet in the streets, on stoops, and in or in front of such places of business as bars or restaurants, sometimes owned or managed by a member of the clique. Sometimes men who were not born or raised in a certain town are included in the clique from that town, but the core of the group is comprised of those who are from the same town. This type of clique is of particular importance in understanding the cultural roles of the male, as one of its main functions is to foster and maintain the cultural definitions of the privileges of the male, namely, that he is of the street and free to do as he pleases. Many of the conversations of members of these cliques rotate around the subject of manliness or "maleness" and the affirmation of masculine exploits. The cliques formed by women from the same home town consist as a rule of housewives ranging in age from their early twenties to those around fifty or even older. The members gossip and discuss events, people from their home town, and the neighborhood.

Other cliques in which recent migrants participate are based on interests that relate purely to neighborhood events. One of this type is that of women who meet on the sidewalks and stoops and in the bodegas at various hours of the day and night, stopping there to chat while attending to such *diligencias* ("business") as shopping, waiting for the daily return of the winning numbers in the illegal lotteries, or waiting for the mailman. The women enter into conversations about people in the block, comment on people passing by, complain about the neighborhood, discuss diseases, asking and giving advice, and talk about other matters of immediate concern in their own lives and surroundings. The leadership of the sidewalk cliques is held by migrants who have lived in this country "for many years," and *bodegueras* (women who work in bodegas) are usually recognized as leaders of the cliques of women which meet in the shops.

Another variant of this kind of clique is the one that emerges among neighbors who live in the same building. It revolves around making protests and learning how to cope with the problems that arise in connection with the institutional services of the larger society. This kind of group is centered on a leader who is articulate in expressing protest against injustices of landlords and building superintendents. He speaks English, calls the police, and writes letters to the mayor of New York, the housing offices, the health department, and other authorities to complain about living conditions. These individuals are recognized as having the know-how needed to get things done in this country, and they themselves boast of their abilities and accomplishments. In addition to the battles with the landlords they undertake, they also advise and serve as interpreters to persons who have difficulties in dealing with American officials in hospitals, courts, and so on. They lead others into action against injustices, particularly people who live in their building. The relationship is between the leader and each particular individual: the helper and the one needing help. Even if many different individuals are involved with the leader, there is no apparent identification of aims among them as a group. The distinctive focus is on the dyadic relationship between the leader and each particular follower, although occasionally the leader may manage to involve a number of tenants in a joint protest. It is not a difficult task to get them to sign complaints to be sent to the proper authorities, as almost everyone in Eastville lives in an apartment where the fixtures do not work, painting is needed, the walls are cracked, and heat is not provided when it is included in the rent. After a number of verbal complaints to the superintendent, he and the tenants are likely to become personal enemies. Then the lack of repairs and the neglect increase. It is at this point that the leader organizes the tenants to protest. Since problems like these are not solved by tenants' protests, however, sequences of letters continue to be sent until eventually the enthusiasm for action wanes, only to rise again with increasing friction between tenants and superintendents.

Know-how, or having the social skills to deal effectively with practical problems in New York, is highly valued. It includes being successful not only in communicating with "Americans" in professional or official roles, but also in not letting anyone take advantage because one is a Hispano.

Reyes, a twenty-seven-year-old recent migrant woman who had a few years of grammar school education in Puerto Rico, is such a person. She is hardly literate in Spanish, and her vocabulary in this language is very limited. Together with her husband and daughters, she was living in one room which they had sublet from the tenant of a three-room apartment in Eastville. Her husband was earning twenty-four dollars a week as a laborer, and the family was receiving supplementary welfare aid to make ends meet. Reyes is illiterate in English, understanding only a few words and phrases in this language. Nevertheless, she goes to any government office, hospital, court, or school in New York City either at the request of officials or on her own initiative. If she has disagreements with her welfare worker, she threatens to appeal to his superiors or actually reports him to his supervisor. For this she uses an interpreter, usually a bilingual grammar school child. Aggressive, she boasts that she lets no one abuse her, and she advises others of their rights. Many of her neighbors call on her for advice regarding how to handle problems with the Welfare Department, the police, and medical personnel. She is comother to a number of persons in her building, which suggests the importance of the ways in which she is involved with many of her neighbors, who form a clique around her oriented toward learning about services and the rights to their use to which they are entitled. Her success in obtaining desired ends is rewarded by her neighbors with their admiration, friendship, and dependence on her leadership. The clique she leads is one of persons who share a lack of skills to deal with American institutions and who recognize their need for such skills, regardless of their ability to speak in English.

Hispanos born or reared in New York participate in cliques other than those of migrants. Their groups are not pointed toward Puerto Rico or toward values considered "Puerto Rican"; rather, they are oriented in terms of their own neighborhood and the larger American society. These cliques are organized along age lines and may include both males and females and members of different ethnic groups. The main types of cliques of this kind are play groups of children eight to thirteen; teen-age cliques, the twelve- to sixteen-year-olds; and young men's cliques.

These cliques manifestly have both recreational and defensive purposes. The individual is protected from loneliness and assured of loyal friends, while he is also protected from the aggression of others. A clique offers him a place in a group in which he feels liked, trusted, and accepted and on which he can depend for his own personal protection and self-enhancement. Should a member of a clique be attacked verbally or physically by an outsider, he can expect to be supported and protected by his fellow clique members.

The cliques of children eight to around thirteen consist either exclusively of boys, or of girls, or they may include both. These children play together, visit each other, and spend a great deal of their recreational time in each other's company. If they have to fight, they fight as a group. Dolly Rosa says that when she was in this age group, she organized four different clubs of girls, founding them because they had to fight together the boys that bothered them. Other boys, who were friendly, built them clubhouses in the alleys. Hispano children, like Dolly Rosa, who are second- and third-generation born New Yorkers, are not as restricted by their parents in their play and in choosing their friends, as are recently arrived children, nor do their parents restrict the girls from playing with boys. Among these parents, on the contrary, friendship between boys and girls is regarded as "natural," and is encouraged and preferred, as against the recent migrant ideal that parents should not permit their daughters to play with boys.

A salient characteristic of the patterns of social relations in Eastville is the tendency for individuals to participate in sets in groups. Rather than in pairs or as buddies involving two friends, individuals participate together as close friends in a group or clique. Dating, for instance, seldom appears as an independent activity of two young people, but those who go out together usually go in a group with other couples. The cliques of teen-agers, in addition to purely recreational and protective purposes, have the aim of facilitating relationships between girls and boys. Friends assist each other in breaking the ice between a girl and a boy who are afraid of starting to go out together. Members of a clique advise each other and inform their friends about activities of their girl friends or boy friends.

Because of the social and emotional ties among members of a clique, conflict with nonmembers or with members of other cliques are also tinged with strong emotional overtones. In performing the duty of protecting and defending the members of a clique from its enemies, aggression is discharged, not unlikely in disproportion to the reality of the act itself. Violence may characterize the methods for resolving the tension, while arbitration by word of mouth may substitute. The interclique conflicts serve to discharge the accumulated aggressions of individuals through means that are socially acceptable to one's clique and to the code of clique behavior. For long periods of time cliques may not enter into any conflicts with others that result in violent action. The clique may be, for instance, a baseball club whose members play against another club.

Cliques differ qualitatively with regard to their emphasis and methods of resolving disputes. Social cliques are those that emphasize recreation and that outspokenly make claims of avoiding violence. Fighting clubs may have a recreational purpose but emphasize violence and war as a method of solving conflicts. Both social and fighting clubs may be small units local to the neighborhood or perhaps to one block, but the tendency is to affiliate a small clique with larger units or clubs that exist in other parts of the city. These larger affiliations of clubs are facilitated by the degree of physical moving in the city. That is, children and young adults who have moved out of the neighborhood, or who have made friends from other sectors of the city in school or summer camps, may continue their relationships within a large club or gang that at the grassroots level binds small groups of individuals from a single block or small neighborhood. Social cliques that abhor violence in the settlement of disputes proclaim arbitration and avoidance of conflict with others as a value. Fighting cliques, on the other hand, alternate phases of nonviolence with those of violence precipitated by the urgency to protect or avenge the clique or one of its members. Fighting cliques which are branches of gangs are, together with drug addict cliques, sources of great fear and apprehension for Eastvillers. Because of this, it is worth while to look at them in detail. Neither is local to Eastville; both are segments of larger organizations of the society. Beyond this, however, the purposes, the kinds of activities, and the interests of the gangs versus the addict cliques are different.

Under the caption "gang" a variety of organizations are recognized in Eastville. For recent Puerto Rican migrants, gangs (*gangas, pandillas*) are any cliques of individuals who are associated for any purpose: going to a movie, a dance, or a party, or for playing together. In New York, Puerto Ricans eventually learn that a gang is also a group which gets together for antisocial purposes. Gangs are actually formally organized clubs with ramifications and membership all over the city. As with small cliques, they are of two kinds: social and fighting clubs. The social gangs are oriented toward recreation and sports, while the fighting clubs are oriented toward safeguarding their members from the assaults of others and toward fighting battles whenever these are necessary to insure such protection. Members of a fighting club are expected to learn how to fight, and undergo training for fighting other gangs, for constructing and purchasing weapons, and for entering into planned attacks on their enemies when called upon to fight. A social gang may under pressure turn into a fighting gang in order to settle a controversy, but as a rule social gangs do not promote fighting. The fighting gang, on the other hand, has periods in which it operates only as a social club, and many fighting gangs resort to arbitration to solve problems they have with other gangs.

Walking through the streets of Eastville one can discover clues to the existence of fighting gangs through the marks of their territorial boundaries. About two feet up the wall of a corner building the words "Charmers Territory" are spelled out in red letters. A block away on another corner "Charmers" is scrawled again. On the roof of a building on the same street the name appears in black paint. Near the boys' junior high school two youngsters can be seen walking up and down, patroling an overpass; on one side of the bridge there is the word "Charmers" again. To junior high school students, to boys and girls who have lived in Eastville all their lives, these signs are meaningful. They know the signs indicate the territorial areas that "belong" to a fighting gang, and they know that if the children in that area are members of the gang they are assured protection from aggression by other children and adults, including their own fathers. A child who crosses the boundaries of a gang's territory may "get in trouble," even if he belongs to no gang himself. Children who speak in Spanish may be attacked by gangs in order to keep them away from their schools in retaliation for being newcomers and not knowing English. In fact, this sort of thing may happen to any child who is readily identifiable because of his speech or skin color in a school or neighborhood in which a particular gang holds "control." In the case of recently arrived Puerto Rican children thus attacked, the net effect is to force them to learn English and to become "American." Using violence, a disapproved form of social behavior in American society, the gangs that attack individuals on account of their race or language, are in fact trying to conform by enforcing the goal of assimilation for all in the society. The story of Pedro serves to illustrate this situation.

Pedro was fifteen when he came to New York. His father, Juan, brought him from Arecibo with two main aims in mind: first, to allow him to complete his high school course, and second, to have him get a part-time job in order to assist his father in helping the rest of the family in Puerto Rico. Juan himself had come to New York several years earlier and had lived in rooming houses while working to support his family. He makes annual trips to the island, and through the years he has lived and worked in New York his family has grown. He now has nine children, and, in his opinion, Pedro at fifteen was old enough to help him financially without having to give up his education by coming to New York. However, Pedro still needed to live "in family" and Juan arranged with one of his sisters who lives with her own family in Eastville for Pedro to stay there. Pedro procured a part-time job as a messenger boy in one of the near-by supermarkets and registered in the Bulova High School. Soon he started to miss school. "One day," he said, "a bunch of Italian fellows ran us [Hispanos] with knives. We were speaking in Spanish." His cousins, who were present when Pedro told this story, laughed and added that Pedro was a coward, because the following day he had taken a kitchen knife to school and hid it inside his notebook. "When he saw the Italian boys coming, he ran so fast that he dropped his notebook and knife." Pedro then volunteered in self-defense that he had Italian friends in school and that they were nice to him, implying that while some Italian boys gang up, not all of them do so, and that he has been able to find friendship and acceptance from a number of them.

Stories like Pedro's repeat themselves so often in Eastville that teachers can keep junior high school boys in line by threatening them with exposure to gangs. Mr. Dick, principal of one of the junior high schools attended by Eastville boys, told a fieldworker that the Bulova High School was held up as a threat to many of his students. "The Italian boys there . . . gang up on Puerto Rican boys. 'If you don't work we'll send you to Bulova High.' They don't want to go there at all." He continued, "There are a lot of gangs. The boys from this area stay away from Avenues A and B and don't go north of Fifth Street."

Children who are not members of gangs or street clubs are "outside" the available peer group structure of the slum. Many boys and girls, however, do not belong to fighting gangs or to any other youth organization. Among these are the children who are "kept upstairs." They may be American Negroes, Italians, Puerto Ricans, West Indians, or others, whose parents enforce their isolation and succeed in discouraging play, recreation, and having friends in the neighborhood. Some of these children remain "upstairs" all during their childhood, while others, as soon as they have learned the ropes, manage to gain acceptance in some sort of youth organization, with or without their parents' approval.

A boy moves into the gang or club gradually through his years of association with others in the neighborhood. He early learns that his movements in the neighborhood, his recreation, and his play with other children are restricted by the fact that play groups are organized and one must be a member to join in the fun. Furthermore, he learns that he has to rely on his associates for his personal defense. Life in Eastville is said to be "tough," and boys and girls who belong to some kind of group find that this assures them of protection from the aggression of others.

A gang is unlike a clique for it is a large organization with officers and hierarchies of groups that incorporate individuals according to their age and sex. Cliques are not necessarily parts of gangs, but at the base of a gang are multiple cliques which form divisions that intergrade within the hierarchy of the gang. The top leader of a gang with divisions and cliques in Eastville may live, for example, in the Bronx, and it is not likely that he will know personally all the members of his gang. But, like a general in the army, he knows his councilors, division leaders, and other high officers. The gang members, however, wherever they live or whichever division they belong to, can recognize each other by their uniforms, hats, pants, or jackets.

On the neighborhood level, the gangs operate as cliques— the clique members being boys or girls of the same age group who live on the same street or block and who have close friendship ties with each other. These individuals may be either of different ethnic groups or of the same one, and a particular clique of girls may be the debutantes of a boys' gang or they may be independent of any boys' organization.

Both social and fighting clubs have names and emblems of gang membership. It is known, for instance, that boys who wear a narrow-brim hat called the "stingy brim" or the "hippy dippy" in or around the neighborhood all belong to the same gang. Or when members of a clique appear in public, such as at a dance, all dressed alike, outsiders are aware that they belong to a particular gang.

Like the social clubs, the fighting clubs may hold their formal meetings in community centers in the neighborhood. Members of fighting clubs also allege that they sometimes use some of the school shops to manufacture the zip guns and other weapons they use in fights.

Debutantes are the girls' branches of the boys' clubs in the neighborhood and are friends of those boys. The boys and their debs engage in group recreation together and flirt with each other. If the club is a fighting one and there is a war, the girls carry the weapons which the boys will use in the fight. Debutantes of a given club have their own special meeting places—specific sidewalks, stoops, or candy stores—and hold their formal meetings in one of the girls' homes. A club member who "gets serious" about a debutante is supposed to ask her to leave her club to insure that she will not "run around" with other club members. After a man gets married he is expected by his club brothers to settle down and to leave the gang. However, in Eastville some men continue to be active in fighting clubs after marriage, even though they are criticized for this by other gang members.

In both social and fighting clubs individuals are usually organized by age. That is, in a particular club the age-range will

be from boys and girls eleven or twelve years old to adults in
their twenties, but the clubs are graded according to age, and
individuals in the same age-set form subdivisions of the club.
The Regals, a social gang that engages in sports activities primarily, illustrates this. Bert, an eleven-year-old boy of Puerto
Rican parents, was born and reared in New York City. He
is a member of the Regals, but he is a Regal Waif, while his
older brothers are Juniors and Seniors in the same club. The
Waifs are boys between eleven and twelve who live in the same
block. Explained Bert, "After this we go to Regal Juniors at
fourteen and fifteen, and then Regal Seniors at sixteen, seventeen, and eighteen." The members of the Regals are "mostly
Spanish," with a few Italians, but no "colored boys." There are
no girl-debs associated with them. Boys are invited to join and
then voted on by the membership. Those asked are "good players" and do not cheat in games. The members do not fight with
other clubs; they compete in games and sports with them. They
play baseball after school during the warm months and football
during the winter, and are helped and refereed by the Regal
Juniors. Members are expected to pay dues, which are used to
defray such expenses as uniforms, hats, and trips to broadcasting
studios, movies, beaches, and parks. The Regals have no club-
house, but the Juniors and Seniors have formal meetings in a
local community center.

In a fighting club, the various age groups are also separated,
but the duties and obligations of members are of a different nature from those of sporting club members. The Charmers, for
instance, have three age-sets: the Tots, boys from twelve to
fifteen; the Juniors, sixteen through eighteen; and the Seniors,
nineteen up.

A former War Councilor of the Charmers explained why the
boys are separated by age. "They use that in order to keep the
fellows away. You find some young fellows sixteen years old,
fifteen, trying to hang around with fellows eighteen, nineteen,

and twenty. So this way they keep them down, like that, Tots or Juniors and Seniors, so they can stay around with the boys there too, their own age; so that there won't be some guys fifteen years old hanging around with guys nineteen, twenty years old. . . . Well, the fellows in the other clubs, if they see younger fellows in the other clubs, if they see younger fellows hanging out with the big guys, they figure that's a pushover, them guys can be easily taken, if they see younger guys with them. You see, usually the Juniors, if they can't finish a fight like if they go out fighting, club fighting, and they can't win the battle, some older fellows from the other club jumps in—all the fellows. Well, the Juniors come back and get the Seniors. . . . [The Tots] they fight also. And if someone older jumps in, like if one of the kids' fathers comes down and jumps in, well, the Seniors come around and take care of the father."

To both children and adults who have lived in Eastville for a number of years, "the heat's on" means one must be cautious in the streets and in recreation areas. The phrase indicates that one fighting club is due for a battle with an enemy club; that conversations between club representatives to prevent the outbreak of "war" have failed to maintain the peace; and that club members have been called to fight. The word spreads around the neighborhood that "the heat's on," and the expectation of trouble keeps many people who know about gangs— although they do not participate in their activities—off the streets. The fight may be between two cliques of the same block or street; or it may involve a series of neighborhood cliques belonging to a "division" of a gang; or it may involve several divisions from different parts of the city. Trouble may, for example, be provoked by a boy who trespasses against another gang by flirting with a debutante of an enemy gang, or by avenging an individual who was victimized by a member of another gang. Eastville cliques and divisions may also be called by other divisions of their gang to participate in a war to be held in some other part of the city, such as a West Side or a Bronx park.

Residents of the neighborhood say that it has changed over the past two decades, and the changes have been assessed variously, both for better and for worse. There is more agreement now as to Eastville's being a "bad" environment, but what is wrong with it has been blamed on all sorts of things—on the new arrivals from Puerto Rico, on the American Negroes, on the Italians, on drug addicts, on the landlords, the apartment shortage, the churches, the candy stores, the streets, on the ways in which youth have changed, on neglectful parents. In short, a host of explanations of different sorts are offered to validate the point that Eastville is a "bad" place. In any case, the way the residents define the neighborhood points to their dissatisfaction with living there. Furthermore, it suggests some of the basic kinds of social patterns that can emerge under such conditions of life. Adults who grew up in Eastville and became involved in the web of neighborhood gang action, which called for such behavior as stealing, making weapons and using them, and so forth, consider themselves "tough." They say the neighborhood was tougher during the years of the Second World War and before than it is now. For newer arrivals, nonetheless, Eastville is a tough place to live in. Tom, a twenty-five-year-old heroin addict, of Puerto Rican migrant parents, who was born and raised in Eastville, expressed the first point of view to a field-worker.

"When I was a kid, I mean, the East Side was pretty rough, rougher than it is now. And, all you had was prostitutes, and Lesbians, and drug addicts, and thieves, and various types of people on the East Side. Kids living in this environment didn't have much of a chance, you know, in growing up."

Tom also says that when he was a boy in Eastville he joined one of the clubs because "[I] didn't have very many friends and

I always felt lonely . . . and guys I used to associate with weren't the type of guys that I wanted to be with . . . these guys from the club. And I had to belong to the club for the feeling of protection and security . . . I didn't always want to be getting in trouble and stealing, I felt that I wasn't cut out for this type of thing, but always seemed to get in trouble. . . . We used to go to the movies, used to go to Coney Island, we played games in the street, we played stick ball and softball, and we used to go swimming in the East River." He also talked of smoking marijuana cigarettes at thirteen with the members of his street clique. Drug addiction, however, prevented him and other addicts from fulfilling gang duties and they quit.

Another drug addict, also in his mid-twenties, born and reared in Eastville, commented on the change in the neighborhood and particularly the change in the nature of gangs or clubs over the past several years. "There ain't hardly much club fighting in . . . in Eastville. . . . There's a few gangs that wants to steal, gang fight, and that there . . . but hardly much of them goes in for that. Unless someone really looks for trouble, there's like a lot of quiet guys in Eastville now, but they're like the reserves. If anything should happen to someone they know well, they'll right away go into club fighting . . . [but] they'll try to stay sociable as long as possible."

One of the most powerful clubs in Eastville today is a social club. These are the Dukes, feared and respected by the fighting gangs. "Today, regardless of where you come from, or where, what country you come from, if you come to Eastville here, and you get in the know, and in a couple of years, well, you find out that the Dukes are the Dukes. Their standard is 'United we stand, divided we fall.' " The Dukes have debutantes, and the debutantes are either the wives or girl friends of the Dukes. The Dukes and their debs, "well, they get together, the guys' wives hang around together, they know one another. They'll come around, they'll meet one another, and if they throw a dance, they dance at the Dukes' dance—they throw a dance twice a year."

The fighting clubs are said "not to bother" the Dukes. "They all respect the Dukes . . . because the way they're organized. They're not like us . . . well, they got all organized system—they're just like a company. They're not just like a group of fellows that they get together. They know each other; they was brought up with each other. In case that some club gets wise and they want to fight, they send their War Councilor."

Many intergang problems are now settled by arbitration. Besides some Youth Board workers, civic and religious leaders who have gained the trust of gang leaders may work with them in settling disputes.

The fighting gang, like any other institution in New York, requires a Puerto Rican migrant to learn different modes of social relations and different sets of values in order to fit into the social contexts in which he carries on his life activities here. Recently arrived Puerto Ricans are not regarded as suitable recruits for gangs. "They're not in the know. They don't do what they do over here [in New York]. . . . They call them squares because they don't know nothing—what's really happening here in New York [and] they ain't got the time to teach him." Among other things, knowledge of New York society, English, and the argot in fashion are necessary to qualify for gang membership.

Gang membership is also disapproved by Puerto Rican parents. Thus recently arrived children are likely not to participate either in social or in fighting clubs. The two elements then that combine to leave them out are the self-imposed, limited participation of recent migrants in the life of the neighborhood, and the social rejection of recent migrant children on the part of New Yorkers in Eastville. These two factors isolate the children from their peer groups in terms of both healthy and unhealthy social outlets. As time passes and the parents and the migrant children start to "learn the know-how" of Eastville life, the children are either allowed to participate in some organizations, or prevented from participating in neighborhood organizations altogether out of fear of the threat it represents to parental ideals of good behavior in their children. When parental control of the child's behavior is effective, the child is likely not to participate in gangs or undertake other antisocial activities, but parents cannot always prevent such participation as other social forces counteract parental wishes.

While the local clubs of both social and fighting gangs are fairly numerous in Eastville, cliques of drug addicts are not at all numerically important, nor, for that matter, are the number of addicts. Nonetheless, addict cliques are even more dreaded by the residents of Eastville than are gangs. It is frequently said among Eastvillers that one of the scourges of the neighborhood that makes living there so bad is its undisclosed numbers of drug addicts and the amount of trade in drugs that takes place there. When an Eastviller describes drug addiction in the neighborhood, he is likely to blame it on "others" and not to identify with any ethnic group ostensibly associated with drugs. Hence, one hears that "Puerto Ricans" (not Hispanos), or "Negroes," or some other group are addicts. In defending the moral values of the people of the neighborhood Eastvillers may also say that addicts are not from Eastville but that they come from the Bronx, for example. When making a derogatory remark about an individual or his ethnic group, an individual may also include that "he" or "they" use drugs. This implies that accusations of drug addiction are not infrequently made on the basis of one's objections or prejudices against an individual, an ethnic group, or even a place of residence. Addiction was found among members of different ethnic groups.

There are drug addicts in Eastville, but the preoccupation with this phenomenon among Eastvillers is relatively much greater than the number of addicts in the neighborhood. Although an exact figure cannot be given, my estimate is that substantially less than one percent of the population there is engaged in the use or sale of drugs. This estimate can be made on the basis of the social organization required for drug addiction, namely, informal cliques in which addicts participate to obtain and use drugs in the neighborhood.

Drug addicts in Eastville are defined by nonaddicts as a group, and the drug addicts also speak of themselves as a distinct group. Actually this group of addicts is involved in the very complex network of the illegal drug business, which is not local to the neighborhood nor a function of any ethnic group in particular. As neighborhood addicts, however, they share a social identification that excludes nonaddicts and that fosters in them a strong *esprit de corps,* a "we feeling,"—a sense of unity and belongingness. They share secrets of addiction, secrets of sources of drugs, and secrets about illegal means of obtaining money fast, and they undertake joint activities directed toward that aim. All these factors put together are of aid in insuring addicts their regularly needed supply of drugs, and thus they protect the illegal flow of drugs.

The members of the addict cliques consist of both men and women in their mid-twenties. The core of this group centers on addicts who have known each other since childhood, when they attended public school and played together in the Eastville streets. Other individuals, also "hooked" in the use of narcotics, have come to live in the neighborhood as adults, or they are residents of other parts of the city but travel to Eastville to meet with other addicts and get their "fixes" of drugs. The social interaction among addicts in the neighborhood is of an interpersonal nature, and they frequently meet together to the exclusion of nonaddicts. They tend to form subgroups in restaurants, on stoops, in alleys, or on sidewalks in various blocks of the neighborhood, but the subgroups frequently change members from within the larger group of addicts.

Addicts, then, form cliques and within these cliques partial fragmentation occurs, largely in response to the organization needed by individual addicts to obtain drugs at a particular time. The clique organization provides a social framework through which addicts relate to the pushers and connection men in the hierarchy of the drug trade both inside and outside the neighborhood. In addition, the cliques represent an available source from which addicts can obtain cooperation for activities necessary to getting money to pay for drugs. Addicts get together as a group, talk boastingly about themselves, express a desire for drugs or a desire to stop using drugs, and praise the potency of particular drugs. When necessary, they can count on each other for protection from the police. Leadership of the clique is not permanent, for leadership is the province of the man or woman who engineers the action designed to obtain drugs. The man or woman who has access to drugs or can plan means to get them rapidly acquires a following. The subgroups or part-cliques form around individuals in need of a "fix," and these then discuss immediate possible drug sources, plan and undertake either a robbery or some other activity to raise money to meet their emergency needs. They continue their association during the preparation of the equipment necessary to "cooking" and taking the drugs, as well as during the administration of the drugs. They may inject their veins from the same dropper and needle and stay together while "high" (under the influence of the drugs). "Off the stuff," addicts may be seen participating in conversations and games with nonaddicts in the streets, but relationships between nonaddicts and addicts are deemphasized when the addict again starts to crave drugs. Then he returns to associations with other addicts within the addict cliques.

Addicts are publicly known as such, and even children of preschool age can identify them. People determine who is addicted from observation of the behavior of addicts in the streets and by information passed around by word of mouth, as well as by admission of a habit on the part of addicts themselves. Individuals who associate with the informal groupings of addicts either are considered to be users or are suspected of peddling. Among themselves, addicts employ an argot that is not used in conventional conversations of nonaddicts, but nonaddicts can nonetheless recognize by their behavior when addicts are expecting a peddler or when they are under the influence of drugs. Secrecy is maintained as to the identity of particular places or persons robbed, the names of fences or peddlers, and the time when the "stuff" is delivered, but addicts speak freely about drug addiction as a habit, its effects on the individual, and the activities they have to undertake in order to raise money to pay for drugs.

While addicts do not disclose the names of fences and always claim that the fences are outside the neighborhood, it was found that actually there are fences in the neighborhood to whom addicts sell some of the take from their robberies, and that these items, in turn, are resold right in the neighborhood at very low prices. Robbery is intricately connected with drug addiction, although it is not undertaken exclusively by addicts. Nor is robbery the only way addicts have of raising cash on short order to pay for drugs. A woman addict may engage in prostitution and male addicts may help to provide her with customers. As a reward, the woman addict will give a free fix to fellow addicts who have helped her. Close family members of an addict, recognizing that he may steal or get into trouble with the police when he needs a fix, will cooperate by giving money to the addict, even if they disapprove of the habit. Other ways of obtaining money for drugs are by securing temporary employment, by selling drugs at a profit, by shooting craps, or by other kinds of chance gambling. Heroin and other drugs must be paid for in cash by the addict, but the drugs become readily available as soon as the money is. As one addict said, "The problem is not getting drugs, [it] is in getting the money to pay for them."

Thus, money is a major preoccupation among addicts, and to obtain it an addict will go to any length or take any chance. Another addict put it this way: "I became desperately in need of money, I used to take things from home, things that were pawnable, such as the radio and suits. . . . Whenever I needed money and [my mother] had it, which she . . . which wasn't very often, she'd give it to me when I told her I was sick and needed the stuff. But she understood pretty well that I was hooked and all she could do was sympathize with me, that I was hooked. . . . [My wife] on a number of times, she has given me money for drugs, but like I told you, she wants me to get off it, very badly, because at present I'm unemployed and there isn't any money coming in, you know, the bills pile up, and . . . a drug addict can't work if he's got the habit, because he needs the money for drugs, and if he's got the drugs in him he can't work because he is always nodding and he feels too high to work, and he isn't good either way."

The wife of Elliott Thomas, a drug addict, discussed some aspects of the behavior of her husband and the effects addiction was having on their relationship and their lives. "What I noticed most of all that I really couldn't take any longer . . . [was] that . . . it led him to be completely dishonest. . . . He would lie to me to get money from me to use for drugs, or he would go to his mother to get money [his mother was an unemployable woman suffering from a lung ailment] . . . or he would tell me he was not using drugs any more. . . . [He] finally broke down my trust in him. Yet it was something he was forced to do because of his habit. . . . He realizes that we're not going to have much of a family life, or much of a marriage either, if he can't kick his habit, and he knows that I don't want him to support the family if he can't kick his habit

and work. . . . We have to have money to live on, and that
he has to work, because now I have a baby, and I'm unable
to work. And, even if I was working, I wouldn't be able to support the family and support him too, and his habit. And he
knows that I don't want him to support the family by stealing
and by other illegal means and that if this is the way he wants
to live, though, that then we won't live together because I just
won't . . . won't live this way."

Only occasionally do addicts have to leave the neighborhood
to buy drugs, for drugs can be purchased there either from
pushers or from other addicts who themselves "push." Transactions between peddler and addict take place in the street,
in restaurants, in bars, on roofs, in corridors, or in alleys. It is
through the peddler that the addict cliques are directly connected with the grapevine of the drug trade in the city. The
drugs the peddler brings to deliver in the neighborhood are in
various stages of processing, ranging from pure drugs to those
in a highly diluted form. The retail peddler obtains his product
from connection men, and runners may intervene to deliver the
drug from the connection to him. Somewhere "on the water-
front" a "big man" or "kingpin" heads the organization. Connection men, runners, and pushers frequently change their de-
livery areas to avoid being identified by the police or accused
of peddling. An addict who "crosses" a pusher or a connection
man by not paying for drugs or by acting as a stool pigeon ex-
poses himself to retaliation, it is said. The story among addicts
is that welchers and squealers may be beaten up and that "some
guys are never heard of again if they cross a connection," that
they may be thrown into the river or given a "hot shot" consisting of a mixture of lye and strychnine instead of heroin.

The neighborhood addict knows that there is "an organization" but his personal contacts within it are restricted to the
peddler, his runner, and perhaps a connection man. Drugs
which reach the neighborhood undiluted, or still strong, are

"cut" in "shops" or "plants" located in basements or on roofs
of the neighborhood buildings. In the shops, quinine and milk
sugar are added. The quinine is obtained from the pusher and
the milk sugar is bought in drugstores as are the capsules in
which the drug is packaged. Cellophane bags of the sort used
for protecting stamps and purchased in school-supply or stamp
collectors' stores are also used for packaging drugs. Addicts
test the drug strength by injecting the mixture intravenously until the desired strength is obtained. Pure drugs sold in the neighborhood for as much as $500 an ounce, and one pure ounce
could be cut into seven or eight ounces with quinine and milk
sugar to retail for $100 an ounce. A shot of heroin retailed for
about $4.00, and an addict might need an average of $90.00, or
more, a week to support his habit.

Addicts are not born, nor is any individual predestined to
become one. What is clear among the addicts of Eastville is
that they had painful and lonely childhoods, according to their
own admissions. Their parents had less education than they;
mothers were described as kind and understanding; and fathers
either had abandoned the mothers or had not been steadily
employed and in the eyes of the children unsuccessful. The gap
between parents and children, the sense of loneliness and isolation from parents, was counterbalanced in their school years
when they started to participate in groups with fellow schoolchildren. As children going through grade school in the neighborhood, they grew close to each other, played together, and
occasionally engaged in petty stealing and fights together. Not
all members of such groups, however, became addicts; rather,
there was a selective process over a period of years by means
of which only a few of these children turned into addicts in
their early adulthood.

Several stages in becoming an addict were distinguished. The
first stage occurred in the early teens, between thirteen and
fourteen, when smoking marijuana was tried as a group ex-

perience by boys. To smoke marijuana, a number of boys share cigarettes, several drawing from the same one. Cigarettes are either provided directly by an adult pusher of drugs or are stolen by the boys from "shops" or from neighborhood hiding places, such as roofs, alleys, or staircases, where the reefers have been casually stashed. An addict related that when he was fourteen, "I used to see them [marijuana smokers], how happy they was, and they used to say, 'You need a reefer,' or stuff like that, and I figured I was old enough to feel the same way."

Smoking marijuana, like smoking tobacco cigarettes, was undertaken as an experiment by these boys. From this the way was opened to becoming drug addicts. Some of those who used marijuana in early adolescence, however, did not become addicts regardless of the opportunities open to them for obtaining drugs in the neighborhood. Tom, a twenty-five-year-old addict, who had smoked marijuana in his teens, described how he "got hooked" into the use of heroin and points to the facilities available for it to any individual on New York's East Side.

"Well, on the East Side there are a bunch of dope runners, and we used to hang around in these yards. And one day a guy comes up to me and asks me did I want to make a half dollar. Well, that was a lot of money to me, so I tell him yes, so he tells me to bring this package over to a certain address. And, I brought it over there, and he told me to pick up some money for it; and I picked up the money and brought it back to him, and he give me a half dollar. And every day he used to come around at the same time and give me this package, and I'd go and bring it over. So one day . . . it was a package of capsules . . . and I never knew what it was, and one day the guy who I delivered it to asked me did I know what I was bringing over. So, I told him, 'No, what was it?' and he told me it was junk, and . . . it was heroin, and it made you get high. So I told him, 'Heroin?' He showed me, 'Sniff,' how you get high, and this was the process: that you emptied the heroin on a book, or on a mirror, or anywhere, and you sniffed it through your nose. And this guy showed me how to do it and I sniffed it. I began vomiting and got a violent headache, but I found that the more I vomited, the greater the sensation got. And, I had gotten a sensation such as I had never received before. It was such a pleasure and good sensation—I mean a warm feeling all over your body, it's one such as I can't express, but it was something like I'd never had before. I knew that I would take it again. While delivering the stuff for this guy I used to take one or two out for myself and began sniffing and sniffing and sniffing. And then one day I didn't run for this guy and I became quite ill. So at the time that I was taking this stuff to . . . running this stuff, I become associated with a number of people that I had taken this stuff to, which were drug addicts, and one of them—I was sitting down on the stoop and my nose was running and my back was hurting, and a guy comes over to me and asks me, what are you . . . what's the matter? I told him, 'I don't feel good, I'm sick,' and all, so he tells me, 'You're hooked.' I asked him, 'Hooked, what do you mean "hooked?"' And he says you need junk to feel better, and he says. . . . I told him I didn't need any of that—that would be the last thing in the world I'd want. I'd guessed I'd go to the doctor and he told me, 'No. Just take a little bit of junk and see what I mean.' So, I went into the hall and I sniffed some junk, and all those illnesses went away. And, I found that my nose stopped running, that my head stopped hurting, that I didn't get cramps in my stomach, and I knew then what the meaning of the word 'hooked' was. And I never looked back from there, I just went on."

The transition from marijuana smoker to drug addict took Tom three months. "And, I graduated from sniffing to shooting. Shooting, you know, is injecting heroin."

Other preaddict stages besides marijuana smoking were also reported. There are the "drug-hoppers," who sniff or do "skin-popping," that is, injecting heroin into the muscles rather than the veins. Explained one addict, "He is fooling around until that stuff will get him . . . skin pops is for a drug-hopper. . . . He might only take heroin on the weekends, but sooner or later he will become a junkie." A sniffer of heroin is referred to as a "horsehead." But it is the one who uses a hypodermic —the man who sees himself hopelessly "hooked"—who is called the "junkie."

Hypodermic needles are obtained either by stealing or by purchasing them from illegal sources. Two years ago, one of the neighborhood grammar schools was broken into, but the only things stolen were the hypodermics from the school clinic. The equipment necessary for intravenous injections are the hypodermic needle, a burner, and an eyedropper (used as a syringe). These are kept in the "plant," "stash," or "workshop." A narrow piece of rubber hose may also be part of the equipment as some addicts tie it around the arm in order to catch the vein.

Drugs may be taken by an individual alone, for addicts usually own their own paraphernalia and the drugs can be self-administered. However, it was not always done this way, as using drugs seems to be part of a social situation in which clique members participate together. Two common types of social gatherings of addicts are the "session" and the "shooting party." At a session they start "mainlining, or skin-popping, or snorting." At a shooting party they all inject intravenously. "We'd steal together, and we'd share whatever we had together. We'd share the money, and buy junk together and get high together."

The "getting high together" seems to be the climax of a set of organized activities which begin when a robbery or hold-up is planned in order to obtain the money for the drugs, continue through the disposal of the goods stolen and the actual purchase of the drugs, and end with administering the drugs together. Sometimes a party of addicts share the same equipment, and in cases when an addict is "sick," that is, in need of the drug, he may get a fix free of charge from other members of the clique with whom he has cooperated in robberies and to whom he has given fixes before. The free fixes are limited, however, and thus the individual who is an addict must participate in a social clique that operates to fulfill his needs.

While addicts profess a desire to "kick" the habit—and may in fact discontinue the use of drugs for a time, they nearly always return to them. During the winter, many Eastville addicts seek voluntary commitment for treatment through one of the social agencies of the neighborhood, and occasionally addicts undertake self-cure measures and forge prescriptions of curative drugs. "Cold turkey," or total discontinuance of drugs, is considered undesirable and painful. Yet, there are times when addicts volunteer for cold turkey treatment in an effort to reduce the need for the drug, at least temporarily. If while in prison under mandatory cold turkey, drugs can in some way be obtained surreptitiously, addicts may use the "pin shot" method of injecting. This consists of puncturing a vein with a pin and feeding heroin into the opening with an eyedropper.

Addicts claim that the presence of other addicts in the neighborhood and their influence encourages the "kick-happy" who is "dozing off" drugs to go back to using them. Eastville addicts define themselves as being trapped and unable to "kick" the habit. In the words of Jack Campos: "They are around, and they are offering me drugs and I have some money in my pocket and they say, 'Hey, Jack, do you want to get high? Come on, how about a fix. Come on, let's cop some drugs.' And I'll tell them, 'No, I don't want to use it.' And they say, 'This guy got some real good drugs,' and I'll say, 'All right, let me try it.' And one leads to two, and two to four, and four to six, and one's too many and a thousand is not enough."

Addicts regard the habit-forming drugs as something they cannot escape. They say, "Once an addict always an addict."

For even if the habit has been checked for any period of time, it is believed that any individual who has ever been an addict can never be fully emancipated from his need for heroin. Some of the names given heroin—which addicts regard as the drug that causes the worst habit—are indicative of this thesis. They include "white goddess," "junk," "stuff," and "dope." The effects of heroin in comparison with those of marijuana were described by an addict as follows.

"It's [heroin] worse than marijuana. . . . It's habit-forming. I know so many people who have been smoking marijuana, and they . . . they not looking like the ones that take heroin. Marijuana is . . . it's you that makes marijuana so bad, I mean the person. Because he be smoking marijuana, and he be looking for a different kick. But if you want to stay on marijuana yourself, you can stay on marijuana. Marijuana is just something that will make you happy, gay; and heroin is . . . after the first couple of times, it makes you feel good and all that, but after a while, it becomes a habit. You have to have it like you have to eat. With marijuana you can stop whenever you want."

Another addict discussed the causes of addiction, placing them in "the environment," and connected this to the emotional and mental illness of addicts. "I've always placed my addiction on my environment. I've never been able to get away from it when I'm in the neighborhood. All my old friends. . . . And I'd break the habit and take the cure and come out and maybe get a job for a week or two, and become bored, and I'd always feel a sense of insecurity, so I wouldn't feel right, well, doing anything unless I was using drugs, so I'd always go back to using drugs.

"Drug addicts receiving psychiatric treatment can get at the basis of their problem—enabling them to understand. They can cope with their problems and understand better. They can stay off drugs . . . if they understand their emotions and their problems, and different things like that. I mean they can really get at the basis of what's troubling them in their minds. Because drug addiction, I believe, is a sickness of the mind, and can be cured. And the psychiatrist—this being his business, the business of the mind, curing minds can help.

"[Drug addicts are] all mentally sick, or emotionally disturbed, that they have problems, that all of them should receive psychiatric treatment, that it is a curse. . . . Very few people but the people who are addicted know what it is to go through life being a drug addict; and the majority of addicts that I have met don't want to be drug addicts. And, it is just something that they can't help, that they have no will power of their own. That they try desperately to get away from, but they just can't seem to get away, because they're caught in this snare. No matter what they do, they're always coming back to their old ways, their old environment, their old friends and associates, and picking up where they left off—maybe they've had a cure—using drugs again."

Hispanos and the larger society

LIVING in Eastville, Hispanos are unavoidably involved in the stream of the larger American society and its culture. As the neighborhood is a part of New York City, its residents, like all New Yorkers, depend on the vast battery of resources of the entire city for their existence—for employment, goods, medical care, transportation, education, social services, police and fire protection, and so on. Among Hispanos the most characteristic and the preferred relationships are those with family, kin, and other small groups, which are based on mutual affection, assistance, and social equality. The usual relationships between Hispanos and white-collar and professional workers who represent the services of the larger society are, however, of a somewhat different nature. In the latter, Hispanos are invariably in a position subordinate to that of the official or the professional, and the relationship between them is based on the service the professional or official renders and which the Hispano needs. Rarely do they consider each other friends. The official is in a position that gives him authority over the Hispano, and he furthermore enjoys a higher social status and greater prestige than does the Hispano in the society. It is usually as a job seeker, an applicant to a social agency, or in some other status of the underprivileged of the society that Hispanos appear to the professional or white-collar worker.

It would be practically impossible to describe and analyze every pipeline of the relationships Hispanos have with the greater community of New York. Because of their general interest, however, a few will be examined subsequently in the context of the cultural ideals that guide the behavior of Hispanos, particularly recent migrants, in their relationships with officials and professionals.

Recent migrants seek and exchange with their friends and relatives advice and warnings about how to cope with American institutions and their personnel. Friends, relatives, or casual acquaintances with some reputation in the neighborhood of "knowing this country" are asked for information regarding specific problems, such as the names and addresses of "good" lawyers, "good" doctors, or even "good" *trabajadores* (caseworkers or social investigators). Further, it is considered desirable that one be accompanied by someone else when it is necessary to transact some business with an official, regardless of whether the individual wanting the service knows how to speak English or not. It is also desirable that the person who accompanies one be a fluent speaker of English and well dressed, that he have good manners and a large vocabulary. These individuals are considered to create a good impression and to be convincing. Thus the intermediary is expected to do more than simply translate. He is supposed to say, on his own initiative, the right thing and to protect the interests of the person he accompanies.

Among professional interpreters are found individuals who learned how to make the rounds of New York City social agencies, physicians' offices, hospitals, courts, and so on in connection with problems of their own. Even their knowledge of English and ability to communicate with Americans with relative ease were acquired when they were trying to tackle personal problems of their own in New York.

More often than not, a schoolchild goes with his mother or father, his aunt or a neighbor to "do these businesses" with "Americans," and if the results are not satisfactory, the child is said not to have *capacidad*. An adult friend or relative may be asked to accompany a person to attend to some business, but a fee is expected in return for such a service. Although migrants speak of helping their friends in such matters as taking them to a courthouse or a hospital, the obligation is not cleared unless payment is made for the service. Fees for interpreters range from three to five dollars for part of a day. Interpreters are also hired to make telephone calls to lawyers, social agencies, or schools. Yet the payment of money to an interpreter is not considered to be purely a business transaction. It is subordinated to the relationship of friendship or kinship between the two parties. An interpreter who is a good person is expected to show his goodness by acknowledging his sense of obligation to be helpful to the person whom he accompanies to see an official or professional and for whom he will interpret. He is also expected to initially reject the payment, while the party served is to press the offer until it is accepted. But the acceptance of fees by interpreters also creates anger and criticism on the part of those who have to pay. They claim that in this country one must pay for everything and that interpreters are not really friends but simply do this work for their own selfish ends. If an adult interpreter does not achieve the desired results when acting in behalf of someone else, it may be said that he failed because "Hispanos here are not worth a hoot," or because he is "afraid of Americans," or because he "does not know what he says."

Where the services of an interpreter or some other favors are needed from somebody else, and the persons are not involved in the kind of mutually expected obligations just described, the approach to obtain the favors may be the direct offer of money. If not that, the transaction will, nonetheless, in such cases, be exclusively on a monetary basis. A logical extension of this pattern are the attempts to pay professionals for their services. These may be interpreted, in turn, as bribery by the professionals, for they also respond according to their own cultural expectations, rather than to the accepted ways of behavior of lower-class Puerto Rican migrants. A clergyman we knew was approached in the street by a Hispano migrant woman who, without any introductory social formality, said to him in Spanish, "I pay you three dollars for a letter of good conduct." The clergyman looked rather perplexed and asked a fieldworker who was present what the woman meant. The woman explained that she needed the letter of good conduct for the police on behalf of her son so that he could get a driver's license, and she again offered to pay the clergyman for such a letter. Looking at his surprised face, hearing no reply from him, and misunderstanding his reaction, she emphasized once more that she would pay him for the letter.

While it is tempting to go further, really, only a few cautious generalizations can be made about the cultural ideals recent migrants and professionals hold about each other and about the nature of the interpersonal relations between them. Some of these have to do with stereotypes on both sides. To recent migrants, professionals and officials are "the Americans." They are powerful, represent the law and the government, and have authority to make decisions that can affect the lives of Hispanos in a fundamental way. Americans are different from Hispanos, and many times fail to understand them. They are "cute," "nice," and "kind," but they are strangers, as one never gets to know anything about them, their families, or their friends, and often one does not even find out their names. Some are "shameless" and hate all Hispanos. On the other side, in the context of New York City, many stereotypes about Puerto

Ricans also prevail, and it is not unusual to find sophisticated professionals and officials sharing them. One often hears professionals unwittingly speak of Puerto Ricans as a "race," as being "all on welfare," as "all carrying knives," and as being responsible for the slums of the city. Others have stereotypes of a more favorable nature, but nonetheless stereotypes, such as, "They have special ability for music," "They are a musical people," or "They have special talent for working with their hands." While these appraisals are more sympathetic, they are hardly applicable to Puerto Ricans as a group either, for although some Puerto Rican individuals may and probably do excel as musicians, or for that matter, carry knives, these are not characteristic of the group but of particular individuals. There are other officials who recognize that Puerto Ricans have different cultural backgrounds than "Americans," but many of these tend to overemphasize the differences to such an extent that they block their own chances of discovering common understandings with Puerto Ricans, which also do exist and which, if seen, could facilitate their relationships. In addition, they overlook or discount the facts that length of time in the United States, as well as age of migration and socioeconomic status, are important factors in the cultural adaptations of Puerto Ricans to life in New York. In an effort to communicate with Hispanos, professionals who know some Spanish, for instance, try to use this language even with Hispanos born or reared in this country, who often have difficulty in understanding and speaking Spanish and who are fully conversant in English. All in all, stereotypes provide group images that are misleading, either because they are wholly false or only partly true when applied to a group. When applied to individuals, they easily lead to interpersonal tensions and misunderstandings, preventing sound and mutually satisfactory relations.

Guiding the relationships of recent migrants with institutions of the larger American society are many preconceptions

Hispanos acquire about the United States in Puerto Rico. A prime preconceived idea is that American citizenship provides those who hold it with boundless rights, boundless opportunities for employment, and boundless security and protection denied anyone who is not an American citizen. Freedom of speech is for Hispanos a fundamental quality of individual freedom, summarized by the cliché, "In this country one can say anything one wants about the President and the government; this is not the Dominican Republic." Freedom of speech is interpreted as the power of the individual to defend himself through verbal protest against any abuse of authority.

When, for example, Lala and her husband were having financial difficulties to the point where the finance company took away their furniture and Con Edison discontinued their electric and gas service, Lala went to the Red Cross to request that her son in the army be discharged so that he could go to work and help the family out of their financial troubles. In recounting the story of her visit to the Red Cross headquarters where she went to present her claim, Lala said the official she talked with told her that her son could not be discharged on these grounds and that she got so angry she started to blame the President of the United States for the draft. At this, the Red Cross worker became very upset, Lala continued, and told her to quiet down because she would be taken for a Communist. Lala continued, "I told her, 'What! a Communist? I just want my son back. Nonsense (*pocasverguenzas;* literally, lack of shame)!' and I laughed."

A Puerto Rican schoolteacher in Eastville interpreted the set of beliefs underlying actions like Lala's as meaning that "the Puerto Rican has more sense of freedom than any other people on the continent. . . . He is used to expressing his ideas freely, what he feels, because he takes literally, 'at the foot of the letter,' that there is freedom of speech. So many 'continentals' [1] do not understand why a Puerto Rican can say that Eisenhower is a son of a 'bla-bla.' It is because in the public schools of Puerto Rico freedom of speech is taught, although its limits are not."

The laws of the United States are also seen as inviolable, otherwise severe punishment will be administered to the offender. They are designed in the eyes of Hispanos to protect the poor from the rich, women from men, children from their parents, in short, to protect those who are weaker from those who are stronger, creating thus a balanced scale of fairness and justice. "The law," it is said among Puerto Ricans, "favors the poor, the worker," as an extension of the ideals of protection and social justice which they associate with American democracy. Yet, concurrently, one must also have "fear of the law," and not "get into trouble," as one is helpless before its power and its instruments.

Voting and participating in the elections and other political activities of this society are regarded as other valuable rights which American citizens hold. But either on grounds of failing the literacy examination in English and being embarrased by it, or because of lack of information about the issues, or on account of anger against the content and kinds of appeals made by political parties and leaders to Hispanos during political campaigns, among other reasons, individual Hispanos are deterred from casting their votes. Many political appeals that have worked successfully in Puerto Rico to deliver the vote do not find approving response among Hispanos, who consider them derogatory and harmful to their status in New York. When one of Puerto Rico's most popular political leaders addressed Hispanos over the radio as *jíbaros* (country folk) who

[1] "Continental" is a term used to refer to persons born in the Continental United States by the Puerto Rican press. The term is seldom used by Puerto Ricans, although Americans use it with reference to themselves when in Puerto Rico.

should act civilized and vote, the responses in Eastville were annoyance and disgust. It was claimed that this kind of speech was detrimental to Hispanos, and the leader was described as "stupid" for using such words.

Self-appointed Hispano political leaders, or leaders appointed by the various political organizations active in Eastville, may not be recognized and accepted as such by the local public. This, too, may stop Eastville Hispanos from performing their electoral duties, or some local neighborhood controversy may be the stumbling block. Once, for example, several Hispanos refused to register because the office of the Board of Elections was established in the home of a Hispano who was very much disliked by his neighbors, and as Julia Cantres said, "Who is going to go to his home?"

In coping with the institutions of the larger society recent migrants tend to personify them, assuming that the particular individual to whom they speak is responsible for the institution itself. Seldom do they know nor can they find out what the name, title, or responsibilities of the person they talk to in the Department of Welfare or some other large organization, like a hospital, are. Often, they are seen by different officials each time they need attention, even for the same problem. This impersonality makes it difficult for Hispanos to deal with such personnel and such institutions, since the preferred way of establishing meaningful, acceptable relationships rests on a one-to-one, interpersonal basis, which requires knowing something personal about an individual in order to set up a working relationship with him in which one can have confidence. Though they get lost in a maze of incomprehensible red tape and in the anonymity of interpersonal relations, Hispanos are nevertheless drawn into firsthand contacts with all sorts of officials and professionals. Of these contacts, perhaps the most important and frequent are those they experience with the job market, welfare agencies, the medical profession, the schools, legal institutions, and religious organizations.

In the vast job market of New York, Eastville Hispanos compete for employment all over the city, in jobs considered unskilled or semiskilled. Though recent migrants prefer to obtain jobs through personal channels, it is not unusual for them to consult the want ads of Spanish dailies. Going to the agency or the place of employment listed may involve someone else, the one who accompanies the prospective worker. For Hispanos who grew up in New York, the matter of seeking jobs is a personal and individual task. As a rule, they go directly to an employment agency, or find out about jobs through the English dailies, and then the individual proceeds by himself to apply for a job. Recent migrants prefer those jobs in which knowledge of English is not essential and in which the "boss" (that is, their immediate superior) speaks "a little Spanish" and has paternalistic relationships with his workers. Employing enterprises are usually referred to as "the company" and the company itself cannot be trusted, since it is only interested in its own welfare and not in that of the workers. Labor unions in the States are considered not to care for the workers either, for they do not appear to be active in obtaining the concessions Hispanos want. They, too, seem too big, impersonal, and uninterested. Thus while admitting to union membership, Hispanos often express disappointment in the unions.

Being employed is the preferred manner of living, and work is an end value in itself. A good man is expected to work, and to work hard in his job. Yet unemployment and underemployment, low and unsteady wages are common and real facts of life for Eastville Hispanos. Having to collect unemployment insurance or receive welfare aid funds are sources of embarrassment and shame to an individual who, many times, will prefer to face severe economic hardship, quietly hiding his financial needs

from others, rather than apply for aid or claim his unemployment benefits.

In Hispano terms, only a sick man can justify receiving welfare aid, and in many cases the man claims that his wife is the
one who receives it, or that it is for the children. Rarely does
the man himself admit that he receives welfare aid. A healthy
man who lives without working is considered lazy and a smart
aleck, or *listo,* and is suspected of being engaged in illegal activities, or of being a man who profits from women. In Eastville
such men are sharply criticized by their neighbors and so are
the women who are said to support them.

A woman is more justified than a man in wanting and receiving welfare aid, and a wife is likely to convince her husband that he should accept assistance by telling him that their
children must eat and be clothed and that he is not providing
the necessities of life for them. When couples have to apply
for either home relief or supplementary aid, it is the wife and
the children who are expected to "get into welfare" and not
the man, even if he benefits from such an income. A man is
likely to phrase it, "My wife is receiving welfare." He, however,
can be expected to do whatever errands and legwork are necessary in order for her to communicate with the Department of
Welfare to meet the requirements of the department for the con-
tinuance of aid.

A work accident will lead a man to apply for workmen's
compensation and, under these circumstances, to draw supplementary aid from the Welfare Department himself, but even
in these cases the welfare assistance is only uneasily accepted
by a "man of work." If an indemnization should be won in a
case taken to court, the plaintiff receiving welfare aid has to
repay from the indemnity whatever he has received from the
Welfare Department. This procedure causes disgruntlement on
the part of Hispano families, for welfare aid is not considered
a loan, but a form of charity, and one which it is "difficult to

get out of." Having to turn back indemnizations to the Welfare Department is regarded as further reducing one's chances of getting out of welfare, because then an individual still lacks any financial resources of his own to fall back on and may still have to accept welfare aid to subsist.

The following letter, a copy of one that a migrant wrote to the Mayor of New York, illustrates some of the conflicts of values that arise for a man who has become an invalid and cannot work.

Letter to the Honorable Robert Wagner
Your Excellency:
Please be informed that due to illness I have been forced to accept home relief aid for myself and my wife for the past four or five years. I am a merchant marine by occupation, and before I was forced to go on relief I sustained some injuries aboard a ship. Naturally the case was handled by attorney John Litz, of New York, and when the case was settled for over $3,000, out of which the attorney charged a fee of $1,000, the rest was turned over to the Home Relief authorities.

When this money was turned over to the Dept. of Welfare, they promised that if I was willing to go to Puerto Rico, they would refund it to me. Now, due to the fact that I am having a great deal of trouble with the Investigator who handles my case, and I am badly afflicted with arthritis all over my body, I would like to have this matter settled once and for all with the Dept. of Welfare authorities, and if the balance of this money is still in their possession ready or any time I am willing to get out of New York. I will very sincerely if thru your influence you will get in touch with them so I might leave the City for the benefit of my health and my wife's, who is almost completely blind.

I am a religious man. You will understand that in my position, I am a man of excellent character, and reputation. Your interference in my behalf will be deeply appreciated, and your

cooperation as soon as you may have the time, will have our
blessings for the rest of our lives.

Thank you sir, and may the Good Lord bless you and your
family.

Respectfully yours,

Luis Pio

Mr. Pio's letter points out the socially justified rationales for
accepting welfare aid. First is an emphasis on physical inability
to work due to a work accident. The second is an emphasis on
respectability and reliability of character. Third is the emphasis
on being "forced" to accept welfare aid because of having nothing else to rely on. In the light of migrants' value orientations
and motivations for coming and settling in New York, welfare
aid is accepted by them without apparent conflict and with
minimal dissatisfactions only under those conditions where
the individual can socially justify his inability to be employed.

Recent Hispano migrants do not as a rule hide from their
neighbors and friends the fact that they are receiving welfare
aid. On the contrary, they are likely to talk of it openly, telling
their friends all about it and the reasons why they must receive aid. Often, too, they will remark, by way of being com-
plimentary to the United States, that it is an advantage to be in
this country where "at least one can get welfare" if things do
not go well, as when one has a long illness or cannot go to work,
because that would mean depriving the children of food and
clothing. This sort of statement provides a socially acceptable
rationalization. It is a mark of personal self-esteem to make
clear that one has been "forced" to obtain welfare aid, that one
really does not want it, but has no other choice. This is the
social technique used to resolve the dilemma of "having to accept" something unacceptable—that is, "help"—among individuals who stress the value of work as an end in itself and con-
spicuous consumption as the expression of the product of their

work in a social context where the display of material goods and generosity toward others represent the harvest of success.

Welfare aid, or any other form of public assistance, or even taking advantage of group health insurance under labor union contracts are, in principle, disapproved of, except under the special conditions of life just described. For a working man with no physical incapacities but with inadequate wages to support his family, welfare aid is likely to pose conflicts both for himself and his family. Miguel, who does not earn enough to support his family, does a lot of running around to Welfare Department offices and protests against the amounts of the checks he receives because they do not cover expenses. Said he to one of the fieldworkers while they were taking a walk together, "In Puerto Rico I earned half of what I earn here [fifteen dollars a week], and I could always support them [his wife and children]; she is the one who wants welfare; we could get along with what I make." Families on welfare may claim that when they had an income from employment, which was smaller than what they receive from welfare, they had savings, they ate better, and they had no debts, because they managed their own funds at their discretion. The conflict of values regarding acceptance of welfare or other social aid is then not resolved merely by obtaining an insured minimum income from welfare sources. Even if this income is essential to rounding out one's livelihood in New York, troublesome social and emotional consequences may accompany and follow the satisfaction of economic needs through aid rather than work.

Because of the disapproval of dependence on welfare aid, a great deal of gossip in Eastville revolves around who receives aid and what he does with the funds. Volunteering that one receives welfare aid, in a sense protects the individual from malicious gossip and criticism. Yet anybody receiving such aid, even if he publicizes it, can easily be a target for accusations of misusing welfare funds or of not deserving the assistance. While it is said that some people "can get anything" out of the Department of Welfare "and live like kings," others are said to receive such small allowances that they can hardly make ends meet for the barest necessities. Those "who live like kings" are criticized for taking advantage of their situation, while those who live in extreme poverty despite the assistance they receive from the Department of Welfare are encouraged to talk firmly to their caseworkers and to "go higher up," "to the office downtown," and to "complain about him." People said to "live like kings" from welfare aid incomes may in reality live in quite poor circumstances, their status of "kingship" referring, for instance, to having received enough money to buy overcoats for themselves and their children when winter starts. In other ways, too, those on welfare may be vulnerable to jealous criticisms from their neighbors. For example, if one individual's work wages are lower than welfare aid for another, jealousy and anger may be fostered, because work is not being remunerated properly in comparison to income not worked for. When individuals receiving home relief or supplementary aid are considered to be "making money," they may be reported to the Department of Welfare by their neighbors. These reports, often exaggerated, are made to get revenge for one thing or another. Luis Marcos converted a dilapidated baby carriage into a cart equipped to prepare and sell shaved ices. It was the first warm weekend of the year when he started his business in a near-by park. He boasted of having sold eight dollars worth of ices on an expenditure of only four dollars for the syrup ingredients and the ice. The following day the welfare worker who handles the case of the Marcos family came to visit them, and Luis's wife said he told her that "somebody" had called him and reported that her husband had a business. He had come to warn Luis that either he discontinue his business or the family would lose their supplementary aid.

If one is receiving welfare assistance, he should not tell Americans or strangers, even about supplementary aid to match one's income from a low-paying job. But schoolchildren whose families receive welfare aid inform their parents that they have to tell because their teachers ask the whole class what their parents' source of income is, and then "everybody in school knows."

Obtaining welfare aid is regarded as involving an invasion of one's privacy, for family matters must be discussed with the welfare worker who is a stranger—*un particular*—and the authority in a family partially shifts to the caseworker assigned to the family. He plans the family budget; the family is required to report any other sources of income, including presents and gifts; and the worker checks up on the family with other strangers, such as teachers, causing embarrassment to family members and exposing their financial status. In the context of their family values and ideals of self-esteem, Hispanos find this hard to take, and the welfare worker is usually blamed personally for the procedures required by his job.

When official channels do not function to meet the needs of Hispano welfare clients, they may try other means for fulfilling them, such as going into debt, doing some kind of work in their homes, or perhaps exaggerating the nature of their need to induce the welfare worker to comply with their requests. For example, Dolores Roman told her caseworker she needed a crib for her baby who was sleeping in a doll's bed given her by a friend. Dolores said that the crib was on loan and that she had to return it, but when the money was allotted by the worker for a new crib, Dolores did not buy one; instead, she used the money to pay off some debts.

When a need cannot be met, it may be said that the "need takes care of itself," or one must just live with one's needs and forget they exist, as in the case of Julia, a pregnant woman receiving supplementary welfare aid. She was hospitalized for a few weeks for malnutrition, and then a special diet was prescribed for her on which she was to continue until she was due to give birth. The hospital social service department was to request an extra three dollars bimonthly from the Welfare Department starting in April to help pay for the diet. In June, Julia still had not received any payments for her diet despite her repeated requests to her caseworker, and for those two months she was not on the diet because she "had not been paid for it." On June 4, her welfare worker said that Julia would get her diet supplement in fifteen days, and the worker's supervisor verified his statement, but warned that she ought to check with the hospital. The social service department at the hospital informed her that they had passed the request on through channels to the hospital dietician, but the dietician said that if the social service department had referred the case to her department at all, they probably had never sent the petition to the Department of Welfare. She continued, "It is too late now, anyhow, because it takes two weeks at least to get Welfare to approve a referral and send the money and her baby is due in one week."

As has already been hinted, relationships between caseworkers and their clients are not always satisfactory. A discreet worker who shows understanding of the problems presented by his client and who does not undertake to direct a family in its affairs is considered "a good person." A worker known to discuss matters of welfare assistance and problems of a client with other persons, or one who overtly shows his distrust of a client's words or tells him directly how he should manage his home problems, is disliked and considered nasty. Once a member of the field team was visiting a family when their welfare worker came to call and unsolicitedly started to discuss his clients' character and problems with the fieldworker. Although the fieldworker was shying away from the topic and trying to change the subject, the welfare worker insisted on contributing his appraisal of the family. The family members watched quietly and nervously until the welfare worker said that the children were doing well in school. In a tense voice, one of the children then interrupted to ask him how he knew. He replied smilingly that he had written to the school to inquire about them because he was interested in them. In an outburst of anger the child demanded of him, "You mean you have written them? How do you dare?" "We must find out," the worker replied, while the tension mounted. Behavior like this only serves to exacerbate for Hispanos the conflicts generated by having to accept welfare aid. For them, receiving things or services for nothing is acceptable only from friends and kin. To depend and rely on free services or gifts from strangers or institutions is considered demeaning of one's dignity, for the migrants cannot reciprocate, which is necessary for compliance with their ideal of mutual obligations. And this extends to areas other than welfare, including, for example, medical care.

The story of Teddy, a fifteen-year-old high school student whose family was on home relief and who had had a toothache for days, bears this out. His mother went to visit a friend of hers from the same home town in Puerto Rico to inquire about the procedure to be followed in going to see the dentist. She wondered whether their welfare card had to be shown in order to obtain the service because her son would not want to indicate that he was on welfare. The neighbor told Teddy's mother that the boy did not have to show the card, that instead the mother could go make the appointment and show the card to the nurse then so that Teddy himself would not have to acknowledge that his family was securing public assistance.

When medical attention is sought, private medical care is preferred to public on the assumption that physicians want to be paid directly by the patient for care and prescriptions, and will see the patient sooner and do a better job if they are. "Private doctors" are said to examine everything and prescribe, whereas one often hears that "Welfare Department doctors are no good," that they do not act promptly in the face of illness.

Even persons receiving welfare aid may therefore go to see physicians privately, if they can possibly scrape together the fee. New York hospitals and medical care for the poor are considered better than those in Puerto Rico, although it is also said that Hispanos in New York are not treated as well as other people on account of anti-Puerto Rican prejudice on the part of some physicians and nurses. Medical services in clinics and hospitals are, however, sought after and used as a rule either in preference or as a complement to home remedies. Often migrants in need of medical services simply cannot afford to do otherwise than go to low-cost or free clinics.

One of the areas of misunderstanding and tension between hospital personnel and patients is that concerning the scheduling and keeping of appointments. The hospital expects patients to be available for scheduled appointments and the patients expect hospitals to keep appointments as scheduled. The discrepancy between these expectations rests in the fact that while the hospital routine is based on the organization and scheduling of the services of the hospital itself, that of the patients is based on the organization and scheduling of their work and family activities. One frequently hears doctors and nurses complaining that Puerto Rican patients do not keep appointments, while Puerto Ricans reciprocate with the same complaint about doctors and nurses in hospitals and clinics. Among migrants, it is said that when one has an appointment with a hospital clinic, it is necessary "to lose the whole day there," meaning that the patient has to wait around until a doctor is available to see him, regardless of how long this may take beyond the scheduled appointment—and it may take many hours. As Moncha said, she went to the hospital one day for a 10 a.m. appointment, having been told not to have any breakfast. By 3 p.m. she had not yet been seen by a doctor and, being hungry and dizzy, she left. Keeping appointments is considered responsible and "good" behavior, and individuals boast about their faithfulness in keeping hospital appointments despite the inconveniences this may entail for them. Yet there is no disapproval or concern for breaking appointments, the rationalization being that a hospital is always so crowded that it does not matter to the doctor whether he sees a particular person or not.

Objections to clinic hours that coincide with hours of employment, as they usually do, are also heard. Going to the hospital implies "losing the day" among working Hispanos, for an employed person must miss work to keep a medical appointment, both because this is a time-consuming process and because the time it consumes is working time. One of the solutions to the problem of "losing the day" needed to keep medical appointments is to go to the hospital as an emergency case, for under such circumstances one can see a doctor with little waiting and without an appointment. This is why one sees so many Hispanos in hospital emergency rooms late at night.

In the case of illness when immediate hospitalization is desired for a patient, a relative, a friend, or a child who speaks English is asked to telephone the police to request them to send an ambulance. An adult who performs this service may receive a cash payment for it. An alternative is to call upon a neighbor, a friend, or a relative living near by who owns a car to drive the patient to the hospital in the company of a well member of the family. Payment to the driver is expected for this service.

Another important area of communication Hispanos have with the larger society is connected with the legal system. Recent migrants have a strongly legalistic orientation and are very much concerned with such matters as using the legal system to protect their rights—"taking it to court"—or obtaining legal protection when accused of violating the laws. Lawyers in this country are said not to be like those in Puerto Rico. Here, it is claimed, "a criminologist is not good at handling a compensation case," pointing to an awareness on the part of recent migrants of the specialized nature of the legal profession in this country. People who "know this country" are asked about "good" lawyers "who don't sell out" and "who talk in court." A good lawyer is a good speaker, a man who by his verve can persuade the judge to favor his client. In the field of civil law, cases pertaining to claims for accidents suffered on the job are common. Operating on the general premises that in this country "the law is for the worker and the poor," that since injuries at work may prevent a man from becoming employed again, and that large cash indemnizations are made to workers who have suffered injuries, a person who has suffered a work injury is likely to become involved in a maze of complex procedures. He will often follow the advice of different lawyers and laymen indiscriminately and even miss the legal channels and opportunities actually available to carry on a legitimate litigation.

On the neighborhood level, relations with the law and utilization of its channels are represented for Hispanos in the relations they have with the police. Recent migrants see the police in this country as agents of the law, which protects women from men and children from their parents, who are on hand in case disputes between neighbors, fights and quarrels, and other expressions of interpersonal aggressions erupt. On the other hand, it is also said that the police are not interested and do nothing when Hispanos are robbed, and that one must protect his own home from robbery himself by keeping it locked and by requesting all those who knock to identify themselves before the door is opened. The police are also said to abuse innocent people by suspecting them of crimes and searching them in public, causing them embarrassment, and by doing nothing when people really need protection. Yet recent migrants do resort to the police for help and protection—and this at the same time they are afraid to have anything to do with the police if they have been accused. "I will have you summoned" is a routine menace resorted to by recent migrants angered at a neighbor. The individual who wants to make trouble for another with the police watches for some "legal technicality," such as throwing garbage or water out of the window, on which to have his enemy delivered a summons. However, one is not supposed to accuse one's friends or the relatives one likes of violations of the law; rather, one is expected to ignore their illegal actions. One also does not accuse individuals who can retaliate and cause harm to those who accuse them, because a person should avoid getting into trouble, even if he disapproves strongly of the actions of others. Children who are rebelling against their parents' punishment for infractions of their rules may threaten to tell the police, while children themselves may be threatened with being sent to the police for some action or words considered disrespectful by adults outside their family's circle of friends or kin. Yet to many an unwanted child who wanders over the streets of Eastville the policeman is kind and nice because "he takes me by the hand and gives me ice cream."

When a quarrel or dispute may possibly lead to a *compromiso* (a tough situation in which life or personal freedom may be risked, as when one would be compelled to fight and violate the law), the police are called to prevent the *compromiso* from burgeoning. Thus a lovers' spat may be reported to the precinct if it is interpreted as leading one of them to suicide. One morning Jack proposed to a girl who turned him down; he walked out. By 11 p.m. he had not returned to his home, so his mother went to the girl friend's home and told her she had to come to the police station because the mother was sure her son had killed himself or done some other *disparate* (nonsense) on account of the girl. The girl friend reported that she was very upset and accompanied the young man's mother to the station. There the mother accused her to the policeman at the desk of being responsible for the boy's disappearance. Jack's girl friend said that while she was explaining the details of the quarrel to the policeman through her tears, he started to laugh loudly. When the girl had finished, the policeman told both women to go back to their homes and that if by midnight Jack had not returned to telephone the police. Jack did return by midnight, hungry and tired, for he had been walking the streets for hours. The following day the girl accepted him as a *novio*. She explained to one of the fieldworkers that she was afraid he might kill himself if she did not.

The idea that the police protect women is extended to relations between husband and wife. It is a widely accepted viewpoint that the wife has the favor of the law in any controversy with her husband, even though a husband is entitled to privileges with his wife that no other man has, regardless of whether they are legally married. It is also held among Hispanos that a child belongs to the mother and that the father cannot take it away from her, that if he tries, the law will restore the child to the mother. In the case of Antonio and Maria, who had lived together for a year and had had a baby girl, this idea was proved false, at least temporarily. After the baby's birth Antonio abandoned Maria, who kept the child, remaining with her where she and Antonio had lived previously—in his aunt's house. Then at the end of another year Maria and her daughter moved across the street into a friend's home. Antonio quickly discovered that Maria had left his aunt's home, and one day he came to the house where she was living while she was out. He demanded of the landlady that she give him his daughter. The landlady later reported, "I gave the *beba* to him because he is the father." When Maria came home and found the baby gone, she turned to the police for help to make Antonio return the child, but the police told her that Antonio could keep the child until the case was heard in court because he was the father. Antonio then became angry at Maria for "putting the cops on him" and watched her home for a whole day, sending in messages that he was going to stab her in the back for what she had done to him.

Maria was afraid he would carry out his threat and did not dare go out, even to her job. The landlady's husband did not go to work either "in case something happened." All day long Antonio either patrolled the sidewalk in front of the house or drove by slowly in a car. Yet neither Maria nor the family she lived with would ask for additional police protection, so afraid were they of Antonio's vindictiveness.

Both the story of Jack and that of Maria and Antonio serve to illustrate the mutual misunderstandings that exist between Hispanos and the law.

Besides the functions of the schools already discussed, they are also important in the relationships between Hispanos and the larger society. To repeat, education for one's children is vigorously pursued as an important goal. Since the relationships between the schools and the neighborhood are extremely limited, it is rare to hear of a teacher, principal, or other school officer, except the attendance (formerly called the truant) officer, who visits the homes of any of his students in Eastville or who has any other relationship to a parent than that of being his child's teacher. The relationships between recent migrants and the teachers and personnel of the school attended by their children are still more limited than those of Hispanos who have lived in New York for a number of years. The latter are not frightened of visiting a school and of finding, perhaps, that the teacher disapproves of them and their children. Visits to schools as required of parents have become a matter of routine involving no major difficulties for them.

School organizations, such as the parent-teacher associations in Eastville have their gears in the schools and are run by school personnel. In a PTA meeting at one of the schools of Eastville the principal's assistant encouraged the parents present to write letters to the Board of Education urging the board to buy window shades for the school "because they pay more attention to parents than to us." Yet despite such pleas for active participation by parents, no leaders from the neighborhood took an active part in the PTAs. An Eastville school principal describing the activities of the PTA in his school said, "[It is] not very active. . . . The members have no incentive or initiative. They meet once a month and always in the evenings since most of the members have to work in the daytime or just couldn't come. . . . One of the main things the PTA does is contribute money. These funds are spent mostly for repairing things that otherwise wouldn't be repaired for quite a while by the Board of Education." A schoolteacher in Eastville paralleled the principal's comments when he told a fieldworker his opinion of parent-teacher organizations. He said, "You must remember that parents in the city do not take the same interest in the parents' organization as in suburban areas. They have so many other things to take their attention that they give little of it to the school and the parents' organization." Actually, given the kinds of relationships that exist between the school personnel and parents and the attitudes displayed by many teachers and principals toward the neighborhood and its people, one could not expect the development of a vigorous and active parents' organization.

In trying to close the gaps between recently arrived Hispanos and the New York community as a whole, the Board of Education of the city has been actively attempting to meet the special needs of its Spanish-speaking population, as described earlier. Other needs of the community met by the schools in Eastville are not exclusive to Hispanos. The offering, for example, of school facilities, such as gymnasiums and playrooms for children to play in after school hours, is extended to all. However, recently arrived children from Puerto Rico do not, as a rule, make use of these facilities.

Hispanos come in contact, too, with religious organizations, but these organizations often fulfill a different function for them than do other institutions of the larger society. Neighborhood churches frequently play an important role as mediator for Hispanos with those other institutions. Many local churches are active in community social welfare work and frequently step in to aid recent migrants in coping with some of their difficulties attendant to living in New York. While less effective when trying to contend with matters considered private family affairs, church personnel are considered reliable and influential in dealing with other institutions of the larger society. This role of mediation was played in the past by political leaders and ward heelers. Actually, the personnel of some of these churches now also take an active part in the political issues and campaigns of the city and even of the nation.

The churches of Eastville vary with the kinds of services they render their congregations and with the kinds of relationships their clergy have with congregation members, as much as they do in denomination, religious orientation, social viewpoint, and ethnic composition. For recent Hispano migrants, the clergyman is a symbol of authority to be recognized by his dress and his manners. He is somebody "of respect," but not necessarily "of trust." The relations of Hispanos with their Catholic priests are formal and limited to areas of religious concern. Clergymen of the Protestant denominations have closer, more personalized, and neighborly relationships with their congregations, though this at times brings criticism on the part of Hispanos, who conceive it proper for clergymen to restrict themselves to the formalities of religion. Relationships between Pentecostal clergymen and their congregations are characterized both by the use of formal address and titles, and by the minister's use of his authority to correct, warn, and scold a member of his church who has stepped out of line. The relationship is not democratic in the sense that the minister is an unchallenged authority, but it has elements of democracy in the sense that the minister is socially one with his flock, since he is usually a Hispano himself, a man who like his parishioners migrated to New York in search of a better life.

For recent migrants the role of the church is to be concerned with the spiritual and social conduct of man. Churches are regarded as a powerful source of social control, a source of control that comes to man from beyond himself, from God and other divine or sacred creatures. It is not considered proper for them to sponsor recreation programs or social affairs, but in New York Hispanos accept as a part of their function their role in facilitating relations with the larger society.

Clergymen may be asked to write letters of recommendation for jobs, to welfare officers, as certificates of good conduct, or to telephone some official and make a firm request or protest on behalf of a recent migrant. The role of the clergyman in facilitating relationships with professionals and officials is not, however, seen as one binding the individual to the clergyman's religious ideas.

Because of the multiple social services many small Eastville churches already render their congregations and the roles they are able to play in securing more direct channels of communication between the neighborhood and the agencies of the larger society, they stand as examples for the potential role that small organizations—social, political, or religious—could play in developing a closer rapprochement between New York's most recent newcomers and the larger community.

Health and life stress

"HEALTH is the most important thing to have." So goes a common saying among recent Hispano migrants. It summarizes the role they assign to health and suggests their preoccupation with disease. Health permits a person to work, and work is both a virtue in itself and a means for carving out one's future. Being healthy is at the base of all well-being, and forms the bed of the path leading to the fulfillment of one's life aims. Hence it is a necessary condition to a good life. The social value of health is tied up with many other aspects of life, and many anxieties and fears about the present and the future are expressed in terms of health and illness. Health is conceived of as a gift from God, and sickness quite often as a punishment for wrongdoing, a work of evil, or a trick of fate. The prevention of illness and the goal of better health are two realities with which man has to contend, but health itself as an absolute quality is beyond man's control.

All societies, primitive and modern, have developed cultural modes of appraising health and dealing with illness. Modern medicine is one of these many cultural modes, but it is by no means the only one followed to maintain and restore the physical and emotional condition of man. In modern society we find that while scientific medicine has become a highly specialized and skilled activity in the health field, many old, prescien-

tific ideas about disease and methods of healing have continued to operate, though modern medical concepts and methods
are continually fed into their frame of reference. Popular medicine, or the medical ideas and practices undertaken by laymen
in any society, is of great importance to the welfare and general
health of the society's population. An understanding of the concepts and methods of the popular medicine of a society is rele-
vant to more adequate and satisfactory medical care of the members of that society. The ways in which people take care of their
sick, their attitudes and beliefs about disease are primary forces
in the control of illness and a field of human behavior that lies
within the scope of study of the social sciences.

Eastville Hispanos are familiar with and acceptant of the
modern physician as the trained specialist on matters of health
and illness, and of clinics and hospitals as the institutions where
the sick are taken care of. Beyond this they fall into two different
categories regarding their views and attitudes toward health
and disease. These cluster around age-groups rather than length
of residence in New York. Young adults, regardless of whether
they were reared in New York or in Puerto Rico, rely more on
the resources of scientific medicine and pharmacopedia than do
older folk, for whom many prescientific medical ideas have
remained valid and acceptable. Older migrants are also more
preoccupied with illness than are younger adults of similar
backgrounds. This preoccupation with disease leads to widespread and intensive use of all the sources of healing available
in the society, including hospitals and other modern medical
services.

Great concern with health, however, is not confined to Hispano migrants in Eastville. There, one of the common themes
of interest among people of different ethnic groups centers on
questions of health. Illness is an everyday matter which impinges
at all times on the problems of daily living. It creates such concern on all sides that it forms a basis for human sympathy and

cooperation and is an effective means of getting people together and stimulating their charity. Feelings about illness and the dread of disease bind together people in Eastville who under other circumstances would perhaps be hostile and unfriendly to each other. It is not unusual to see and hear of people of different ethnic groups whose friendship started with some illness that aroused sympathy between them. Even people who profess strong feelings against members of other ethnic groups than their own can be moved to sympathy and to going out of their way to visit or assist a sick child, an old woman, or a feeble parent, either in a hospital or at home.

Health is a topic that can both spark and enliven a conversation among adult migrants. In fact, the ability to discuss coherently the health condition of some person or persons makes for good and captivating conversation. News of symptoms of illness, home remedies, patent medicines, and health advice in general are exchanged, and these, together with anecdotes about hospitals, nurses, doctors, and patients, are among the favorite conversation pieces that one hears when visiting the homes of Hispano migrants or when meeting them in the street. Greetings of "How are you?" lead easily into rich interchanges of health information. It is rare to meet an adult Hispano migrant who does not have at his command a grand array of general and specific, common and esoteric items of information about hospitals, diseases and methods of curing them, patent medicines, and home pharmacopedia. But Hispanos who have grown up in New York as a rule disclaim this knowledge, for they regard it as being the "ancient," superstitious, and ignorant ideas and beliefs of "Spanish people" (meaning Puerto Rican migrants). For them physicians, books, and druggists are the authorities on health problems. Illness is not to be cured at home with remedies and medicines which migrants would prescribe; rather, prescriptions should be given by those who have studied and who are therefore considered competent to deal with illness. Yet an adult raised in New York, who does not believe in the effectiveness of remedies recognized by migrants as proper and good and who would shy away from using them if he himself were a patient, might very well prepare such medicines for a sick migrant parent in order to please the parent.

Among recent migrants the ideals of good health are summarized in their desire to be strong, to have good color (pink cheeks), to be plump, and to have no pains. It is said that a healthy person is "strong and fat like a cannon." An individual who is not thus is under the pall of illness, and is not considered very attractive physically either, for beauty is an adjunct of health. A skinny woman is not pretty and a handsome man is neither weak nor puny. A beautiful child is fat—like Gerardito, "who was such a fat baby that his skin popped open in the rings around his arms and legs."

In New York there are more ways and more possibilities than in Puerto Rico for realizing these health aspirations. Here the air is good, the food and milk better and more abundant than they were back home. One also has fewer worries here, and this, too, is good, for too much worrying makes people sick and prevents them from gaining weight and looking plump. Further, one can afford to see more physicians, healers, and druggists, and can buy more medicines and remedies to gain health. Thus one can become healthier in New York than in Puerto Rico. The idea of self-improvement and progress which is polar in the explanations of recent migrants for coming to New York involves implicitly and explicitly questions of bettering health. The standards of health and the preoccupation with losing one's health are connected with the frustration of hopes and aspirations that Hispanos build on their migration and settlement in New York. While sickness and ill-health may have been an accepted part of their lives in Puerto Rico, in New York, Puerto Ricans regard disease as a major threat against the realization of the kind of life and desires for which they came. Conversely, good health comes to be viewed as the condition that will permit such realization. But soon after migration unexpected and apparently unresolvable conflicts and dilemmas of adaptation start to take their toll. On a psychological level, it can be said that frequent and intensive frustrations and feelings of being threatened are likely to be expressed in terms of illness as well as in overt preoccupation with health.

In recent years modern medicine has been giving a great deal of attention to the effects of life stress situations on the human organism and to their role in physical and emotional illness. Undeniably, such situations are present in the living experience and growth of all human beings. When life stresses become too strenuous and intolerable for the organism, however, illness is one of the responses it may make. Because the human organism must live in a social milieu and develop as a person within it, its psychological adaptations to living like a human being are of a social and cultural nature. An individual's feelings are conditioned by his society and the systems of values and cultural norms that the society provides.

The life stresses of Hispanos in Eastville that result from their social conditions are not unique to them. Underprivileged people throughout American society, who have to struggle to maintain their dignity and even their lives within a social system in which the goals and values given them by society are at odds with the opportunities available to them for achievement, are similarly beset. However, the social and cultural stresses of recent migrants are reactions to qualitatively different circumstances of life from those met by Hispanos or members of other ethnic groups who have grown up in this country and who are acculturated to American society. For recent migrants the main areas of stress are those connected with the realization that the social techniques they learned in Puerto Rico to cope with their social needs and goals do not work in New York. Language barriers are only one aspect of this, and perhaps not so important a one as it has often been assumed, because in the social world in which recent migrants operate in New York, English is not essential either to work, to play, or to live. Furthermore, recent migrants who can manage in English may refuse to speak it on grounds that they do not speak it correctly and may therefore be ridiculed.

The struggles of recent migrants are common to Hispanos who have grown up in New York to the extent that they, too, are the recipients of social disapproval and discrimination on the part of the larger society, despite their being English-speaking and oriented to American culture. Hispanos who have grown up here speak of themselves as being both Spanish and American, as two unintegrated aspects of themselves. This translates itself into ambivalence and self-rejection for being identified as Puerto Ricans, whom they reject, and for being denied the identification as Americans, which they seek.

Since among recent migrants it is held that "too many worries make one sick," to be healthy, one cannot take life too seriously, nor can one let troubles take over, nor should one suffer the troubles of others. Otherwise one will become skinny and nervous, have headaches, develop wheezes, age fast, and acquire *achaques*—general malaise or pains "here and there and everywhere." To prevent illness and to insure recovery from disease, a person must forget about other people's troubles, and "not take the unpleasant actions of others to one's chest." Sufferings and worries, nonetheless, are unavoidable; they are part of being a good person as well as part of just being alive. The individual always suffers, because that is the nature of life itself, particularly for the poor, whose life is solely one of suffering. The only people who do not suffer are the selfish and those who have such a "special kind of character" that "nothing kills them" or bothers them. Very few good people possess such a special character; the other good people must suffer. Delia Inclan had been complaining to her neighbor Antonia of being sick. She made up her mind to go see a physician and returned from the consultation in despair and disappointment. He had found "nothing wrong" with her, only that she "worried too much." On the premise that Delia is a poor and good person who does not possess the special character necessary to those who do not worry or suffer, she could not see the value of the physician's opinion, and both she and Antonia were critical of his statement.

Since human life is subject to fate, fate ultimately predestines its path. One does not know what destiny he is to have in life, and fate may unexpectedly catch up with an individual. The acts of fate can mean an improvement in life which was never suspected possible, but they can also mean unexpected and intense suffering. One form of such suffering is illness. Since it is those who act wrongly who are expected to pay with suffering, chronic illness or a sudden major illness in an individual or those he loves will lead him to wonder what wrong he has done that he must pay for. An incapacitating chronic illness that cannot be cured, regardless of what is done for it, is looked upon as the work of fate, and faced with fate's work one may only feel hopelessly resigned.

While the ultimate cause of illness, like other human suffering, lies in powers beyond man's control, there are also more immediate and more controllable reasons for falling sick. Taking worries too seriously and suffering on account of the actions of others are examples of these, but not the only ones. A person may also happen into an accident or do some nonsense—*disparate*—such as walking in the rain, overeating "heavy" (rich) foods, sitting in a draft, getting chilled, or being just plain careless. An infection, for instance, is incurred by such behavior, as in the case of Tomas, a boy of nine, who played in the water disposal unit of a sanatorium for the incurable in Arecibo and fell violently ill. One should also be cautious about eating in some people's homes, because "one never knows" what might be wrong with them, or they may not be clean, and dirt also produces illness. And one may, in addition, fall sick as a result of the envy of others through magic and witchcraft.

Accidents are harmful injuries that happen casually to incapacitate a person to a greater or lesser degree for life. An individual may have made an error—a *disparate*—that made the accident possible. This happened to Ramon Lino, a man in his late forties, who for many years earned a living working as a chauffeur in Ponce. He made a *disparate* and collided with another vehicle. Hurting his back, he was treated medically in Puerto Rico but did not recover. He came to New York in the hope that he could be cured, but as of now he is still suffering pain in his back and is unable to work although he protests that he wants to regain his health. Too hard physical labor, like hauling and carrying heavy loads, will also eventually incapacitate a person, for hernias develop and "the waists open" internally, depriving the body of proper support. Pains follow and one can no longer bend or do any heavy labor. Jobs in New York all require hard labor of men and women, and after the "waists open" or a hernia develops it is not possible to become employed. In New York City it is said that workers are easily hurt in the performance of their duty, and are inevitably exposed to accidents. A compensating factor is, however, that if one becomes disabled as a result of a work injury, he can sue the employer and obtain a large financial reward as an indemnity. It may take years to "win" a case, but the effort is worth while because the indemnity will enable the injured party to start a business in Puerto Rico or perhaps to buy an apartment house in New York, furnishing thus support for himself and his family. Yet stories are frequently told about people who had job accidents as a result of which they were injured permanently and who, while they "won" their cases in court, were prevented by the insurance company or the government from receiving any indemnity when they became unemployable.

Envy is considered a powerful destructive force that whether employed intentionally or not may bring illness to its object. A beautiful child may be the victim of the evil eye, an adult, the victim of directed envy or revenge. One can take revenge on an enemy by invoking spirits and ghosts or the devil himself to harm the enemy. To counteract these powers, a person can pray to God, the Virgin, and the saints, as well as to the spirits whose task it is to shield their wards from unhappiness and illness, and one can also use charms and amulets for this purpose.

Should a person fall ill, he must try to discover the cause before he can be cured. Since diseases have ultimately either natural or supernatural causes, the methods to be followed in combating them depend largely on the causal factors. Physicians cannot cure supernaturally caused illnesses. Rather, this is a job for *espiritistas*—spiritualists. There are also diseases that only Hispanos suffer, which American physicians do not know how to cure, and then there are diseases attacking Hispanos in New York that are never found in Puerto Rico. Some diseases can be cured only in New York, whereas for others one may have to return to Puerto Rico to get well again.

Diseases are classified not only according to their causes or origins, but also on the basis of their symptoms and their effects on the organism or on particular organs. With regard to the effects of illness on particular organs or areas of the body, diseases are specified as those of the stomach, the intestines, the chest, brain, kidneys, gall bladder, heart, liver, uterus, legs and arms, throat, teeth, blood, bones, nerves, and the senses of sight and hearing.

Symptoms of illness are phrased in terms of having either localized or general body pain, becoming skinny, losing strength, having bad color (paleness), experiencing dizziness, vomiting, swelling, diarrhea, constipation, excessive sweating, fever, and chills. The term *achaques* is applied to a conglomerate of symptoms—pains and physical discomforts that are repetitive but do not prevent a person from carrying on his expected normal roles, such as working or being active. He who complains of too many symptoms is said to be *achacoso.* An aged person is justified in having *achaques,* but younger people who complain of general malaise and pains are considered annoying. An apprehensive individual may say that everyone in his family is having *achaques* when asked about their health so as to protect them from possible envy of their good health and also to prevent fate from striking them ill because he has boasted of their good health. Good health is so greatly desired, so subtly changed, and so far beyond one's control that a person cannot afford to feel and voice confidence about it, because it is a value that can easily be lost.

To restore one's health one may resort to the care of a physician, a healer, or a druggist, follow the health advice of friends or that offered in the newspapers, on the radio or television. Generally, care of the sick starts with home remedies, next a physician is tried, and if medical treatment fails, then it is time to assume that the disease is probably the work of spirits and ghosts. Home remedies, consisting primarily of patent medicines and herbs, are considered sound for taking care of illness produced by natural agents, and simple illness can be handled completely at home. Common colds, for instance, can be cured at home, even if it takes months to effect the cure. Chicken pox is one of the diseases of children that can be cared for better by the family than by physicians, for it requires only a touch of a mixture of baby's urine and alcohol on each pox to cure an afflicted child. Measles is disposed of easily by taking warm milk with raisins. In either case the child must stay home until he is well. There are some contaminating diseases, such as tuberculosis, mouth infections, and venereal diseases, that require segregation of the dishes, towels, and other personal objects of the sick person.

While disease may be classified thus according to origin.

symptoms, and effect, some diseases, particularly those associated with internal organs, are described in terms of "hot" and "cold." Conversely, "fresh" and "cool" are expressive of conditions of health and well-being. These qualities are independent of physical temperature, and are assessed independently of sensations of fever, chill, or normal temperature. Popular in the medical knowledge accepted during the Middle Ages, these concepts were brought to the New World by the Spanish and Portuguese conquerors and settlers. They are still widespread today in the medical lore of countries of Iberian tradition in the Western Hemisphere. Among Eastville migrants they are important guides in the case of certain illnesses. Observation of the skin, location and description of pain, and inspection of urine and feces are the main elements considered by migrants in diagnosing a disease in terms of "heat" or "cold."

Skin and mouth rashes, skin abcesses, and eczema are "hot" and due to "irritation" of an internal organ. A patient with such an irritation should take only "fresh" or "cool" medicines and food and not anything "cold" or "hot." So an individual taking vitamin pills to supplement his diet would probably discontinue them if he developed an irritation, for vitamins are considered hot, and hence could be harmful with a condition of irritation. The designation of food and medicine as hot, cold, fresh, or cool is also independent of the physical state of heat, cold, freshness, or coolness of the product or of its temperature. Rather, in the case of freshness or coolness, it refers to the potential of certain foods and medicines for neutralizing hot or cold and restoring a balance of freshness and coolness necessary to the well-being of the human organism. One should not take cold medicine or cold food for a condition which is either hot or cold itself, for cold medicine and food by themselves never restore health. Hot food and medicine are antidotes for cold diseases, while cool and fresh food and medicine are antidotes in cases of heat. A pregnant woman must take cool or fresh medicine and after her child is born she is to continue so doing, for in the state of pregnancy, or postnatally, irritations are easily provoked as a result of which mother or baby may develop rashes. Medicines used to induce miscarriages are "hot," so if a woman tries them and fails to have the miscarriage, she will develop irritations that can be neutralized only by taking fresh or cool medicines and foods.

Tropical vegetables, such as plantains (Musa paradisiaca), yams (Dioscorea species), dasheens (Caladium colocasia 1.), cassava (Manihot manihot 1.), and yautías (Xanthosoma), are fresh foods. Dried codfish is also fresh, and so are some kinds of spices, while sweet potatoes (Ipomea batatas 1.) are cold, and chocolate is hot.

Nasal or chest colds may be cold or hot depending on whether and how the digestive and other internal organs and the skin are affected by them. The presence of a rash or the loss of desire for hot foods are clues that a cold is hot. During the winter and in the cold—as in summer when one sleeps or sits in a draft, or the temperature drops suddenly—one can catch a cold that is described as "cold." With it the internal organs become cold, a condition that is opposed to both freshness and irritation.

Empacho is one of the common illnesses of the stomach, due to improper digestion. This occurs when food "has not fallen well in the stomach," which means the food has remained there and formed a "ball," digestion having stopped short. *Empacho* is a cold disease. Eating non-Hispano foods or leftovers, eating in a restaurant, or eating food that once before did not agree with oneself may provoke this kind of indigestion. The presence of an *empacho* in one's stomach may produce fever and swelling of the belly, affect the intestines, cause loss of appetite, and evoke "pains in the stomach and intestines." The home remedy for this condition is a purgative, such as castor oil, which is hot, or milk of magnesia, which is fresh. An enema may also be administered in case of an *empacho,* and this may be composed of either hot or fresh ingredients. Because an *empacho* is "cold," it is thus different from an irritation, which is a condition with similar symptoms but hot, as it is produced by hot foods and medicines.

Actually, whenever one is sick, one should take a purgative, for the disease may be "thrown out" of the body that way. It is also good for one's health to take a purgative before embarking on a trip or going to a place where it is necessary to change one's food habits or drink different water. Mary Silos told one of the fieldworkers that when she arrived in New York from Puerto Rico she could not avoid taking a purgative, and that in the "old days" one took his purgative a few days before leaving the island. It is also common in Eastville to give small children purgatives when their diet is being changed to include new foods in order to prevent their getting sick.

Knowledge of hot and cold diseases and foods is considered not to be possessed by physicians, and in many instances physicians' prescriptions fail to work favorably for the patient because they violate the rules of heat and cold that apply to particular illnesses and the constellation of nutritive and medicinal products that are necessary to their control. The ideas about heat and cold in illness, the role of spirits in disease, and the subtle ways in which fate plays with man's health are regarded as being part of a different set of beliefs and ideas than those held by physicians and by the "modern" as acceptable. In fear of being disapproved and ridiculed for such ideas, those who believe in them keep them secret from those who do not.

Most diseases that come from suffering and worries involve pain in the chest and around the heart and throat, as well as difficulties in breathing. The nerves are also "altered" by suffering and worry. Among the home remedies used to treat these ailments are numerous patent medicines, either self-prescribed or prescribed by druggists. Orange-flower water is considered most helpful for soothing the nerves. A druggist in Eastville remarked that "orange-flower water is one of the hottest numbers among Spanish people."

From "bad nerves" one loses weight and cannot regain it. Worries may also affect the brain and turn a sensible person into an insane one, but an insane person may be one who became "sick in the brain" in early childhood and has remained *anormal* the rest of his life. Mental illness—defined as sickness of the brain and nerves—may be either a concomitant of syphilis or a disease induced by supernatural action, fate, or too many worries. There are also diseases that make persons act as if they were mentally ill when they really are not, and physicians in New York fail to recognize this. They believe the person in question is "crazy." For example, the disturbed behavior of a woman after labor is not a genuine mental illness. Rita, a recent migrant, told one of the fieldworkers that a woman who had the "labor bug" (*la pulga del parto,* meaning purge) had been sent by her doctor to an "asylum for the insane" on Long Island. The woman's mother wrote a letter to the governor of Puerto Rico explaining to him that her daughter was not crazy but had the labor bug and that she wanted her out of the hospital. Her daughter, she said, was all right, for when she spoke she "made sense." Yet she was still in the hospital. There her mother while visiting her had been treating her real illness, the labor bug. Rita said that she herself had had the labor bug two days after she gave birth to her fourth child, because her husband went out of the house that Saturday night when she, needing help to feed the baby and take care of other things, had no one to aid her. She got a fever because the blood—the bad blood—which should all have been thrown out of her body after labor, stayed in. When that happens, the woman becomes crazy-like, because instead of going out the bad blood goes "up to the head." This is what happens with the labor bug, until it finds its way out of the body, but it is not a form of mental illness.

People who are nervous or have bad nerves may have fits or

seizures known as *ataques* under conditions of severe strain, such as in a major crisis, at "bad moments," or in sudden fright (*susto*). A person may have a fit when there is severe illness, death, or some other major tragedy in his family. A small child may be said to have fits when he has severe temper tantrums. This child is said to be "nervous" or to act as if he had rabies (*rabioso*). The word *ataque* is also used with reference to any sudden form of illness in the sense of an "attack of illness," or with reference to a seizure that is due to a particular kind of illness, as when referring to epileptic attacks (*ataques epilépticos*). If one has fits for no apparent "natural" reason, however, they are explained as being due to possession by spirits.

Among the diseases that affect breathing are asthma and wheezing (*fatiga*). Both children and adults may suffer from either condition. Asthma and wheezing both "attack" or appear and reappear often, becoming chronic conditions. Wheezing is associated with "suffering," worries, anger, and "colds that are not well cured" which have impaired one's breathing. In New York this condition is translated into English as asthma; yet the distinction between wheezing and asthma remains in Spanish referring to two separate but related conditions. Asthma, as Carmen Gomez, who has suffered from it for over ten years, says, is produced by dust and sudden changes in the weather, and wheezing or *fatiga* is one of its components.

The bones, legs, and arms are affected by rheumatism and arthritis. Syphilis and gonorrhea are disorders of the blood, and men give them to women and women to men. In a man these are referred to as illnesses of women, and in women, as illnesses of men. They are curable by doctors even if one is ashamed of them.

Being host to tropical parasites is not considered an illness unless the parasite is affecting the body with loss of weight, fever, or other symptoms of ill-feeling. Parasites may be given as explanations for certain conditions of ill-health in children, for which other explanations are given should similar symptoms be found in an adult. Children are said to have parasites, particularly Ascaris l. (roundworm), because the Ascaris is produced by eating too many sweets. Parasites such as Uncinaria (hookworm, referred to as *la uncinaria,* or anemia), Ascaris, and taenia (tapeworm) are said to eat the child's blood, making him pale and preventing him from gaining weight, even if he is frequently hungry and eats a great deal.

The illnesses and symptoms considered most difficult to cure and most often fatal are heart diseases, diabetes, tuberculosis, cancer, double pneumonia, hemorrhages, malaria, and "internal tumors." Seldom does one recover fully from surgery, and if there has been surgery of an internal organ, one may "never be again what one was before." One is an *operado,* and this means he must watch himself and be careful about undertaking physical activities. Surgery of an internal organ prevents a person from "exercising force," moving around, and doing heavy work.

Bad color is associated with lack of blood and implies that the person has anemia, tuberculosis, malaria, or other diseases considered fatal. Anemia is looked upon as a stage in the development of tuberculosis, and if one conquers anemia, he is protecting himself from becoming tubercular. Surgery or any ailment which causes bleeding leaves the individual weak, and weakness is a symptom of anemia. "The blood that one loses is not gotten back again for years," commented Julio Dante, discussing the importance of blood to the body. When one feels weak, medicine is needed, perhaps injections of liver, or vitamins, or a medicinal wine with "many things" in it, including vitamins, for these are body and blood rebuilders (*reconstituyentes*). It is good to have "a lot of blood," with high hemoglobin content, and a person should not give away his blood, unless it is to someone he loves very much, such as his mother or his child. For them he may risk his own life by giving of his own blood, but he should not do this for others.

The treatment of disease is related to the fundamental assumption that sickness revolves about having too much or too little of something in the organism, on account of which it cannot function properly. Hence, something must be taken out of or put into the diseased body to restore it to health. The most accepted methods are surgery (which only a physician-surgeon can perform), drinking medicines that cleanse the organism (e.g., purgatives), taking enemas, and taking medicines such as vitamins that build up the organism. Hot baths with aromatic herbs are good for diseases induced by the supernatural for they wash away the spirits that made the body sick.

Only those who believe firmly that spirits have the power to produce and cure illness can really be made well by supernatural treatment. Among older people, both old and recent migrants, supernatural beliefs about disease are more currently accepted than among younger adults. Belief in spiritual causes of illness is regarded by young people as old-fashioned. For those who believe in spirits and ghosts these beliefs are ingrained in their conception of man and the universe. They are regarded as means of reaching into powers and mysteries beyond the understanding of man. Thus they are a part of religious experience.

The victim of a disease induced by magic or spirits is supposed to obtain a prescription from a spiritualist—an *espiritista* —in order to become well. One may consult a spiritualist in person, by mail, or may send another in his stead to visit the spiritualist. The spiritualist may be in Mexico, in Puerto Rico, or in some other state than New York. It is necessary to pay a spiritualist for the service rendered, otherwise the prescription will not work.

It is said that many spiritualists now are racketeers who "know nothing," that all they want is to make money. Individuals who really do possess the gift of seeing and communicating with spirits and ghosts and who obtain prescriptions and advice from them may do this as a full-time occupation, receiving patients for treatment regularly. Others, however, practice only occasionally as a gesture of conciliation to the spirits who have endowed them with such power.

Miguela Mendez remarked one day that there is a Hispano physician with a medical office near Eastville who believes in the existence of spirits and their power to restore health, and who knows when the patient is a victim of an illness caused by spirits. Once she accompanied a friend of hers to see him "as a doctor." He singled them out from the other patients, telling them, "Both of you wait in that other office." After a while, he came back and said to Miguela, pointing to her friend, "That woman is not sick. She has spirits (*seres*), and what she needs is a herb bath. Tell her to go see So-and-So who can cure her, an *espiritista,* not me."

Prescriptions from *espiritistas* include patent medicines, injections, tablets, and powders obtainable in drugstores, as well as amulets, prayers, and herbs. The herbs can be procured in any of the many herb stores known as "botanical gardens" that are scattered all over Manhattan, the Bronx, and Brooklyn and which often advertise in the telephone directories. Some prescriptions call for ingredients that are not sold in New York City and that must be imported from Puerto Rico, Mexico, New Jersey, other foreign countries, or other parts of the United States. Medicines prescribed by *espiritistas* may cost a good deal of money. Jose Gontan, for instance, wears a gold chain around his neck to which is appended a small cloth bag of "medicine." An *espiritista* prescribed to Jose's wife that he wear the bag as a preventative to illness. Jose paid twenty dollars for the bag, which ostensibly has the magical power to protect him from any disease.

Some patients suffering a major illness for which no improvement is obtained regardless of the treatment followed must first repent of their wrongdoings before they will be able to notice any favorable change. This repentance involves confession of one's evil doings, but the confession need not be made to a priest or minister. It is more important and more effective for these people to obtain the forgiveness of their victims, for their illness has been a punishment of God for their evil lives. This act of contrition is a manifestation of belief in an ethical value that requires the recognition of humility and goodness toward others as necessary requisites for men to live in health, since health is basically a gift granted by God to man for which he must pay with kindness to his fellows.

Linda Roman was spoken of as a quarrelsome woman by her neighbors, who complained of her blasphemies and insults. She had accused several of them to *la hara* (the police) for making too much noise, for throwing water out of the windows, and for disposing of garbage bags on top of the lids of the building garbage cans. Then Linda started to feel sick. She became very pale, lost weight, and ultimately was taken to a hospital, where she claims to have undergone a major operation. She says that while in the hospital she "almost died," but that she underwent a religious conversion and became an "Alleluyah," although previously she had been a regular and active member of another church in Eastville. She claims that it was after her conversion that she got well. When she returned home, she went to visit each neighbor with whom she had fallen out and asked forgiveness for her past wrongdoings. Maria de Leon, who had had several exchanges with her, remarked that it had taken a serious illness (*una gravedad*) to put some "shame" (sense of decency) into Linda, with whom she had renewed her friendship after Linda's repentance.

Believing that there is an interplay of supernatural action and disease does not, however, exclude the acceptance of rational and scientific explanations of disease. This is consonant with theories of disease which view illnesses as painful and uncomfortable experiences that threaten life not only with death but also with living in sickness, and that must be combatted actively if

one is to save one's life and live in health. The most important
factor to be considered is the restoration of health, and whatever
will help to achieve this, one has to do. So explanations and
treatments of one kind or the other of disease are seen as supplementary to each other, rather than as conflicting.

Hispanos use modern medical services, frequent low-cost and
free clinics, and also go to the offices of physicians as private
patients and pay standard fees. Doctors are called privately for
home visits, and calls are also made to the police to send an
ambulance with a doctor on a home call or to take a patient to
the hospital. Individuals who pay for health insurance may not
take advantage of it, but instead may visit a physician recommended by a friend. A patient is considered to be better treated
and cared for by a physician if he pays the physician a regular
fee himself, rather than if "the company" (the insurance company or his employer) pays for it. One may be feeling very
sick and not dare to go see a doctor because there is no money
to pay the fee. In such instances one may have to be reassured
by family members and neighbors that it is all right to go to
the hospital and not pay a fee "because one's health is the most
important thing to have." Going to a clinic for any medical
reason may be postponed until "emergency" hours, that is,
nights and holidays, since then the wait to see a doctor is shorter.
A doctor who is on a house call for a particular patient may be
asked to attend several patients in the same apartment, or perhaps others in different apartments of the same building. When
Dr. Givol, a physician who has a large number of private patients in Eastville, was called to come and see Jose Droz's daughter, a neighbor, Maria Santos, waited restlessly for him in the
corridor of the building. Her son was sick and she wanted to
take the opportunity to consult the doctor while he was at hand.
Dr. Givol obligingly responded to her and went to see the boy.

"German physicians" are said to be the best doctors, and if it
is remarked that "a German doctor," no matter what his na-

tionality, prescribed a certain medicine or treated a certain patient, the abilities and knowledge of German doctors may be praised. A good doctor is one who before giving a prescription makes a complete examination, continuing until he finds out "what is wrong." Specialists are sometimes underevaluated because they do not make such general examinations. One goes to a doctor, a druggist, or a healer to get medicines (*a recetarse*), as prescriptions or medicines are essential to a cure and a detailed examination is a prerequisite to reliable treatment.

Medical treatment requiring several visits to a physician during which the patient can find no evidence of change in his condition may be suspected of being an experiment with the patient because the doctor does not really know what is wrong. A good doctor keeps a patient informed as to what is wrong with him and tells him what he must and must not do, warning and advising him as to what can happen if he does not follow orders. A patient may seek care from different physicians without their knowledge or advice, all within a few days, in his anxiety over an ailment, and may take their various prescriptions simultaneously, continuing those which make him feel better and eliminating those that do not seem to help. Other members of the family may take some of the medicines prescribed for one family member by a doctor to control similar symptoms. Injections are considered the most effective kind of medicine for recovering from any disease. Next to these are emulsified liquids and wines with vitamins, iron, and meat. Pills and capsules are not considered so effective, but worst of all is to have no medicine. Patent medicines with Spanish, French, or Italian names are considered "good" for one's health and are taken regularly either to improve health or to cure disease.

While "medical examinations" are highly desirable, standards of behavior considered to be proper—as those in the areas of personal modesty—enter to affect the patient-physican relationship. These ideals of modesty are taught as part of the social training that individuals receive from early childhood, and they express some of the preferred and undesirable ways of behaving in social relations. A good woman is not to undress or expose her body. She is to avoid being touched and to refrain from discussing sex or physiological problems connected with sex with men. She may not discuss them with other women either with whom she does not have a close personal relationship of trust.

A girl is expected to be a virgin at marriage and to be ashamed of having lost her virginity before. One who has lost her virginity and keeps this a secret is likely to act with greater restraint with a physician than one who is publicly known to have lost her virginity. Women are supposed to maintain their modesty even with women doctors, for modesty is one of the most important indices for judging whether a woman is good or bad. Thus a woman can be expected to show reticence in undertaking a pelvic or breast examination. A woman may also refuse, or show considerable embarrassment, if requested to undress in front of a nurse or other women patients. These preferences about modesty are reflected in the marital relations of a man and a woman, for not even with her husband may a good woman volunteer a discussion of sexual problems or matters pertaining to her body. If she is a good woman her husband will expect her to maintain the desirable standards of modesty with him too.

The problem is somewhat different for men. A man can show his body to other men, but he is expected to show his body only to a woman with whom he has a sexual relationship. "He is ashamed" that he may become sexually excited in front of a woman doctor, or else that he may not. This problem relates to his conception of himself as a male and to the restrictions that a good male must impose upon himself: namely, that since nakedness is equated with sexuality, a good male cannot be naked before a woman doctor, for sexuality is barred in a relationship between patient and doctor. Thus a woman doctor who is going to examine a man around erotic zones raises a problem of shame in the patient that may prevent completion of the medical examination.

The Sick Person

When a person is sick, he should be able to rely on the sympathies and offers of cooperation of his friends and relatives. A sick person is supposed to receive visitors who will ask about his health and show their consternation. Close kin are expected to demonstrate their concern with expressions of grief and offers of help. When a person who is not close behaves as a member of the family in making offers of help, he is likely to become "as if a member of the family" and a person of trust.

One can be sick and remain on one's feet (*de pie*), or one may have to stay in bed (*de cama*). Diseases that require bed rest are considered to be worse than those in which one can remain active, regardless of the actual intensity or degree of illness. Several states of illness are recognized, including "half-sick" (*medio malo*), "sick" (*malo*), "very sick" (*malísimo*), and "at the verge of death" (*grave*). A patient who is half-sick, sick, or very sick can be treated at home or as an out-patient of a hospital, but one who is *grave* must be hospitalized. Adults as a rule, take being sick themselves more lightly than they take the sickness of their children. Still, illness is a major preoccupation and is seen as a threat that can become a reality at any time. Worries about falling sick or not feeling well are often expressed.

Being sick and feeling sick are not identical conditions, for admittedly one may be sick and not feel it, and vice versa. If a person is sick and does not feel it, he may ignore the disease or postpone its treatment indefinitely, but if he feels sick, regardless of what the medical dictum may be, he must do something to recover. A physician who tells a patient that there is nothing wrong with him when he feels sick is likely to be considered to have poor judgment. If the feeling of illness persists, the patient is likely to enter into a series of treatments and consultations with other physicians, try prescriptions from druggists as well as self-prescribed medicines, or visit healers. One should not be stingy or passive when feeling ill, nor should one neglect the care of those one loves when they claim to feel ill. Illness must be attacked.

The sick person is not to be alone and away from his family, and a sick person who still has friends and relatives on whom he can rely in Puerto Rico may return to the island for medical care. Conversely, a sick person in Puerto Rico may come to New York because the friends and kin he can rely on are here. Roberto Tigler, who lives in Arecibo, Puerto Rico, and who has a sister living in Eastville and other brothers and sisters near by, flew to New York when he found that he was sick and needed major surgery. He was admitted to a hospital here and operated on. While he was in New York, his sisters, brothers, in-laws, nephews, nieces, and friends here from his home town visited him regularly. After he recovered a few weeks later, he returned to his home in Puerto Rico.

A sick person is in a special position in his home and in relation to his family. While the illness of a child is a matter of great concern to his brothers, sisters, and parents and can partially disrupt the life of the family, it is the illness of a parent, the breadwinner, or someone in charge of the household, that can disrupt family life in many ways. A severe illness of a parent calls for mobilizing family members to do things they normally would not undertake and may involve decision-making by individuals who were previously subordinate and not allowed to make decisions without consultation or approval of the central authority of the household. This is particularly true if the father becomes ill and impaired, as then the mother or oldest child has to shoulder many of his functions. Should the mother be sick and incapacitated, the father may assist in the care of the children and the house. But, for a man who has been trained in terms of seeing a sharp difference between what men do and women do and for one who has been taught throughout his life to avoid many of the activities that women undertake and which supposedly men cannot learn, the illness of the housewife may create unresolvable problems. It is perhaps in response to life-situations in New York that migrants have started to modify their conceptions of what men and what women can do. Among Hispanos born or reared in New York, it is acceptable for a boy to help his mother in her household chores, and there is no stigma attached to a man who helps his wife in their own household. Among recent migrants, however, a man who helps his wife or a boy who helps his mother in such chores as cooking or cleaning the house, is likely to be criticized by others. When Maria Colon was severely ill, her children, who ranged from seven to nine, took over the care of the household and their mother. Her son Ralph, a boy of nine, helped his sister by doing the dishes and selecting the daily food to be consumed by the family. When he went to shop at the bodega, recent migrant men, who were hanging around talking and shopping for items assigned to them by their own wives, would tease and ridicule Ralph, calling him "sissy" for doing household work with his sister. Nonetheless, one may hear young recent migrant fathers and mothers say that in this country it is important for a man to learn how to change a child or how to take care of a home in case the wife falls ill.

A sick person needs special food for recovery; he may have to be "on a diet," that is, taking only certain foods. (The term diet is not used in reference to regular meals.) Among the foods termed "diet" is hen soup, which is considered highly nourishing and easily digestible and to be fed to a patient who is weakened by illness. Even patients in hospitals may be brought a container or thermos bottle of hen soup by a visitor. Other foods considered diet for the sick are boiled foods, such as rice cooked with milk and sugar, cream of wheat and cream of rice, corn meal, corn starch, a punch of black malt or wine with an egg or two added, mashed potatoes, and mashed tropical vegetables. In addition, a patient is entitled to *antojos,* or foods and aperitifs which he considers to "fall well" in the stomach. With the exception of black malt, foods of a diet are "fresh." Black malt is "hot" but is good for gaining strength, blood, and weight, and one takes it after surgery or labor.

When a person is severely ill (*malísimo* or *grave*), his wrongdoings are to be forgiven. Good persons "forget" their grievances when an enemy is very ill and may renew the relationship by visiting him and expressing sympathy. Illness, or the threat of illness, is a powerful mechanism in fostering social relations, in securing approval and forgiveness, and in reestablishing and solidifying social bonds that have been strained or disrupted. Juana Homero gave a party in her home to which she did not invite one of her downstairs neighbors, Pedro Ramos. The following day Juana came downstairs, and from the hall shouted to Pedro that he was a coward because he had called *la hara* and complained about the noise. Pedro retorted in shouts that she was noisy and disorderly. Then he screamed that he had something aching in his face, and Juana changed her angry tone to ask him what was wrong, recommending that he use an *unguento* or pomade of sulphur to cure the condition. He thanked her, and by this time the quarrel was over as they continued to discuss illnesses related to facial pains.

Migrants: transients or settlers?

MANY Hispanos see their lives and those of their children as unfolding in this country. To them, Puerto Rico is something of the past, and for many of the children who are growing up or have grown up in the United States, Puerto Rico is less than an echo; it is a land they have never visited, a "foreign country." Some migrants consciously decide at some point or other to make their homes here, to stay in this country permanently, never again turning back to look at Puerto Rico. These are to be found even among recent migrants. They are the people who view their future as being tied up with whatever life in New York may offer. We can call these Hispanos settlers, and can distinguish them from transients or those who regard their future life as gravitating toward Puerto Rico and who hope to return to live there later on, after their children have grown up or when they have enough savings to buy a house or start a business.

Settlers who have migrated to New York as adults are those who have lost or who give little importance to their relationships with their home towns, their friends and relatives who are still in Puerto Rico or are recent migrants to New York. They

have cut off their emotional ties with the homeland, but they
may still have significant interpersonal relationships with their
kin and within cliques that may consist largely of persons from
their own home town who are residents of New York. The settler
fulfills or expects to fulfill his social needs in relation to living in
New York.

One sort of settler has in his formative years moved away
from his home town, rural or urban, in Puerto Rico to another
town or city in the island itself. He started to break away from
the primary relations and bonds of his home town then. By
the time he comes to New York, he has already experienced life
situations in which primary groups derived from his home town
contexts have no longer operated for him, in which he has developed new social bonds, wherever he may have been. The primary group relationships of this kind of settler lack the continuity and history of those of the settler who, throughout his
life, whether in Puerto Rico or New York, has been able to continue depending and relying on persons known to him for many
years.

The consequent social adjustments that the settlers here
have made are the outcome of a gradual process of adaptation
to living in New York, and of recognizing that home, friends,
and other interests are here and not in Puerto Rico. The settler
may be oriented within the ethnic group of Puerto Ricans in
New York, partially by his participation in the cliques and
other small groups of people from his home town and in those
of his New York neighbors. But the one who has lost his primary ties with a home town and has been exposed to a greater
variety of group experiences in Puerto Rico through moving
about there is likely to become involved in New York in groups
and cliques that are not derived from any particular home town
context. The kinds of adjustments he can make to these changing group situations is related to his own background experiences
as a migrant in Puerto Rico itself. There he may have reacted

to and resolved the social stresses of the uprooting he underwent as a migrant, acquiring as a result the social techniques for making it easier to establish satisfactory social relationships outside of home town and family settings.

The migrant who is essentially a transient, on the other hand, still maintains ties with the homeland: he has a strong feeling of having a country in Puerto Rico, a national identity there, and there he has friends and relatives whom he writes, visits, and can rely upon. "If things get bad" (*si las cosas se ponen malas*), he can go back to Puerto Rico and get sympathy and help from those he grew up with. The transient migrants can be expected to feel obligated to their Puerto Rican friends and relatives, should these come to New York. The settler, on the other hand, is likely to say that he will "not return to Puerto Rico even if I have to eat stones in New York," and he will feel less bound to friends and relatives left in the island.

But becoming a settler does not necessarily involve a conscious decision. Transients may change into settlers as life orientations and social relations that are satisfactory and meaningful to them become part of their life in New York. The fundamental difference between settlers and transients is that the settler's life is organized in New York, while that of the transient is both in New York and in Puerto Rico.

In New York the lives of Puerto Ricans must, obviously, undergo profound changes. For those who learn American life in a slum like Eastville, the experience is one thing. For Puerto Ricans who were in better circumstances and had better life-chances in the island, it is another: they can begin life in New York as members of the middle class and avoid the particular cultural and social difficulties that beset the residents of Eastville. Yet all have their difficulties. Many overcome them. Many Eastvillers have made their way out of the slum into satisfactory fulfillment of their aspirations for themselves and their children. Others have returned to Puerto Rico.

One of the matters that concern Eastville Puerto Ricans is what has happened and is happening to Puerto Ricans in New York. Among migrants, social and cultural changes among Hispanos are a conscious preoccupation. They see the results of change in their own lives and in those of their friends. It is on this basis that they evaluate social behavior. Their awareness also reflects the conflicting values, orientations, and ambivalence of New York Hispanos.

True, old migrants and Hispanos who have grown up in New York regard recent migrants as representing a departure from their culture and as being socially inferior; on the other hand, recent migrants, in turn, express discontent with the ways Hispanos "are"—behave—in this country. George Espino, a New York-born man of Puerto Rican parents voiced a sentiment frequently heard from others who like himself have grown up in New York: "The Puerto Ricans that are coming over today, well, they're the most hated people . . . the most hated people." Migrants, particularly those who have come as adults, contrast and evaluate the changes they experienced in their lives in Puerto Rico with those they are experiencing in New York. To them, changes here in family life, in the expectancies of what family members can demand of each other, in the ways children are brought up, in marital behavior, and in the behavior of men, women, and children—all these factors that govern daily life— are of concern. Migrants are conscious of these changes and speak of how they have something to do both with modern life and with living in New York. Some of these changes are acceptable and "good," while others are disapproved of and considered "bad."

Migrants write of their experiences in New York, tell of them on visits to Puerto Rico, or show in their behavior the new ways they have adopted. In Puerto Rico some of these types of behavior are considered to be for the best, others for the worst. Potential migrants in the island know their future life in New

York is going to be different from their life in Puerto Rico. How, and to what extent, however, is part of the adventure and "changing environment" they will find in New York.

The impact of New York life on Puerto Rican migrants is described in fact and popular fancy, but whether it is described glowingly, soberly, or depressingly, depends on the aspirations, frustrations, hopes, and anxieties of the one who is speaking. Men, women, and children change in New York, it is said. How?

Clara Fredes, now a mother of three, who migrated after the Second World War when she was a teen-ager, replied to a member of the field team when asked if there were any differences between "the way people act here and in Puerto Rico," that "when women get here they act too free. They go out and stand in the street and don't cook dinner or anything. Puerto Rican women in New York City are bad. They talk to other men beside their husband, and just aren't nice. They boss the men. In Puerto Rico a wife obeys her husband, and keeps house, and takes care of her children. But here they run wild. [They are] all day long in the candy store talking and forgetting about their houses. Men here don't always support their wives and children. They are too free too. They think they can get away with everything, but I think it's the woman's fault. They are so bad. They don't take care of the children right. The children [are] out on the streets at all hours of the night."

Another informant, Gina Ortiz, said that Puerto Rican women in New York like to go dancing the mambo and drinking and that "they don't do it in Puerto Rico. In Puerto Rico the woman who smokes and drinks is a bad woman."

Rosa Burgos also explained changes in the behavior of women migrants. "[It is] because they work and they have too much freedom. In Puerto Rico the wife is always in the house. Here they go out, they go to work, get together with another girl, drink beer, and so on. In Puerto Rico they don't do that."

Women who want to be rated as "good" do not admit to

having changed in these directions. They would claim that they do not drink, smoke, or work outside the home, though they may acknowledge having changed in such areas as child-rearing, including giving greater freedom to their children.

Among changes that men undergo in New York, Dolores Miro mentioned that "some of them take friends. The friends like to drink and has women in the street. They change. They like to do same thing the friends do. . . . In Puerto Rico they have the same friends always, but here they have friends from other places, other towns. Some of them are good friends, some bad."

Good men are expected not to change in New York, but to continue recognizing their obligations to their wives and children. They may say they do not have friends in New York because friends get a man in trouble.

A couple that consider themselves good and as having a satisfactory relationship with each other and their children may deny changes in their lives in New York. Manuel and Sophia Tres, in telling a fieldworker about themselves, said, "We don't have any change. We still the same." Manuel continued, "Some of them [Hispanos] when they come here they want to go to the bar and drink, are drunk people and have plenty girl friends," to which Sophia added, "because they make more money to spend. We are not changed, we have the same customs."

In New York children also change, in a variety of ways. It is more difficult to make them respect their parents and elders, and one must keep them upstairs in order to prevent their becoming too uncontrollable and bad. For Juana Roman: "In Puerto Rico the fathers don't want the children to do what they want. They are strict; is better there. In Puerto Rico if your kids do anything wrong, the father punishes. Here you can't punish a big boy. . . . One day my boy went with another boy and they took a train and got lost, and when I got to the Children's Shelter, the lady said, 'Don't punish the boy' and I said, 'Oh yes [I will punish him], I don't want him to do it again.' I see many kids that they do what they want."

Antonio Velez, now in her mid-thirties, finds that in this country people are nice to old people, but says that in Puerto Rico old people are more respected. Her children do not respect in the same way she respected her father and mother in Puerto Rico when she was a child. Yet she is acceptant to some of the changes in patterns of respect she finds among her children. Says she, "Everybody is nice with the old people here in this country. They take care better of the old people and the children. I didn't pay too much attention to it in Puerto Rico. They are nice too. Everybody respects old people. The children are more respectful to old people in Puerto Rico than here . . . I know. I never used to argue with my mother in Puerto Rico. If she had a reason or no, I keep quiet. And with my father too. The word that he said was the only word to me. If he said not to go to a movie, I didn't discute [argue] that with him. I didn't go. No here. The children are more free here. Tommy, when I say, do that, and he don't want to and he explains me why, I don't mind that. I think it is better for him. You know, we didn't do that but it was not good inside. I think so, because they are human beings too. I love my father and mother because they are so good to me. If I didn't go to movies they may have the reason to say no, but I don't know it. Maybe that way, if I know it, I would have been better."

Children who have migrated recently at ages when they had friends and were allowed to play in the yards and streets in their home towns and now are being reared "upstairs in the home" speak of their past life in Puerto Rico with nostalgia. Lydia Rios, age twelve, says that "here one cannot do anything," referring to having to remain at home, sitting and watching from a window the play of other children, except when she goes to church or school.

Advantages listed of living in New York are the higher wages and income, better opportunities to educate the children, better medical care, more and better food, more and better clothes, furniture, and material things here than in Puerto Rico. In New York one can even save money to go back to Puerto Rico and purchase a house. Which place is better to live in is contingent on whether the migrant has realized or is on his way to realizing the aspirations and hopes connected with his coming to New York.

For Emilio Cruz it is better to live in New York than in Puerto Rico. "I think life in New York is better. We have better living in New York and can give the children the food they want and need. When we work we have more money. We spend more here but we earn more so we can live better. In Puerto Rico we rent a house [for] $10.00 or $12.00 a month, and here we [pay] so much [more] money and [must have] a lease too, [of] two or three years in New York."

Migrants speak of the future with reference to a good life, and a good life can be realized either in New York or in Puerto Rico, though one must search for it. As Rafael Dorcas put it, "A good life is when we work and we has the things we need for all the family. I think that's a good life."

Index

Boys (*Continued*)
89; clubs of, 224-25; *see also*
Adolescents; Children
British West Indians, 9, 89, 92-93
Business relationships in Eastville,
14

Capacidad (maturity), 107, 185,
192, 251
Case history: of migrant nuclear
family, 134-41; of joint family,
142-47
Caseworkers, *see* Welfare aid
Catholics, *see* Churches
Children, 14-16, 176-89; attitudes
toward, 60, 112; discipline of,
63-64, 149, 177-89; as interpreters, 64, 155, 201-2, 209,
223, 251; of consensual marriages, 65; living away from
parents, 130-32; responsibilities
in the family, 155; food preferences, 157-58; importance of social environment for, 161-69;
activities of, 161-211; teaching
of attitudes to, in home, 165; influence of schools on, 166-67,
168; friendships among, 168-69,
195-97; role of family in lives
of, 169-94; attitudes toward arrival of new babies, 171-72;
ideal of good behavior for, 185-
89; role of neighborhood and
school in lives of, 194-211;
cliques of, 224; illness of, 298;
effect of living in New York
City on, 306-7; *see also* Babies;
Boys; Girls
Churches, 3-4, 10, 18, 66; attitude
toward birth control, 111-12;
attendance at, 139, 197; influence of, 167, 272-74; and poli-
tics, 273
Civil rights, 53, 84
Class structure: of Hispano society in New York City, 27-28,
33, 50, 75, 211; in Puerto Rico,
33, 72-75

Clergymen, 273-74; *see also*
Churches
Clinics, use of, 5, 137, 172, 173,
266-67, 294
Cliques, 12, 93, 212-48; home
town, 215, 218-21, 302; importance of, 217; recreation
and, 218, 219, 223-24, 225; participation in, 220; of men, 220;
of women, 220-21; of neighbors,
221-23; leadership in, 221-23,
238; of children, 224; of teen-
agers, 224-25; conflicts in, 225-
26; social and fighting, 225-26;
ethnic groups and, 228, 229,
230; differentiated from gangs,
229-30; of drug addicts, 236-48;
see also Gangs
Clothing, *see* Wearing apparel
College education, attitude toward,
211
Comic books, 167, 199-200
"Common law" marriage, *see*
Consensual marriage
Communication: between New
York City and Puerto Rico, 50;
language and, 95-100; through
grapevine, 214-15; *see also* Mass
communication media
Community centers, 195, 231
Competitive games, 197
Conflict: solidarity resulting from,
11-12; within Hispano group,
52, 67-68; cultural backgrounds
of, 82-83; resulting from social
racial situation, 77-81; in joint
family, 142; between home and
school, 166-67; interclique, 225
(*see also* Gangs); in value orientation, 304; *see also* Discrimination; Prejudice
Consensual marriage, 65-66, 101-
12, 192
Consensus and solidarity among
Puerto Ricans, 29; *see also* Solidarity
Conservatism, cultural, 52
Consumption, patterns of: apart-
ment-buying, 7, 136; and pres-